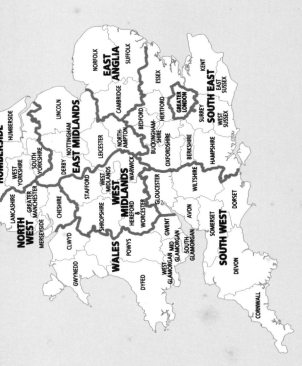

The Economist

POCKET BRITAIN
IN FIGURES

The
Economist

POCKET

BRITAIN
IN FIGURES

THE ECONOMIST IN ASSOCIATION WITH
HAMISH HAMILTON LTD

Published by the Penguin Group
Penguin Books Ltd, 27 Wrights Lane, London W8 5TZ, England
Penguin Books USA Inc., 375 Hudson Street, New York,
New York 10014, USA
Penguin Books Australia Ltd, Ringwood, Victoria, Australia
Penguin Books Canada Ltd, 10 Alcorn Avenue, Toronto,
Ontario, Canada M4V 3B2
Penguin Books (NZ) Ltd, 182–190 Wairau Road, Auckland 10,
New Zealand

Penguin Books Ltd, Registered Offices: Harmondsworth,
Middlesex, England

Published by Hamish Hamilton Ltd
in association with The Economist 1995

10 9 8 7 6 5 4 3 2 1

Material researched and compiled by
Joanna Malvisi, Liz Mann, David McKelvey,
Justene McNeice, Keith Potter,
Sara Pritchard, Nick Wiseman, Anna Wolek

Design and makeup Jonathan Harley

The greatest care has been taken in compiling this book. However,
no responsibility can be accepted by the publishers or compilers
for the accuracy of the information presented.

Printed in Great Britain by William Clowes Limited,
Beccles and London

A CIP catalogue record for this book is available
from the British Library

ISBN 0-241-13464-1

Contents

CONTENTS

CONTENTS

CONTENTS

Notes and glossary

Notes

In this first edition of *The Economist Pocket Britain in Figures* we present a detailed overview of where Britain stands today and how it has changed over the years, how its regions vary and how they have changed, and how Britain compares with other countries. The contents list on the previous pages gives a full list of the hundreds of subjects covered in the 13 main sections.

The research for this book was carried out during the latter half of 1994, using the most up-to-date and most authoritative sources available. The sources used are listed at the end of the book. However, some notes of explanation are necessary.

What is Britain?   Technically, Great Britain includes only England, Wales and Scotland, whereas the United Kingdom includes Northern Ireland as well. In this book we have often used Britain in a broad sense to mean either the United Kingdom or Great Britain, but we have endeavoured to make it clear how much and which parts of the United Kingdom specific data refer to. Statistical data are often collected by region. The map at the beginning and end of this book shows which counties are included in the regions that are most commonly referred to.
Does it all add up?   The simple answer is "No, not always". Because of rounding, individual amounts do not always add up to the totals given. Similarly, percentages may not add up to 100. However, the differences are usually small and of little significance.
Historical quirks   Over time the methods of collecting or reporting data have changed. Collection of data has generally improved, so more recent statistics should be more reliable than those reported decades ago. In some instances the method of reporting data has changed, which makes it inappropriate if not impossible to compare what has happened since the change with what happened before. Where major changes in the method of reporting data have taken place we have, to the best of our knowledge, indicated so in a footnote. In general, the historical data included in this book give as clear a picture of how trends have developed as is possible, but should not be used for strictly accurate comparisons.

Glossary

Balance of payments   The record of a country's transactions with the rest of the world. The current account of the balance of payments consists of visible trade (goods) and invisible trade (income and expenditure for services such as banking, insurance, tourism and shipping, together with profits earned overseas and interest payments). Imports include the cost of "carriage, insurance and freight" (cif) from the exporting country to the importing. The value of exports does not include these elements and is recorded "free on board" (fob). Balance of payments statistics are generally adjusted so that both exports and imports are shown fob; the cif element is included in invisibles.
Confidence indices   CBI: The difference between the percentage of firms (as surveyed by the CBI) reporting an increase in general business optimism in their industry compared with four months ago, and those reporting a decrease. Gallup: A survey of consumers' optimism.

CSO: A longer leading indicator that helps to identify in advance peaks and troughs in the UK economy. It is derived from five indicator series.

Crude birth rate   The number of live births per 1,000 population. The crude rate will automatically be high if a large proportion of the population is of child-bearing age.

Crude death rate   The number of deaths in one year per 1,000 population. Also affected by the population's age structure.

Current prices   These are in nominal terms and do not take into account the effect of inflation.

Enrolment   Gross enrolment ratios may exceed 100% because some pupils are younger or older than the standard primary or secondary school age.

EU   European Union. At end 1994 members were: Belgium, Denmark, France, Germany, Greece, Ireland, Italy, Luxembourg, Netherlands, Portugal, Spain and the United Kingdom.

Fertility rate   The average number of children born to a woman who completes her childbearing years.

G7   The Group of Seven. Members are Canada, France, Germany, Italy, Japan, UK and USA.

GDP   Gross domestic product. It is the sum of all output produced by economic activity within that country. GNP (gross national product) includes net income from abroad eg. rent, profits. In measuring GDP, market prices are normally used to value outputs and so include indirect taxes. When GDP is "at factor cost", indirect taxes have been subtracted.

Infant mortality rate   The annual number of deaths of infants under one year of age per 1,000 live births.

Inflation   The annual rate at which prices are increasing or decreasing. The most common measure is the change in the consumer price index. The underlying rate is usually arrived at by excluding mortgage interest payments. The producer price index tracks the prices of domestically produced goods when they leave the factory.

Life expectancy   The average length of time a newborn baby can expect to live.

Marginal tax rate   The rate of tax paid on extra units of income.

Money supply   A measure of the "money" available to buy goods and services. Various definitions of money supply exist. Those used here are narrow (M0): notes and coins in circulation, and broad (M4): notes and coins and sterling deposits at at all UK banks and building societies.

OECD   Organisation of Economic Cooperation and Development. The "rich countries club" established in 1961. Now has 25 members.

Population density   The total number of inhabitants divided by the surface area.

Real terms   Figures are adjusted to allow for inflation.

Reserves   The stock of gold and foreign currency held by a country to finance any calls that may be made for the settlement of foreign debt.

Trade-weighted exchange rates   This measures a currency's depreciation (figures below 100) or appreciation (figures over 100) from a base date against a trade-weighted basket of the country's main trading partners.

Part I
THE LAND AND THE ENVIRONMENT

Regions and counties

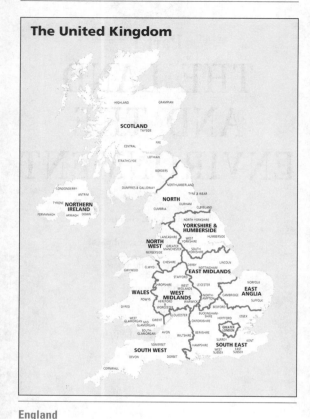

The United Kingdom

England

Sq km

North		
Cleveland	597	
Cumbria	6,824	
Durham	2,429	
Northumberland	5,026	
Tyne & Wear	540	

Yorkshire & Humberside		
Humberside	3,508	
North Yorkshire	8,309	
South Yorkshire	1,559	
West Yorkshire	2,034	

North West		
Cheshire	2,331	
Greater Manchester	1,286	
Lancashire	3,070	

Merseyside	655

West Midlands	
Hereford & Worc.	3,923
Shropshire	3,488
Staffordshire	2,715
Warwickshire	1,979
West Midlands	899

East Midlands	
Derbyshire	2,629
Leicestershire	2,551
Lincolnshire	5,921
Northamptonshire	2,367
Nottinghamshire	2,160

East Anglia	
Cambridgeshire	3,400

Norfolk	5,372	Kent	3,735
Suffolk	3,798	Oxfordshire	2,606
South East		Surrey	1,677
Bedfordshire	1,236	West Sussex	1,988
Berkshire	1,259	South West	
Buckinghamshire	1,877	Avon	1,332
East Sussex	1,795	Cornwall	3,559
Essex	3,675	Devon	6,703
Greater London	1,578	Dorset	2,653
Hampshire	3,779	Gloucestershire	2,653
Hertfordshire	1,639	Somerset	3,452
Isle of Wight	380	Wiltshire	3,476

Wales
Sq km

Clwyd	2,430	Mid Glamorgan	1,017
Dyfed	5,766	Powys	5,077
Gwent	1,377	South Glamorgan	416
Gwynedd	3,863	West Glamorgan	820

Scotland
Sq km

Borders	4,670	Lothian	1,756
Central	2,627	Strathclyde	13,529
Dumfries &		Tayside	7,502
Galloway	6,370	Orkney	976
Fife	1,308	Shetland	1,433
Grampian	8,707	Western Isles	2,898
Highland	25,304		

Northern Ireland
Sq km

Antrim	2,595	Londonderry	1,998
Armagh	1,441	Fermanagh	1,700
Down	1,962	Tyrone	3,787

Counties: from biggest to smallest
Sq km

1	Highland	25,304	37	Clwyd	2,430
2	Strathclyde	13,529	38	Durham	2,429
3	Grampian	8,707	39	Northamptonshire	2,367
4	North Yorkshire	8,309	40	Cheshire	2,331
5	Tayside	7,502	41	Nottinghamshire	2,160
6	Cumbria	6,824	42	West Yorkshire	2,034
7	Devon	6,703	43	Londonderry	1,998
8	Dumfries & Galloway	6,370	44	West Sussex	1,988
9	Lincolnshire	5,921	45	Warwickshire	1,979
10	Dyfed	5,766	46	Down	1,962
11	Norfolk	5,372	47	Buckinghamshire	1,877
12	Powys	5,077	48	East Sussex	1,795
13	Northumberland	5,026	49	Lothian	1,756
14	Borders	4,670	50	Fermanagh	1,700
15	Hereford & Worcester	3,923	51	Surrey	1,677
16	Gwynedd	3,863	52	Hertfordshire	1,639
17	Suffolk	3,798	53	Greater London	1,578
18	Hampshire	3,779	54	South Yorkshire	1,559
19	Kent	3,735	55	Armagh	1,441
20	Essex	3,675	56	Shetland	1,433
21	Cornwall	3,559	57	Gwent	1,377
22	Humberside	3,508	58	Avon	1,332
23	Shropshire	3,488	59	Fife	1,308
24	Wiltshire	3,476	60	Greater Manchester	1,286
25	Somerset	3,452	61	Berkshire	1,259
26	Cambridgeshire	3,400	62	Bedfordshire	1,236
27	Lancashire	3,070	63	Mid Glamorgan	1,017
28	Western Isles	2,898	64	Orkney	976
29	Staffordshire	2,715	65	West Midlands (Met. County)	899
30	Gloucestershire	2,653	66	West Glamorgan	820
31	Dorset	2,653	67	Merseyside	655
32	Derbyshire	2,629	68	Cleveland	597
33	Central	2,627	69	Tyne & Wear	540
34	Oxfordshire	2,606	70	South Glamorgan	416
35	Antrim	2,595	71	Isle of Wight	380
36	Leicestershire	2,551			

Mountains, rivers and parks

Highest mountains
Metres

1	Ben Nevis	Highland	1,342
2	Ben Macdhui	Grampian	1,310
3	Braeriach	Grampian	1,294
4	Cairn Toul	Grampian	1,292
5	Cairn Gorm	Grampian	1,244
6	Aonach Beag	Grampian	1,237
7	Càrn Mor Dearg	Highland	1,222
8	Aonach Mor	Grampian	1,218
9	Ben Lawers	Tayside	1,214
10	Beinn a'Bhùrid	Tayside	1,196

Longest rivers
Kilometres

1	Severn	354
2	Thames	346
3	Trent	297
4	Aire	259
5	Ouse	230
6	Wye	215
7	Tye	188
8	Neùe	161
9	Clyde	158
10	Spey	158
11	Tweed	155

National Parks

		Area sq km	Established
1	Lake District	2,292	1951
2	Snowdonia	2,142	1951
3	Yorkshire Dales	1,769	1954
4	Peak District	1,438	1951
5	North York Moors	1,436	1952
6	Brecon Beacons	1,351	1957
7	Northumberland	1,049	1956
8	Dartmoor	954	1951
9	Exmoor	693	1954
10	Pembrokeshire Coast	584	1952
11	Norfolk and Suffolk Broads[a]	303	1989

a The broads are given the same protection as the national parks.

Pollution and waste

Emissions
Tonnes, m

	Carbon dioxide	Per unit of GDP[a], £m	Methane	Per unit of GDP[a], £m	Sulphur dioxide	Per unit of GDP[a], £m
1970	182	521	5.09	14.6	6.43	18.4
1971	175	490	5.14	14.4	6.06	17.0
1972	171	464	4.96	13.4	5.79	15.7
1973	181	457	5.20	13.1	6.01	15.2
1974	169	433	5.09	13.1	5.51	14.1
1975	165	427	5.22	13.5	5.37	13.5
1976	166	417	5.13	12.9	5.18	13.0
1977	170	417	5.11	12.5	5.16	12.7
1978	171	407	5.12	12.2	5.23	12.4
1979	180	416	5.16	11.9	5.54	12.8
1980	164	387	5.19	12.2	4.90	11.6
1981	157	377	5.15	12.3	4.44	10.6
1982	154	362	5.12	12.0	4.21	9.9
1983	152	345	5.10	11.6	3.86	8.8
1984	148	327	4.40	9.8	3.72	8.2
1985	154	330	4.85	10.4	3.73	8.0
1986	158	323	5.01	10.3	3.90	8.0
1987	159	310	4.96	9.7	3.90	7.6
1988	159	295	4.91	9.1	3.81	7.1
1989	156	284	4.88	8.9	3.72	6.8
1990	158	287	4.83	8.8	3.78	6.9
1991	159	296	4.83	9.0	3.57	6.6
1992	155	288	4.74	8.8	3.50	6.5

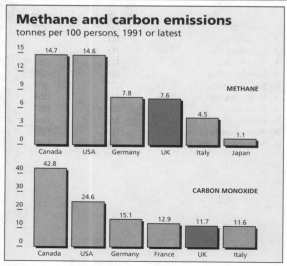

Methane and carbon emissions
tonnes per 100 persons, 1991 or latest

METHANE

Canada	USA	Germany	UK	Italy	Japan
14.7	14.6	7.8	7.6	4.5	1.1

CARBON MONOXIDE

Canada	USA	Germany	France	UK	Italy
42.8	24.6	15.1	12.9	11.7	11.6

a GDP measured at 1990 prices.

Black smoke	Per unit of GDP[a], £m	Nitrogen oxides	Per unit of GDP[a], £m	Carbon monoxide	Per unit of GDP[a], £m
1.03	2.9	2.32	6.6	4.83	13.8
0.92	2.6	2.29	6.4	4.85	13.6
0.80	2.2	2.28	6.2	4.87	13.2
0.81	2.0	2.41	6.1	5.05	12.7
0.77	2.0	2.29	5.9	4.90	12.6
0.67	1.7	2.27	5.9	4.80	12.4
0.65	1.6	2.32	5.8	4.93	12.4
0.67	1.6	2.34	5.7	5.03	12.3
0.63	1.5	2.38	5.7	5.13	12.2
0.64	1.5	2.48	5.7	5.14	11.9
0.56	1.3	2.39	5.6	5.30	12.5
0.53	1.3	2.33	5.6	5.36	12.8
0.53	1.2	2.31	5.4	5.49	12.9
0.51	1.2	2.33	5.3	5.46	12.4
0.47	1.1	2.32	5.1	5.58	12.4
0.55	1.2	2.44	5.2	5.80	12.4
0.57	1.2	2.53	5.2	6.04	12.4
0.53	1.0	2.66	5.2	6.32	12.4
0.52	1.0	2.75	5.1	6.69	12.5
0.50	0.9	2.84	5.2	7.10	12.9
0.47	0.9	2.86	5.2	7.02	12.7
0.47	0.9	2.84	5.3	7.02	13.0
0.46	0.9	2.75	5.1	6.71	12.5

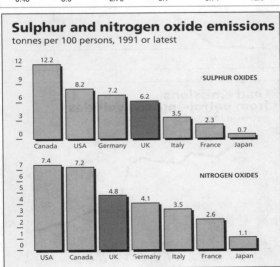

Sulphur and nitrogen oxide emissions
tonnes per 100 persons, 1991 or latest

SULPHUR OXIDES

Canada 12.2, USA 8.2, Germany 7.2, UK 6.2, Italy 3.5, France 2.3, Japan 0.7

NITROGEN OXIDES

USA 7.4, Canada 7.2, UK 4.8, Germany 4.1, Italy 3.5, France 2.6, Japan 1.1

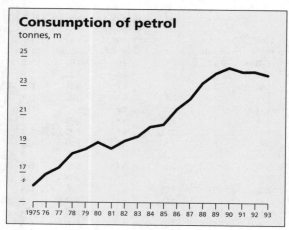

Consumption of petrol
tonnes, m

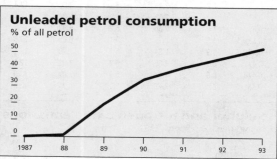

Unleaded petrol consumption
% of all petrol

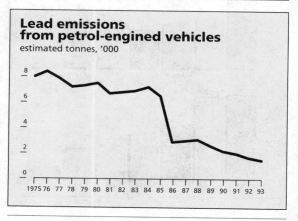

**Lead emissions
from petrol-engined vehicles**
estimated tonnes, '000

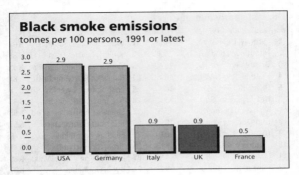

Black smoke emissions
tonnes per 100 persons, 1991 or latest

USA 2.9 | Germany 2.9 | Italy 0.9 | UK 0.9 | France 0.5

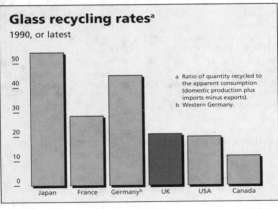

Glass recycling rates[a]
1990, or latest

Japan | France | Germany[b] | UK | USA | Canada

a Ratio of quantity recycled to the apparent consumption (domestic production plus imports minus exports).
b Western Germany.

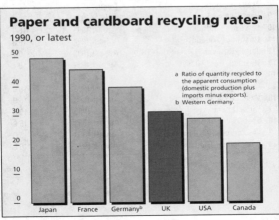

Paper and cardboard recycling rates[a]
1990, or latest

Japan | France | Germany[b] | UK | USA | Canada

a Ratio of quantity recycled to the apparent consumption (domestic production plus imports minus exports).
b Western Germany.

Temperature

Highest yearly average
July 1993–June 1994, °c

1	Torquay, Devon	11.05	21	Waddington, Lincolnshire	9.00
2	Heathrow, London	10.53	22	Whitby, North Yorkshire	8.88
3	Bristol, Avon	10.48	23	Warnall, Nottinghamshire	8.85
4	Ventnor, Isle of Wight	10.42	24	Ringway, Grt. Manchester	8.84
5	Plymouth, Devon	10.37	25	Long Sutton, Lincolnshire	8.76
6	Hastings, East Sussex	10.20	26	Skegness, Lincolnshire	8.69
7	Manston, Dorset	10.06	27	Leeming, North Yorkshire	8.68
8	Bude, Cornwall	10.03	28	Shawbury, Shropshire	8.57
9	Oxford, Oxfordshire	10.01	29	Edinburgh, Lothian	8.49
10	Clacton-on-Sea, Essex	9.91	30	Tiree, Strathclyde	8.41
11	Lowestoft, Suffolk	9.90	31	Bradford-on-Avon, Wilts.	8.38
12	Penzance, Cornwall	9.80	32	Dyce, Grampian	8.37
13	Cheltenham, Glos.	9.65	33	Presteigne, Powys	8.20
14	Hurn, Dorset	9.62	34	Aldergrove, Antrim	8.20
15	Tenby, Dyfed	9.60	35	Dundee, Tayside	8.01
16	Cambridge, Cambs.	9.56	36	Elmdon, Warwickshire	7.95
17	Valley, Gwynedd	9.54	37	Aspatria, Cumbria	7.95
18	Isle of Portland, Dorset	9.36	38	Durham, Durham	7.86
19	Aberporth, Dyfed	9.08	39	Sheffield, South Yorkshire	7.85
20	Morecambe, Lancashire	9.06	40	Abbotsinch, Strathclyde	7.80

Highest monthly average
July 1993–June 1994, °c

1	Torquay, Devon	June 1994	17.5
2	Heathrow, London	July 1993	17.1
3	Heathrow, London	August 1993	16.7
4	Torquay, Devon	July 1993	16.5
5	Oxford, Oxfordshire	July 1993	16.5
6	Manston, Dorset	July 1993	16.5
7	Clacton-on-Sea, Essex	July 1993	16.5
8	Manston, Dorset	August 1993	16.4
9	East Malling, Kent	July 1993	16.4
10	Lowestoft, Suffolk	July 1993	16.3
11	Heathrow, London	June 1994	16.3
12	Torquay, Devon	August 1993	16.1
13	Hastings, East Sussex	August 1993	16.1
14	Bristol, Avon	August 1993	16.1
15	Cambridge, Cambridgeshire	July 1993	16.0
16	Ventnor, Isle of Wight	August 1993	15.9
17	Hurn, Dorset	July 1993	15.9
18	East Malling, Kent	August 1993	15.9
19	Clacton-on-Sea, Essex	August 1993	15.9
20	Cheltenham, Gloucestershire	June 1994	15.9

Lowest yearly average

July 1993–June 1994, °c

1	Braemar, Grampian	4.46	21	Shawbury, Shropshire	8.57
2	Lerwick, Shetland Islands	6.30	22	Leeming, North Yorkshire	8.68
3	Buxton, Derbyshire	7.18	23	Skegness, Lincolnshire	8.69
4	Cleethorpes, Humberside	7.36	24	Long Sutton, Lincolnshire	8.76
5	Inverness, Highland	7.40	25	Ringway, Grt. Manchester	8.84
6	Stornoway, Western Is.	7.63	26	Warnall, Nottinghamshire	8.85
7	Dumfries, Dumfries	7.69	27	Whitby, North Yorkshire	8.88
8	Bala, Gwynedd	7.78	28	Waddington, Lincolnshire	9.00
9	Abbotsinch, Strathclyde	7.80	29	Morecambe, Lancashire	9.06
10	Sheffield, South Yorkshire	7.85	30	Aberporth, Dyfed	9.08
11	Durham, Durham	7.86	31	Isle of Portland, Dorset	9.36
12	Aspatria, Cumbria	7.95	32	Valley, Gwynedd	9.54
13	Elmdon, Warwickshire	7.95	33	Cambridge, Cambs.	9.56
14	Dundee, Tayside	8.01	34	Tenby, Dyfed	9.60
15	Aldergrove, Antrim	8.20	35	Hurn, Dorset	9.62
16	Presteigne, Powys	8.20	36	Cheltenham, Glos.	9.65
17	Dyce, Grampian	8.37	37	Penzance, Cornwall	9.80
18	Bradford-on-Avon, Wiltshire	8.38	38	Lowestoft, Suffolk	9.90
19	Tiree, Strathclyde	8.41	39	Clacton-on-Sea, Essex	9.91
20	Edinburgh, Lothian	8.49	40	Oxford, Oxfordshire	10.01

Lowest monthly average

July 1993–June 1994, °c

1	Braemar, Grampian	February 1994	-0.3
2	Braemar, Grampian	December 1993	0.3
3	Dumfries, Dumfries	February 1994	0.7
4	Buxton, Derbyshire	February 1994	1.1
5	Braemar, Grampian	November 1993	1.3
6	Braemar, Grampian	January 1994	1.5
7	Durham, Durham	February 1994	1.7
8	Bradford-on-Avon, Wiltshire	February 1994	1.9
9	Leeming, North Yorkshire	February 1994	1.9
10	Inverness, Highland	December 1993	2.1
11	Presteigne, Powys	February 1994	2.1
12	Sheffield, South Yorkshire	February 1994	2.1
13	Dyce, Grampian	February 1994	2.2
14	Aspatria, Cumbria	February 1994	2.3
15	Dyce, Grampian	December 1993	2.3
16	Waddington, Lincolnshire	February 1994	2.3
17	Dumfries, Dumfriesshire	January 1994	2.4
18	Abbotsinch, Strathclyde	February 1994	2.5
19	Dundee, Tayside	February 1994	2.5
20	Lerwick, Shetland Islands	February 1994	2.5

Rainfall

Highest monthly average
July 1993–June 1994, mm

1	Penzance, Cornwall	124	21	Dyce, Grampian	84
2	Bala, Gwynedd	124	22	Aspatria, Cumbria	84
3	Buxton, Derbyshire	122	23	Isle of Portland, Dorset	82
4	Plymouth, Devon	115	24	Long Sutton, Lincolnshire	79
5	Lerwick, Shetland Islands	107	25	Aberporth, Dyfed	79
6	Tiree, Strathclyde	103	26	Hastings, East Sussex	79
7	Torquay, Devon	100	27	Sheffield, South Yorkshire	78
8	Tenby, Dyfed	100	28	Inverness, Highland	78
9	Hurn, Dorset	97	29	Cheltenham, Gloucestershire	75
10	Braemar, Grampian	95	30	Aldergrove, Antrim	75
11	Abbotsinch, Strathclyde	94	31	Warnall, Nottinghamshire	72
12	Stornoway, Western Is.	94	32	Valley, Gwynedd	71
13	Elmdon, Warwickshire	93	33	Lowestoft, Suffolk	69
14	Dumfries, Dumfries	88	34	Ringway, Grt. Manchester	69
15	Bude, Cornwall	86	35	Cleethorpes, Humberside	67
16	Morecambe, Lancashire	86	36	Oxford, Oxfordshire	65
17	Bradford-on-Avon, Wiltshire	85	37	Skegness, Lincolnshire	65
18	Ventnor, Isle of Wight	85	38	Durham, Durham	62
19	Bristol, Avon	85	39	Whitby, North Yorkshire	61
20	Presteigne, Powys	85	40	Shawbury, Shropshire	60

Highest monthly total
July 1993–June 1994, mm

1	Bala, Gwynedd	December 1993	361
2	Buxton, Derbyshire	December 1993	270
3	Elmdon, Warwickshire	March 1994	262
4	Penzance, Cornwall	December 1993	246
5	Lerwick, Shetland Islands	January 1994	243
6	Dumfries, Dumfries	January 1994	227
7	Plymouth, Devon	December 1993	225
8	Dumfries, Dumfries	December 1993	223
9	Penzance, Cornwall	August 1993	211
10	Tiree, Strathclyde	December 1993	209
11	Bala, Gwynedd	January 1994	209
12	Morecambe, Lancashire	December 1993	206
13	Lerwick, Shetland Islands	March 1994	206
14	Bala, Gwynedd	March 1994	204
15	Torquay, Devon	December 1993	202
16	Tenby, Dyfed	December 1993	201
17	Aspatria, Cumbria	December 1993	191
18	Bude, Cornwall	December 1993	188
19	Buxton, Derbyshire	January 1994	185
20	Plymouth, Devon	August 1993	182

Lowest monthly average
July 1993–June 1994, mm

1	Leeming, North Yorkshire	53	21	Inverness, Highland	78
2	Dundee, Tayside	53	22	Sheffield, South Yorkshire	78
3	Cambridge, Cambridgeshire	54	23	Hastings, East Sussex	79
4	Waddington, Lincolnshire	55	24	Aberporth, Dyfed	79
5	Clacton-on-Sea, Essex	58	25	Long Sutton, Lincolnshire	79
6	Manston, Dorset	59	26	Isle of Portland, Dorset	82
7	Edinburgh, Lothian	59	27	Aspatria, Cumbria	84
8	Heathrow, London	60	28	Dyce, Grampian	84
9	Shawbury, Shropshire	60	29	Presteigne, Powys	85
10	Whitby, North Yorkshire	61	30	Bristol, Avon	85
11	Durham, Durham	62	31	Ventnor, Isle of Wight	85
12	Skegness, Lincolnshire	65	32	Bradford-on-Avon, Wiltshire	85
13	Oxford, Oxfordshire	65	33	Morecambe, Lancashire	86
14	Cleethorpes, Humberside	67	34	Bude, Cornwall	86
15	Ringway, Grt. Manchester	69	35	Dumfries, Dumfries	88
16	Lowestoft, Suffolk	69	36	Elmdon, Warwickshire	93
17	Valley, Gwynedd	71	37	Stornoway, Western Is.	94
18	Warnall, Nottinghamshire	72	38	Abbotsinch, Strathclyde	94
19	Aldergrove, Antrim	75	39	Braemar, Grampian	95
20	Cheltenham, Gloucestershire	75	40	Hurn, Dorset	97

Lowest monthly total
July 1993–June 1994, mm

1	Waddington, Lincolnshire	June 1994	7
2	Abbotsinch, Strathclyde	May 1994	11
3	Braemar, Grampian	May 1994	12
4	Oxford, Oxfordshire	June 1994	13
5	Durham, Durham	May 1994	14
6	Isle of Portland, Dorset	June 1994	15
7	Sheffield, South Yorkshire	June 1994	15
8	Dumfries, Dumfries	May 1994	16
9	Inverness, Highland	November 1993	16
10	Heathrow, London	June 1994	17
11	Torquay, Devon	June 1994	18
12	Whitby, North Yorkshire	June 1994	18
13	Aspartria, Cumbria	May 1994	19
14	Hurn, Dorset	June 1994	19
15	Leeming, North Yorkshire	June 1994	19
16	Presteigne, Powys	June 1994	19
17	Cambridge, Cambridgeshire	June 1994	20
18	Shawbury, Shropshire	June 1994	20
19	Bradford-on-Avon, Wiltshire	June 1994	21
20	Lowestoft, Suffolk	February 1994	23

Sunshine and daylight

Sun patterns
Total amount of sunlight from sunrise to sunset, taken on the first day of each month, hrs.mins

	London	Bristol	Birmingham	Manchester	Newcastle	Glasgow	Belfast
January	7.56	7.56	7.46	7.35	7.18	7.07	7.23
February	9.10	9.11	9.04	8.57	8.45	8.42	8.49
March	10.56	10.54	10.51	10.49	10.45	10.42	10.45
April	12.57	12.57	12.58	13.01	13.04	13.06	13.03
May	14.50	14.50	14.57	15.03	15.14	15.21	15.11
June	16.19	16.19	16.29	16.40	16.59	17.10	16.54
July	16.34	16.33	16.44	16.52	17.16	17.29	17.11
August	15.25	15.25	15.33	15.41	15.55	16.03	15.50
September	13.35	13.35	13.38	13.41	13.48	13.51	13.46
October	11.39	11.39	11.38	11.36	11.35	11.34	11.36
November	9.41	9.41	9.36	9.30	9.20	9.14	9.22
December	8.12	8.12	8.03	7.53	7.37	7.26	7.41

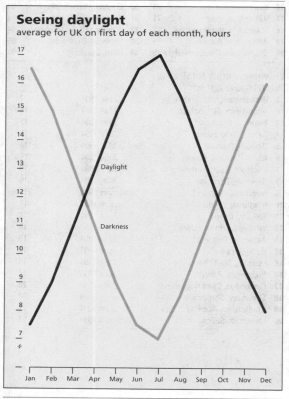

Seeing daylight
average for UK on first day of each month, hours

Daylight

Darkness

=== Part II ===
POPULATION

Regions compared

Where the British live

	1992 Population	1992 Population per sq km
UK	57,999	240
England	48,379	371
Wales	2,899	140
Scotland	5,111	66
Northern Ireland	1,610	119
North	3,099	201
Yorkshire & Humberside	5,002	325
North West	6,400	872
West Midlands	5,278	406
East Midlands	4,062	260
East Anglia	2,089	166
South East	17,703	650
South West	4,746	199

Regional trends
'000s

	1891	1911	1931	1951
UK	34,264	42,082	46,037	50,225
England	27,231	33,649	37,358	41,159
Wales	1,771	2,421	2,593	2,599
Scotland	4,026	4,761	4,843	5,096
Northern Ireland	1,236	1,251	1,243	1,371
North	2,122	2,729	2,938	3,009
Yorkshire & Humberside	3,138	3,896	4,319	4,567
North West	4,585	5,658	6,062	6,305
West Midlands	2,664	3,277	3,743	4,423
East Midlands	1,975	2,467	2,732	3,118
East Anglia	1,105	1,191	1,231	1,381
South East	9,096	11,613	13,349	14,877
South West	2,546	2,818	2,984	3,479

	1961	1971	1981	1991
UK	52,709	55,515	56,353	57,648
England	43,561	46,411	46,821	48,209
Wales	2,644	2,731	2,814	2,886
Scotland	5,179	5,229	5,180	5,100
Northern Ireland	1,425	1,536	1,538	1,594
North	3,120	3,142	3,117	3,019
Yorkshire & Humberside	4,681	4,856	4,918	4,797
North West	6,429	6,597	6,459	6,147
West Midlands	4,758	5,110	5,187	5,089
East Midlands	3,321	3,633	3,853	3,919
East Anglia	1,469	1,669	1,864	2,019
South East	15,994	16,931	16,732	16,794
South West	3,689	4,081	4,327	4,600

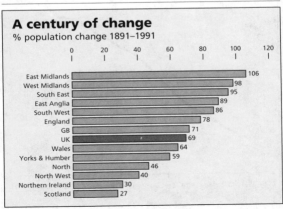

A century of change
% population change 1891–1991

East Midlands	106
West Midlands	98
South East	95
East Anglia	89
South West	86
England	78
GB	71
UK	69
Wales	64
Yorks & Humber	59
North	46
North West	40
Northern Ireland	30
Scotland	27

Growth

UK population
m

	Total	Male	Female
1801	12.07	5.93	6.32
1811	13.76	6.75	7.18
1821	15.47	7.50	7.97
1831	17.84	8.65	9.19
1841	20.18	9.82	10.36
1851	22.26	10.86	11.40
1861	24.52	11.89	12.63
1871	27.43	13.31	14.12
1881	31.02	15.06	15.96
1891	34.26	16.59	17.67
1901	38.24	18.49	19.75
1911	42.08	20.36	21.73
1921	44.03	21.03	22.99
1931	46.04	22.06	23.98
1941	48.22	23.22	24.95
1951	50.23	24.12	26.11
1961	52.81	25.48	27.23
1971	55.93	26.95	28.56
1981	56.35	27.10	28.74
1991	57.80	27.34	29.12
2001	59.72	29.34	30.38
2011	61.11	30.16	30.95
2021	61.98	30.66	31.32
2031	62.10	30.68	31.42

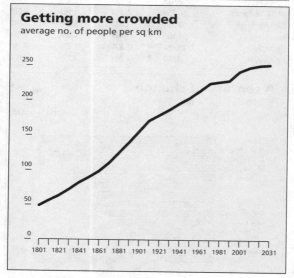

Getting more crowded
average no. of people per sq km

England and Wales
'000

	Total	Male	Female
1821	12,000	5,850	6,150
1841	15,914	7,778	8,137
1861	20,066	9,776	10,290
1881	25,974	12,640	13,335
1901	32,528	15,729	16,799
1921	37,887	18,075	19,811
1931	39,952	19,133	20,819
1951	43,758	21,016	22,742
1961	46,196	22,347	23,849
1971	49,151	23,897	25,254
1981	49,635	24,160	25,475
1991	51,101	24,995	26,106
2001	52,526	25,819	26,708

Scotland
'000

	Total	Male	Female
1821	2,092	983	1,109
1841	2,620	1,242	1,378
1861	3,062	1,450	1,612
1881	3,736	1,799	1,936
1901	4,472	2,174	2,298
1921	4,882	2,348	2,535
1931	4,843	2,326	2,517
1951	5,096	2,434	2,662
1961	5,184	2,485	2,699
1971	5,236	2,516	2,720
1981	5,180	2,495	2,685
1991	5,107	2,470	2,638
2001	5,026	2,449	2,577

Northern Ireland
'000

	Total	Male	Female
1821	1,380	665	715
1841	1,649	800	849
1861	1,396	668	728
1881	1,305	621	684
1901	1,237	590	647
1921	1,258	610	648
1931	1,243	601	642
1951	1,371	668	703
1961	1,427	696	731
1971	1,540	755	786
1981	1,538	754	784
1991	1,594	777	817
2001	1,686	828	859

Age and sex

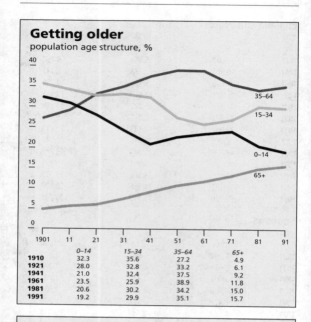

Getting older
population age structure, %

	0–14	15–34	35–64	65+
1910	32.3	35.6	27.2	4.9
1921	28.0	32.8	33.2	6.1
1941	21.0	32.4	37.5	9.2
1961	23.5	25.9	38.9	11.8
1981	20.6	30.2	34.2	15.0
1991	19.2	29.9	35.1	15.7

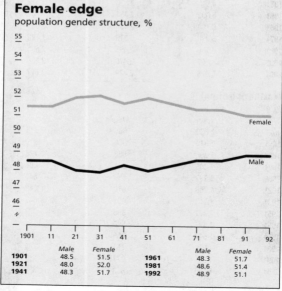

Female edge
population gender structure, %

	Male	Female		Male	Female
1901	48.5	51.5	**1961**	48.3	51.7
1921	48.0	52.0	**1981**	48.6	51.4
1941	48.3	51.7	**1992**	48.9	51.1

Growth and urbanisation

Growing comparisons
population average annual growth, 1960–92, %

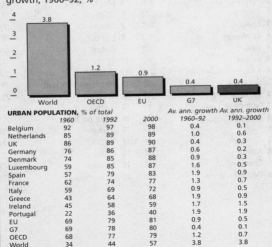

POPULATION, m	1960	1992	2000	Av. ann. growth 1960–92	Av. ann. growth 1992–2000
World	3,000.0	5,348.0	6,113.0	1.8	1.5
OECD	630.0	810.0	850.0	0.8	0.6
G7	514.0	660.0	690.0	0.8	0.2
EU	300.0	350.0	350.0	0.5	0.3
Germany	72.7	80.2	82.6	0.3	0.1
UK	52.0	58.0	59.0	0.3	0.2
Italy	50.2	57.8	58.1	0.4	0.1
France	45.7	57.1	58.8	0.7	0.4
Spain	30.5	39.1	39.6	0.8	0.2
Netherlands	11.5	15.2	16.1	0.9	0.7
Greece	8.3	10.2	10.3	0.6	0.2
Belgium	9.2	10.0	10.1	0.3	0.1
Portugal	8.8	9.9	9.9	0.4	0.1
Denmark	4.6	5.2	5.2	0.4	0.2
Ireland	2.8	3.5	3.4	0.7	-0.2
Luxembourg	0.3	0.4	0.4	0.6	0.7

The move to the cities
urban population as % of total population, average annual growth, 1960–92, %

URBAN POPULATION, % of total	1960	1992	2000	Av. ann. growth 1960–92	Av. ann. growth 1992–2000
Belgium	92	97	98	0.4	0.1
Netherlands	85	89	89	1.0	0.6
UK	86	89	90	0.4	0.3
Germany	76	86	87	0.6	0.2
Denmark	74	85	88	0.9	0.3
Luxembourg	59	85	87	1.6	0.5
Spain	57	79	83	1.9	0.9
France	62	74	77	1.3	0.7
Italy	59	69	72	0.9	0.5
Greece	43	64	68	1.9	0.9
Ireland	45	58	59	1.7	1.5
Portugal	22	36	40	1.9	1.9
EU	69	79	81	0.9	0.5
G7	69	78	80	0.4	0.1
OECD	68	77	79	1.2	0.7
World	34	44	57	3.8	3.8

City living

The biggest cities
Pop. '000

1901

1	London	4,536
2	Liverpool	648
3	Manchester	544
4	Birmingham	522
5	Leeds	429
6	Sheffield	381
7	Bristol	329
8	Bradford	280

1911

1	London	7,160
2	Glasgow	784
3	Liverpool	746
4	Manchester	714
5	Birmingham	526
6	Leeds	446
7	Sheffield	455
8	Belfast	387
9	Bristol	357
10	Edinburgh	320
11	Bradford	288
12	Kingston-upon-Hull	278
13	Nottingham	260
14	Stoke-on-Trent	235
15	Leicester	227
16	Cardiff	182
17	Dundee	165
18	Aberdeen	164
19	Coventry	106
20	Wolverhampton	95

1931

1	London	8,100
2	Glasgow	1,088
3	Birmingham	1,003
4	Liverpool	856
5	Manchester	766
6	Sheffield	512
7	Leeds	483
8	Edinburgh	439
9	Belfast	438
10	Bristol	397
11	Kingston-upon-Hull	314
12	Bradford	298
13	Stoke-on-Trent	277
14	Nottingham	269
15	Leicester	239
16	Cardiff	224
17	Dundee	176
18	Aberdeen	167
	Coventry	167
20	Wolverhampton	133

1951

1	London	8,197
2	Birmingham	1,113
3	Glasgow	1,090
4	Liverpool	789
5	Manchester	703
6	Sheffield	513
7	Leeds	505
8	Edinburgh	467
9	Belfast	444
10	Bristol	443
11	Nottingham	306
12	Kingston-upon-Hull	299
13	Bradford	292
14	Leicester	285
15	Stoke-on-Trent	275
16	Coventry	258
17	Cardiff	244
18	Aberdeen	183
19	Dundee	177
20	Wolverhampton	163

1961			*1971*		
1	London	7,992	**1**	London	7,454
2	Birmingham	1,107	**2**	Birmingham	1,015
3	Glasgow	1,055	**3**	Glasgow	897
4	Liverpool	746	**4**	Liverpool	610
5	Manchester	662	**5**	Manchester	544
6	Leeds	511	**6**	Sheffield	520
7	Sheffield	494	**7**	Leeds	496
8	Edinburgh	468	**8**	Edinburgh	454
9	Bristol	437	**9**	Bristol	427
10	Belfast	416	**10**	Belfast	362
11	Nottingham	312	**11**	Coventry	335
12	Coventry	306	**12**	Nottingham	301
13	Kingston-upon-Hull	303	**13**	Bradford	294
14	Bradford	296	**14**	Kingston-upon-Hull	286
15	Leicester	273	**15**	Leicester	284
16	Stoke-on-Trent	265	**16**	Cardiff	279
17	Cardiff	257	**17**	Wolverhampton	269
18	Aberdeen	185	**18**	Stoke-on-Trent	265
19	Dundee	183	**19**	Aberdeen	182
20	Wolverhampton	151		Dundee	182

1981			*1991*		
1	London	6,696	**1**	London	6,890
2	Birmingham	1,007	**2**	Birmingham	938
3	Glasgow	766	**3**	Leeds	677
4	Leeds	705	**4**	Glasgow	654
5	Sheffield	538	**5**	Sheffield	503
6	Liverpool	510	**6**	Bradford	451
7	Bradford	457	**7**	Liverpool	450
8	Manchester	449	**8**	Edinburgh	422
9	Edinburgh	437	**9**	Manchester	400
10	Bristol	391	**10**	Bristol	372
11	Belfast	314	**11**	Coventry	295
	Coventry	314	**12**	Belfast	279
13	Leicester	280	**13**	Cardiff	277
14	Cardiff	274	**14**	Leicester	272
15	Nottingham	272	**15**	Nottingham	262
16	Kingston-upon-Hull	270	**16**	Kingston-upon-Hull	253
17	Wolverhampton	255	**17**	Stoke-on-Trent	244
18	Stoke-on-Trent	253	**18**	Wolverhampton	241
19	Aberdeen	204	**19**	Aberdeen	201
20	Dundee	180	**20**	Dundee	166

Immigration and race

Ethnic breakdown
% of population

	White		Black		Indian	
	1983	1993	1983	1993	1983	1993
Great Britain	94.2	94.5	1.0	1.7	1.4	1.5
Wales	97.4	98.9	0.1	0.0	0.3	0.0
Scotland	98.2	99.3	0.0	0.0	0.1	0.0
North	97.6	99.0	0.0	0.0	0.2	0.0
Yorkshire & Humberside	94.9	95.2	0.5	1.0	0.8	0.9
North West	94.9	95.9	0.4	0.6	1.0	1.0
West Midlands	91.0	95.2	1.5	0.9	3.2	1.0
East Midlands	94.4	95.9	0.6	0.9	2.3	2.2
East Anglia	97.2	98.1	0.3	0.6	0.2	0.0
South East	91.0	89.9	2.1	3.9	2.2	2.5
South West	97.4	98.6	0.3	0.6	0.2	0.4

Immigration and emigration
Immigration, '000s

	Total	British citizens			
		Country of last/next residence			
		Total	EU	Old Commonwealth	New Commonwealth
1982	201	97	38	10	19
1983	202	94	22	20	22
1984	201	95	24	13	22
1985	232	110	37	12	22
1986	250	120	36	14	25
1987	211	98	32	13	19
1988	216	89	26	15	17
1989	250	104	23	24	18
1990	267	106	28	23	22
1991	267	117	40	23	23
1992	216	99	46	15	13

Emigration, '000s

	Total	British citizens			
1982	257	186	31	60	22
1983	184	121	26	31	18
1984	164	102	26	19	18
1985	174	108	26	21	17
1986	213	132	47	34	15
1987	209	130	40	39	12
1988	237	143	41	48	16
1989	205	122	26	42	18
1990	231	135	34	43	15
1991	239	137	47	36	19
1992	227	133	43	31	15

Pakistani/Bangladeshi		Mixed/other		Total	
1983	1993	1983	1993	1983	1993
1.0	1.3	1.1	1.1	54,118	55,770
0.3	0.0	0.6	0.6	2,777	2,884
0.4	0.0	0.3	0.6	5,056	4,996
0.4	0.5	0.6	0.4	3,057	3,054
1.7	2.4	0.6	0.7	4,846	4,938
1.0	1.9	0.9	0.8	6,321	6,324
2.2	2.0	0.7	1.1	5,126	5,238
0.3	0.4	0.7	0.7	3,833	4,044
0.3	0.6	0.7	0.6	1,912	2,109
0.9	1.7	2.1	2.3	16,825	17,469
0.1	0.0	0.5	0.5	4,365	4,714

		Other EU citizens		
		Country of last/next residence		
USA	Other	Total	EU	Other countries
8	21	18	17	1
11	19	13	11	3
6	30	19	17	2
11	27	21	17	4
10	35	35	31	3
11	23	25	21	2
8	23	26	24	1
12	27	29	28	2
10	22	35	31	4
10	21	31	27	3
8	18	21	20	2
15	58	11	7	4
16	30	12	10	2
12	28	10	7	3
12	33	12	8	3
13	23	10	8	1
18	20	19	16	3
15	23	22	16	3
13	23	21	17	4
22	22	28	25	3
13	23	32	23	7
16	29	16	14	3

Births and deaths

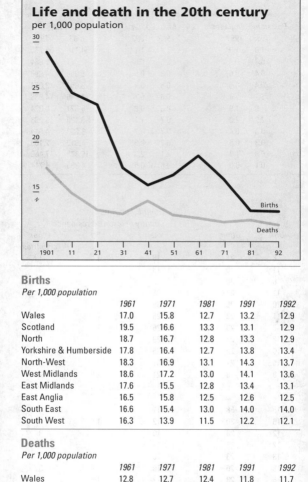

Life and death in the 20th century
per 1,000 population

Births

Deaths

1901 11 21 31 41 51 61 71 81 92

Births
Per 1,000 population

	1961	1971	1981	1991	1992
Wales	17.0	15.8	12.7	13.2	12.9
Scotland	19.5	16.6	13.3	13.1	12.9
North	18.7	16.7	12.8	13.3	12.9
Yorkshire & Humberside	17.8	16.4	12.7	13.8	13.4
North-West	18.3	16.9	13.1	14.3	13.7
West Midlands	18.6	17.2	13.0	14.1	13.6
East Midlands	17.6	15.5	12.8	13.4	13.1
East Anglia	16.5	15.8	12.5	12.6	12.5
South East	16.6	15.4	13.0	14.0	14.0
South West	16.3	13.9	11.5	12.2	12.1

Deaths
Per 1,000 population

	1961	1971	1981	1991	1992
Wales	12.8	12.7	12.4	11.8	11.7
Scotland	11.3	10.6	10.6	9.5	9.3
North	11.9	11.9	12.3	12.3	12.0
Yorkshire & Humberside	12.5	12.0	12.0	11.5	11.1
North-West	13.3	12.4	12.4	12.0	11.7
West Midlands	10.9	10.4	10.9	10.8	10.6
East Midlands	11.2	11.0	11.2	10.9	10.7
East Anglia	11.6	11.2	11.1	10.9	10.6
South East	11.9	11.2	11.1	10.3	10.1
South West	12.4	12.3	12.5	11.9	11.6

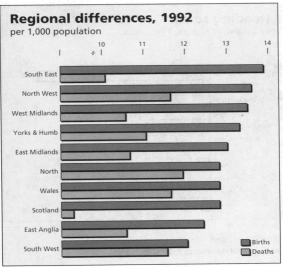

Regional differences, 1992
per 1,000 population

| | 10 | 11 | 12 | 13 | 14 |

South East
North West
West Midlands
Yorks & Humb
East Midlands
North
Wales
Scotland
East Anglia
South West

- Births
- Deaths

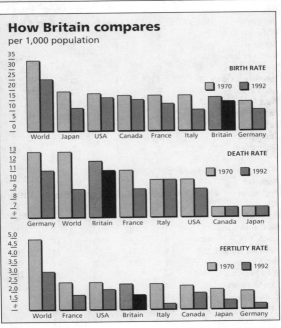

How Britain compares
per 1,000 population

BIRTH RATE

1970 1992

World Japan USA Canada France Italy Britain Germany

DEATH RATE

1970 1992

Germany World Britain France Italy USA Canada Japan

FERTILITY RATE

1970 1992

World France USA Britain Italy Canada Japan Germany

Internal migration

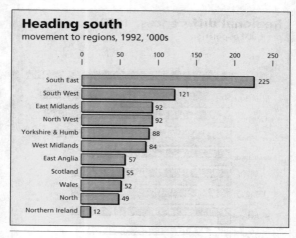

Heading south
movement to regions, 1992, '000s

South East	225
South West	121
East Midlands	92
North West	92
Yorkshire & Humb	88
West Midlands	84
East Anglia	57
Scotland	55
Wales	52
North	49
Northern Ireland	12

Moving around
Inter-regional movements, 1992, '000s

Region of destination	Region of origin				
	Wales	Scotland	N Ireland	North	Yorks & Humb
Wales	–	2	…	1	3
Scotland	2	–	2	5	5
Northern Ireland	…	1	–	…	1
North	1	5	1	–	9
Yorkshire & Humb	3	4	1	10	–
North West	7	6	1	7	14
West Midlands	7	3	1	3	7
East Midlands	3	3	1	4	15
East Anglia	1	2	…	2	4
South East	15	17	4	13	22
South West	9	4	1	3	6

Region of destination	Region of origin					
	N West	W Mids	E Mids	E Anglia	S East	S West
Wales	10	8	3	1	16	8
Scotland	7	3	4	2	20	4
Northern Ireland	1	1	1	…	5	1
North	8	3	4	2	14	3
Yorkshire & Humb	15	8	13	4	24	6
North West	–	11	8	3	27	7
West Midlands	11	–	11	3	28	11
East Midlands	9	12	–	7	31	6
East Anglia	3	3	6	–	31	4
South East	28	27	26	23	–	50
South West	9	14	7	4	65	–

Part III
THE
ECONOMY

Gross domestic product

National trends
GDP, £bn

	UK[a]	England	Wales	Scotland	N.Ireland
1971	52.0	44.1	2.2	4.6	1.1
1972	59.0	50.0	2.5	5.2	1.3
1973	68.9	58.2	3.0	6.2	1.5
1974	77.8	65.8	3.2	7.1	1.7
1975	98.1	82.8	4.2	8.9	2.2
1976	114.6	96.5	4.9	10.6	2.6
1977	133.3	112.7	5.6	12.1	2.9
1978	152.2	129.1	6.4	13.4	3.3
1979	175.7	149.4	7.3	15.3	3.7
1980	203.3	173.5	8.2	17.4	4.2
1981	220.9	188.4	8.8	19.1	4.6
1982	237.7	203.1	9.6	20.1	4.9
1983	261.2	208.0	10.4	22.0	5.3
1984	280.7	221.0	10.8	22.9	5.7
1985	307.9	246.1	11.8	25.3	6.4
1986	328.3	272.7	13.3	27.3	7.1
1987	360.7	299.2	14.8	29.7	7.5
1988	401.4	336.5	17.0	32.7	8.4
1989	441.8	371.3	18.6	35.9	9.2
1990	478.9	402.4	20.1	39.6	10.1
1991	494.8	415.7	20.8	43.5	11.0
1992	514.6	431.0	21.8	44.0	11.6

Regional trends
GDP, £bn

	North	Yorkshire & Humberside	North West	West Midlands
1974	4.0	6.4	8.8	7.0
1975	5.1	8.0	11.0	8.8
1976	6.1	9.3	12.8	10.0
1977	7.0	10.9	14.7	11.4
1978	7.7	12.4	16.9	13.2
1979	8.7	14.0	18.9	14.7
1980	10.0	15.5	21.4	16.3
1981	10.9	16.9	22.4	17.1
1982	11.7	18.4	24.4	18.6
1983	12.6	20.0	26.4	20.4
1984	13.1	20.9	27.8	21.8
1985	14.6	23.4	30.5	24.5
1986	15.7	26.1	33.4	26.8
1987	17.2	28.1	36.2	29.5
1988	18.9	31.0	40.5	33.4
1989	20.9	34.2	44.3	36.5
1990	22.3	37.0	47.7	39.9
1991	23.7	38.5	48.9	41.2
1992	24.8	40.6	50.8	42.9

a Including Continental Shelf.

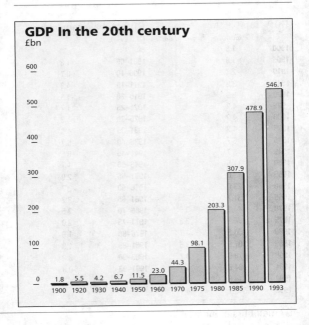

GDP in the 20th century
£bn

Year	GDP (£bn)
1900	1.8
1920	5.5
1930	4.2
1940	6.7
1950	11.5
1960	23.0
1970	44.3
1975	98.1
1980	203.3
1985	307.9
1990	478.9
1993	546.1

East Midlands	East Anglia	Greater London	Rest of South East	South West
4.9	2.3	12.9	14.1	5.4
6.2	2.9	16.3	17.6	6.7
7.2	3.5	18.5	20.6	7.9
8.4	4.1	21.0	24.0	9.2
9.4	4.6	23.9	28.3	10.3
10.9	5.2	27.1	32.7	11.9
12.7	6.2	30.7	37.8	13.9
13.8	6.7	32.9	41.0	15.1
15.0	7.5	33.5	44.1	16.6
16.3	8.2	36.5	49.3	18.3
17.5	9.2	38.3	53.0	19.5
19.5	10.1	42.9	58.9	21.2
21.6	11.3	47.9	65.6	24.3
23.6	12.4	53.1	72.3	26.9
26.4	14.0	59.1	83.0	30.3
29.4	15.7	65.1	91.9	33.3
31.7	17.1	70.7	99.6	36.3
33.2	17.8	72.5	101.2	37.8
34.0	18.7	74.7	105.1	39.4

Economic growth

GDP[a], total

	£bn	% world GDP
1900	1.8	...
1905	1.9	...
1910	2.1	...
1915	3.2	...
1920	5.5	...
1925	4.2	...
1930	4.2	...
1935	4.2	...
1940	6.7	...
1945	8.7	...
1950	11.5	...
1955	17.0	...
1960	23.0	...
1965	31.7	...
1970	44.3	3.9
1975	98.1	3.8
1980	203.3	4.7
1985	307.9	3.6
1990	478.9	4.7
1991	494.8	4.7
1992	514.6	4.6
1993	546.1	4.1

GDP real average annual growth

	%
1901–05	1.8
1906–10	0.7
1911–15	4.9
1916–20	-4.5
1921–25	1.7
1926–30	1.2
1931–35	1.3
1936–40	5.7
1941–45	-0.5
1946–50	1.1
1951–55	2.9
1956–60	2.7
1961–65	3.2
1966–70	2.5
1971–75	2.0
1976–80	1.9
1981–85	1.9
1986–90	3.2
1991–93	-0.3

G7 members compared

GDP, real % change on a year earlier

	UK	USA	Japan	Germany[b]	France	Italy	Canada
1980	-2.2	-0.5	3.6	1.0	1.6	4.1	1.5
1981	-1.3	1.8	3.6	0.1	1.2	0.6	3.7
1982	1.7	-2.2	3.2	-0.9	2.5	0.2	-3.2
1983	3.7	3.9	2.7	1.8	0.7	1.0	3.2
1984	2.3	6.2	4.3	2.8	1.3	2.7	6.3
1985	3.8	3.2	5.0	2.0	1.9	2.6	4.7
1986	4.3	2.9	2.6	2.3	2.5	2.9	3.3
1987	4.8	3.1	4.1	1.5	2.3	3.1	4.2
1988	5.0	3.9	6.2	3.7	4.5	4.1	5.0
1989	2.2	2.5	4.7	3.6	4.3	2.9	2.4
1990	0.4	1.2	4.8	5.7	2.5	2.1	-0.2
1991	-2.2	-0.7	4.3	4.5	0.8	1.2	-1.7
1992	-0.6	2.6	1.1	2.1	1.2	0.7	0.7
1993	1.9	3.0	0.1	-1.3	-0.9	-0.7	2.4

a Factor cost, current prices.
b Western Germany only to 1991.

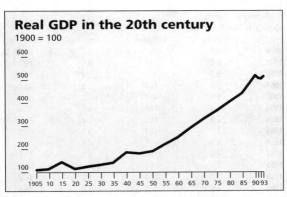

Real GDP in the 20th century
1900 = 100

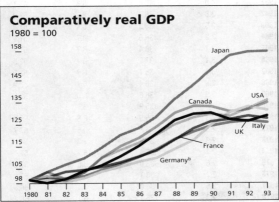

Comparatively real GDP
1980 = 100

North-south divide
GDP average annual growth, %

	1971–80	1981–90	1991–92
UK	14.6	8.9	3.6
Wales	14.0	9.3	4.2
Scotland	14.3	8.6	6.9
Northern Ireland	14.1	9.1	6.8
North	14.2	8.3	5.4
North West	13.5	8.3	3.1
Yorkshire & Humberside	14.0	9.1	4.7
West Midlands	12.9	9.4	3.7
East Midlands	15.3	9.6	3.5
East Anglia	15.4	10.7	4.3
Greater London	13.5	8.7	2.8
Rest of South East	14.7	10.2	2.8
South West	15.1	10.1	4.0

GDP by sector

Post-war change
Origins of GDP, % of total

	Agriculture	Industry	Construction	Services
1948	6.1	39.3	5.4	49.2
1949	6.2	39.1	5.5	49.2
1950	5.7	40.4	5.3	48.6
1951	5.5	41.1	5.3	48.2
1952	5.6	40.7	5.5	48.1
1953	5.4	41.4	5.7	47.4
1954	5.0	41.9	5.7	47.4
1955	4.7	42.1	5.7	47.5
1956	4.5	41.9	6.0	47.6
1957	4.5	42.1	5.9	47.5
1958	4.4	41.6	6.0	48.0
1959	4.2	41.7	5.9	48.2
1960	4.0	41.7	6.0	48.4
1961	4.0	40.6	6.3	49.1
1962	3.8	38.7	6.4	51.0
1963	3.5	38.3	6.4	51.8
1964	3.3	38.6	6.7	51.4
1965	3.2	38.4	6.7	51.7
1966	3.1	37.7	6.7	52.5
1967	3.1	36.7	6.7	53.5
1968	2.9	36.4	6.7	53.9
1969	2.9	36.6	6.6	53.9
1970	2.8	35.9	6.7	54.6
1971	2.8	35.5	6.8	54.9
1972	2.5	33.3	6.5	57.7
1973	2.9	34.9	7.3	54.9
1974	2.7	33.4	6.7	57.1
1975	2.6	33.0	6.6	57.8
1976	2.7	33.1	6.4	57.8
1977	2.5	35.0	6.1	56.5
1978	2.3	35.1	6.1	56.4
1979	2.2	35.1	6.2	56.5
1980	2.1	34.9	6.0	57.0
1981	2.0	33.9	5.7	58.4
1982	2.3	34.9	5.7	57.1
1983	2.0	34.4	5.8	57.8
1984	2.3	33.5	5.9	58.3
1985	1.9	33.8	5.7	58.5
1986	1.9	30.2	5.8	62.1
1987	1.9	29.5	6.2	62.4
1988	1.7	28.0	6.7	63.6
1989	1.8	27.9	7.1	63.2
1990	1.8	26.7	6.9	64.7
1991	1.8	26.4	6.3	65.5
1992	1.7	25.7	6.0	66.6

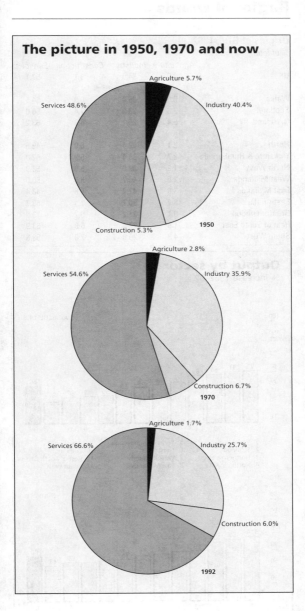

The picture in 1950, 1970 and now

Agriculture 5.7%
Services 48.6%
Industry 40.4%
Construction 5.3%
1950

Agriculture 2.8%
Services 54.6%
Industry 35.9%
Construction 6.7%
1970

Agriculture 1.7%
Services 66.6%
Industry 25.7%
Construction 6.0%
1992

Regional trends

Origins of GDP, 1982
% of total

	Agriculture	Industry	Construction	Services
UK	2.3	34.9	5.7	57.1
Wales	3.6	35.4	6.9	54.1
Scotland	3.6	33.0	7.4	56.0
N. Ireland	5.4	25.1	6.3	63.2
North	2.1	42.4	6.0	49.5
Yorkshire & Humberside	2.7	39.4	5.9	52.0
North West	1.2	39.0	5.9	53.9
West Midlands	2.5	40.7	5.9	50.9
East Midlands	3.8	42.2	5.6	48.4
East Anglia	8.2	30.7	7.4	53.7
Greater London	0.1	21.2	5.7	73.0
Rest of South East	1.9	27.4	6.8	63.9
South West	4.3	29.9	7.0	58.8

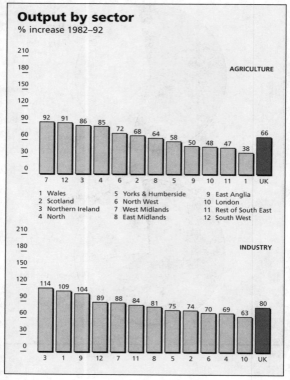

Output by sector
% increase 1982–92

AGRICULTURE

7	12	3	4	6	2	8	5	9	10	11	1	UK
92	91	86	85	72	68	64	58	50	48	47	38	66

1 Wales
2 Scotland
3 Northern Ireland
4 North
5 Yorks & Humberside
6 North West
7 West Midlands
8 East Midlands
9 East Anglia
10 London
11 Rest of South East
12 South West

INDUSTRY

3	1	9	12	7	11	8	5	2	6	4	10	UK
114	109	104	89	88	84	81	75	74	70	69	63	80

Origins of GDP, 1992
% of total

	Agriculture	Industry	Construction	Services
UK	1.8	25.7	6.0	66.6
Wales	2.2	32.4	6.8	58.6
Scotland	2.7	26.3	7.6	63.4
N. Ireland	4.2	22.7	6.3	66.8
North	1.8	33.9	6.9	57.4
Yorkshire&Humberside	1.9	31.1	6.4	60.6
North West	1.0	31.8	5.8	61.4
West Midlands	2.1	33.2	6.1	58.6
East Midlands	2.8	33.7	6.3	57.2
East Anglia	4.9	25.1	7.0	63.0
Greater London	0.1	15.5	4.7	79.7
Rest of South East	1.2	21.2	6.7	70.9
South West	3.5	23.8	6.4	66.3

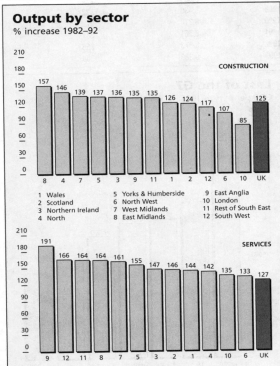

Output by sector
% increase 1982–92

CONSTRUCTION

157	146	139	137	136	135	135	126	124	117	107	85	125
8	4	7	5	3	9	11	1	2	12	6	10	UK

1 Wales
2 Scotland
3 Northern Ireland
4 North
5 Yorks & Humberside
6 North West
7 West Midlands
8 East Midlands
9 East Anglia
10 London
11 Rest of South East
12 South West

SERVICES

191	166	164	164	161	155	147	146	144	142	135	133	127
9	12	11	8	7	5	3	2	1	4	10	6	UK

Living standards

GDP per person

	£	*real GDP per person, 1900 = 100*
1900	44	100
1905	44	105
1910	47	104
1915	69	128
1920	126	108
1925	93	114
1930	92	119
1935	90	124
1940	139	158
1945	177	152
1950	227	156
1955	334	178
1960	439	197
1965	583	222
1970	796	246
1975	1,745	269
1980	3,609	294
1985	5,438	322
1990	8,310	372
1991	8,561	361
1992	8,873	358
1993	9,388	364

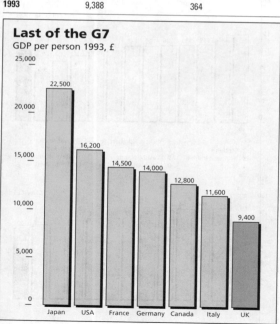

Last of the G7
GDP per person 1993, £

- Japan: 22,500
- USA: 16,200
- France: 14,500
- Germany: 14,000
- Canada: 12,800
- Italy: 11,600
- UK: 9,400

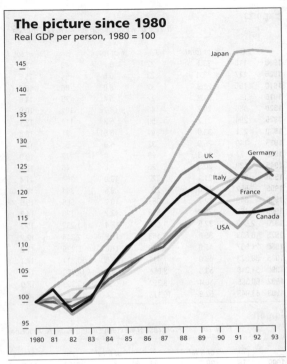

The picture since 1980
Real GDP per person, 1980 = 100

GDP per person, current prices
$

	1960	1970	1980	1990	1993
Japan	477	1,964	9,069	23,801	33,799
USA	2,849	4,933	11,891	21,866	24,316
France	1,333	2,814	12,335	21,014	21,678
Germany	1,300	3,042	13,154	23,658	21,069
Canada	2,257	3,960	10,934	21,273	18,865
Italy	791	2,003	8,023	18,991	17,406
UK	1,382	2,226	9,540	16,968	16,132

Regional growth rankings
GDP per head 1992, UK = 100

Greater London	123.4	West Midlands	92.8
Rest of South East	111.1	Yorkshire & Humberside	92.5
East Anglia	102.2	North	91.2
England	101.6	North West	90.5
Scotland	98.3	Wales	86.1
East Midlands	95.5	Northern Ireland	82.0
South West	94.7		

Trade: partners and products

Exports

	To EU		To rest of western Europe		To N. America	
	£m	% of total	£m	% of total	£m	% of total
1900	118	33.1	22	6.2	48	13.5
1905	117	28.6	23	5.6	64	15.6
1910	155	28.9	32	6.0	86	16.0
1915	156	31.2	27	5.4	73	14.6
1920	486	29.2	144	8.7	181	10.9
1925	294	31.2	50	5.3	114	12.1
1930	221	33.0	44	6.6	71	10.6
1935	140	25.9	32	5.9	54	10.0
1940	77	19.3	28	7.0	72	18.0
1945	139	30.9	25	5.6	46	10.2
1950	476	21.1	227	10.0	257	11.4
1955	552	18.0	296	9.6	344	11.2
1960	849	22.7	381	10.2	596	15.9
1965	1,466	29.8	598	12.2	728	14.8
1970	2,643	32.5	1,090	13.4	1,232	15.2
1975	6,839	35.6	2,453	12.8	2,345	12.2
1980	21,657	45.9	5,476	11.6	5,299	11.2
1985	38,223	49.0	7,411	9.5	13,311	17.1
1990	54,248	53.3	9,054	8.9	14,758	14.5
1992	60,365	56.4	8,392	7.8	13,969	13.0
1993	63,945	52.9	10,178	8.4	17,313	14.3

Imports

	From EU		From rest of western Europe		From N. America	
	£m	% of total	£m	% of total	£m	% of total
1900	178	36.7	22	4.5	163	33.6
1905	172	32.6	40	7.6	144	27.3
1910	188	29.7	44	7.0	149	23.6
1915	116	13.8	51	6.1	282	33.6
1920	287	15.8	135	7.5	666	36.8
1925	336	27.8	73	6.0	321	26.6
1930	327	34.3	67	7.0	196	20.6
1935	165	22.8	53	7.3	146	20.2
1940	…	…	…	…	364	36.4
1945	…	…	…	…	527	75.3
1950	546	23.6	168	7.3	392	17.0
1955	776	22.9	322	9.5	764	22.6
1960	1,039	25.1	430	10.4	950	23.0
1965	1,505	29.1	577	11.2	1,131	21.9
1970	2,673	32.8	1,193	14.7	1,877	23.1
1975	9,380	41.8	2,878	12.8	3,223	14.4
1980	21,701	47.4	6,094	13.3	7,383	16.1
1985	41,650	51.2	12,075	14.8	11,697	14.4
1990	64,289	53.3	14,943	12.4	16,194	13.4
1992	64,022	53.2	13,792	11.5	14,973	12.4
1993	67,899	50.5	15,621	11.6	17,645	13.1

To Japan	
£m	% of total
10	2.8
10	2.4
10	1.9
5	1.0
28	1.7
17	1.8
8	1.2
4	0.7
…	…
…	…
3	0.1
14	0.5
29	0.8
53	1.1
149	1.8
310	1.6
596	1.3
1,012	1.3
2,631	2.6
2,227	2.1
2,654	2.2

From Japan	
£m	% of total
2	0.4
2	0.4
4	0.6
9	1.1
30	1.7
7	0.6
8	0.8
8	1.1
6	0.6
…	…
8	0.3
24	0.7
42	1.0
78	1.5
135	1.7
673	3.0
1,709	3.7
4,117	5.1
6,762	5.6
7,444	6.2
8,536	6.3

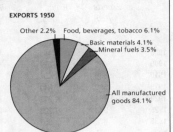

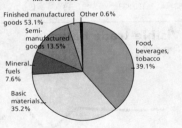
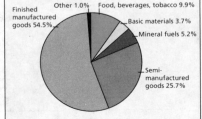

What Britain trades

Trade: balances

Balance of payments
£m

	Exports (fob)	Imports (fob)	Visible-trade balance	Invisible-trade balance	of which services balance
1900	356	485	-129	163	61
1905	409	527	-118	206	86
1910	536	632	-96	270	104
1915	500	840	-340	285	120
1920	1,664	1,812	-148	485	240
1925	943	1,208	-265	317	66
1930	670	953	-283	319	67
1935	541	724	-183	206	25
1940	400	1,000	-600	-200	-350
1945	450	700	-250	-620	-650
1950	2,261	2,312	-51	358	-30
1955	3,073	3,386	-313	158	9
1960	3,737	4,138	-401	164	-1
1965	4,913	5,173	-260	183	-98
1970	8,130	8,141	-11	832	421
1975	19,185	22,441	-3,256	1,732	1,315
1980	47,149	45,792	1,357	1,486	3,653
1985	77,991	81,336	-3,345	5,583	6,398
1990	101,718	120,527	-18,809	541	3,808
1991	103,413	113,697	-10,284	2,632	3,657
1992	107,047	120,453	-13,406	2,867	4,202
1993	120,839	134,519	-13,680	2,799	5,202

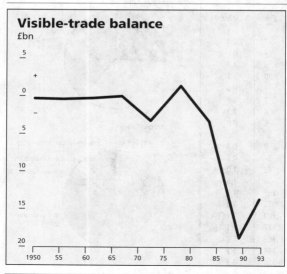

Visible-trade balance
£bn

Current-account balance	Current-account balance as % of GDP
34	1.8
88	4.2
174	7.8
-55	-1.6
337	5.8
52	1.1
36	0.8
23	0.5
-800	-10.6
-870	-8.8
307	2.4
-155	-0.8
-237	-0.9
-77	-0.2
821	1.6
-1,524	-1.4
2,843	1.2
2,238	0.6
-18,268	-3.3
-7,652	-1.3
-10,539	-1.4
-10,881	-1.7

Trade share
Exports as % of world exports

Year	%
1950	10.4
1951	9.6
1952	9.8
1953	9.3
1954	9.2
1955	9.3
1956	9.4
1957	9.0
1958	9.1
1959	8.7
1960	8.1
1961	8.2
1962	7.9
1963	7.8
1964	7.4
1965	7.4
1966	7.2
1967	6.7
1968	6.5
1969	6.4
1970	6.3
1971	6.3
1972	5.7
1973	5.1
1974	4.6
1975	4.9
1976	4.6
1977	4.9
1978	5.2
1979	5.3
1980	5.4
1981	5.1
1982	5.1
1983	5.0
1984	4.8
1985	5.2
1986	5.0
1987	5.2
1988	5.0
1989	4.9
1990	5.3
1991	5.2
1992	5.1
1993	4.9

Invisible-trade balance £bn

The pound in your pocket

Internal purchasing power of the pound
Year in which purchasing power was 100p

	1900	1905	1910	1915	1920
1900	100.0	94.9	106.3	146.8	341.8
1905	105.3	100.0	112.0	154.7	360.0
1910	94.0	89.3	100.0	138.1	321.4
1915	68.1	64.7	72.4	100.0	232.8
1920	29.3	27.8	31.1	43.0	100.0
1925	54.1	51.4	57.5	79.5	184.9
1930	76.0	72.1	80.8	111.5	259.6
1935	76.7	72.8	81.6	112.6	262.1
1940	52.0	49.3	55.3	76.3	177.6
1945	41.4	39.3	44.0	60.7	141.4
1950	33.8	32.1	35.9	49.6	115.4
1955	27.5	26.1	29.3	40.4	94.1
1960	24.5	23.3	26.1	36.0	83.9
1965	20.6	19.6	21.9	30.3	70.5
1970	16.5	15.7	17.5	24.2	56.4
1975	8.9	8.5	9.5	13.1	30.6
1980	4.6	4.3	4.9	6.7	15.6
1985	3.2	3.1	3.4	4.7	11.0
1990	2.4	2.3	2.6	3.6	8.3
1993	2.2	2.1	2.3	3.2	7.4

	1955	1960	1965	1970	1975
1900	363.3	407.6	484.8	606.3	1,117.7
1905	382.7	429.3	510.7	638.7	1,177.3
1910	341.7	383.3	456.0	570.2	1,051.2
1915	247.4	277.6	330.2	412.9	761.2
1920	106.3	119.3	141.9	177.4	327.0
1925	196.6	220.5	262.3	328.1	604.8
1930	276.0	309.6	368.3	460.6	849.0
1935	278.6	312.6	371.8	465.0	857.3
1940	188.8	211.8	252.0	315.1	580.9
1945	150.3	168.6	200.5	250.8	462.3
1950	122.6	137.6	163.7	204.7	377.4
1955	100.0	112.2	133.4	166.9	307.7
1960	89.1	100.0	118.9	148.8	274.2
1965	74.9	84.1	100.0	125.1	230.5
1970	59.9	67.2	80.0	100.0	184.3
1975	32.5	36.5	43.4	54.2	100.0
1980	16.6	18.6	22.2	27.7	51.1
1985	11.7	13.2	15.7	19.6	36.1
1990	8.8	9.9	11.7	14.7	27.0
1993	7.9	8.8	10.5	13.1	24.2

For help with using the table, note that:
- in 1993 the pound was worth 2.2p compared with its value in 1900 and 8.8p compared with its value in 1960;
- compared with its value in 1993, the pound was worth 46.12 times more in 1900 and 11.32 times more in 1960.

1925	1930	1935	1940	1945	1950
184.8	131.6	130.4	192.4	241.8	296.2
194.7	138.7	137.3	202.7	254.7	312.0
173.8	123.8	122.6	181.0	227.4	278.6
125.9	89.7	88.8	131.0	164.7	201.7
54.1	38.5	38.1	56.3	70.7	86.7
100.0	71.2	70.5	104.1	130.8	160.3
140.4	100.0	99.0	146.2	183.7	225.0
141.7	101.0	100.0	147.6	185.4	227.2
96.1	68.4	67.8	100.0	125.7	153.9
76.4	54.5	53.9	79.6	100.0	122.5
62.4	44.4	44.0	65.0	81.6	100.0
50.9	36.2	35.9	53.0	66.6	81.5
45.3	32.3	32.0	47.2	59.3	72.7
38.1	27.2	26.9	39.7	49.9	61.1
30.5	21.7	21.5	31.7	39.9	48.9
16.5	11.8	11.7	17.2	21.6	26.5
8.4	6.0	6.0	8.8	11.1	13.5
6.0	4.3	4.2	6.2	7.8	9.6
4.5	3.2	3.2	4.7	5.8	7.2
4.0	2.9	2.8	4.2	5.2	6.4

1980	1985	1990	1993
2,187.3	3,097.5	4,132.9	4,611.8
2,304.0	3,262.7	4,353.3	4,857.7
2,057.1	2,913.1	3,886.9	4,337.3
1,489.7	2,109.5	2,814.7	3,140.8
640.0	906.3	1,209.3	1,349.4
1,183.6	1,676.0	2,236.3	2,495.4
1,661.5	2,352.9	3,139.4	3,503.2
1,677.7	2,375.7	3,169.9	3,537.2
1,136.8	1,609.9	2,148.0	2,396.9
904.7	1,281.2	1,709.4	1,907.5
738.5	1,045.5	1,395.3	1,557.0
602.1	852.6	1,137.6	1,269.4
536.6	759.9	1,014.0	1,131.5
451.2	638.9	852.5	951.3
360.8	510.9	681.6	760.6
195.7	277.1	369.8	412.6
100.0	141.6	188.9	210.8
70.6	100.0	133.4	148.9
52.9	74.9	100.0	111.6
47.4	67.2	89.6	100.0

The value of the pound: abroad

Annual average exchange rates to the £

	US Dollar	French franc[a]	D-mark[b]	Yen
1900	4.872	25.38	20.72	9.9
1905	4.866	25.31	20.62	9.8
1910	4.868	25.45	20.71	9.9
1915	4.748	26.51	...	...
1920	3.661	52.47	404.59	7.6
1925	4.829	102.54	20.41	11.9
1930	4.862	123.88	20.38	9.9
1935	4.903	74.27	12.18	17.1
1940	4.030	176.62	...	16.8
1945	4.030	203.89	...	60.5
1950	2.800	980.00	...	1010.2
1955	2.800	978.10	11.74	1011.4
1960	2.808	13.77	11.71	1008.2
1965	2.796	13.7	11.17	1013.0
1970	2.396	13.24	8.74	857.8

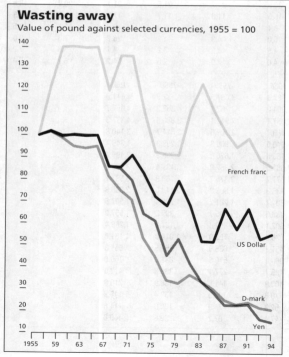

Wasting away
Value of pound against selected currencies, 1955 = 100

a New Franc introduced 1959.
b Reichsmark 1900–1929.

	US Dollar	French franc	D-mark	Yen
1975	2.220	9.50	5.45	658.1
1980	2.328	9.82	4.23	525.6
1981	2.028	11.02	4.58	444.6
1982	1.751	11.50	4.25	435.2
1983	1.517	11.56	3.87	359.9
1984	1.336	11.68	3.80	316.8
1985	1.298	11.55	3.78	307.1
1986	1.467	10.16	3.19	246.8
1987	1.639	9.85	2.95	236.5
1988	1.781	10.61	3.13	228.0
1989	1.640	10.46	3.08	226.2
1990	1.785	9.72	2.88	258.4
1991	1.769	9.98	2.94	238.4
1992	1.766	9.35	2.76	223.6
1993	1.502	8.51	2.48	167.0

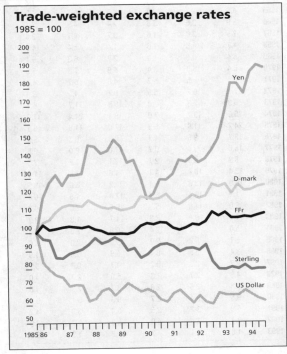

Trade-weighted exchange rates
1985 = 100

For an explanation of trade-weighted exchange rates, see page 12.

Inflation's ups and downs

Consumer price changes compared
% change on a year earlier

	UK	France	Germany[a]	Italy	Japan	USA
1950	3.1	8.0	-6.2	-1.0	-7.1	-1.4
1951	7.3	17.7	7.7	12.5	16.5	8.0
1952	7.2	12.0	2.1	1.9	5.0	2.2
1953	1.5	-1.9	-1.9	1.4	6.6	0.8
1954	1.1	0.4	0.2	2.9	6.5	0.4
1955	4.0	1.0	1.7	2.3	-1.0	-0.3
1956	4.9	4.3	2.6	3.4	0.0	1.5
1957	3.7	-0.8	2.1	1.2	3.3	3.5
1958	2.2	15.3	2.1	2.9	-0.3	2.8
1959	0.0	5.7	1.0	-0.5	1.0	0.8
1960	0.9	4.2	1.5	2.4	3.8	1.6
1961	3.4	2.4	2.3	2.1	5.4	1.1
1962	4.2	5.2	2.9	4.6	6.6	1.1
1963	2.0	5.1	3.0	7.6	7.8	1.2
1964	3.4	3.2	2.4	5.9	3.7	1.3
1965	4.6	2.7	3.2	4.5	6.7	1.6
1966	3.9	2.6	3.6	2.4	4.9	3.1
1967	2.5	2.8	1.6	3.7	4.1	2.8
1968	4.7	4.6	1.6	1.4	5.4	4.2
1969	5.4	6.1	1.9	2.7	5.3	5.4
1970	6.4	5.9	3.4	4.9	7.6	5.9
1971	9.4	5.5	5.2	4.8	6.2	4.3
1972	7.1	6.2	5.5	5.7	4.5	3.3
1973	9.3	7.3	7.0	10.8	11.7	6.2
1974	16.0	13.7	7.0	19.1	24.4	11.0
1975	24.2	11.8	5.9	17.0	11.8	9.1
1976	16.7	9.6	4.3	16.8	9.3	5.8
1977	15.8	9.4	3.7	17.0	8.0	6.5
1978	8.3	9.1	2.7	12.1	3.8	7.6
1979	13.4	10.8	4.1	14.8	3.6	11.3
1980	18.0	13.3	5.4	21.2	8.0	13.5
1981	11.9	13.4	6.3	17.8	4.9	10.4
1982	8.6	11.8	5.3	16.5	2.6	6.2
1983	4.6	9.6	3.3	14.7	1.8	3.2
1984	5.0	7.4	2.4	10.8	2.3	4.3
1985	6.1	5.8	2.2	9.2	2.0	3.6
1986	3.4	2.5	-0.1	5.9	0.6	1.9
1987	4.2	3.3	0.2	4.7	0.0	3.7
1988	4.9	2.7	1.3	5.0	0.7	4.0
1989	7.8	3.5	2.8	6.2	2.3	4.8
1990	9.5	3.4	2.7	6.3	3.1	5.4
1991	5.9	3.2	3.5	6.4	3.3	4.2
1992	3.7	2.4	4.0	5.3	1.7	3.0
1993	1.6	2.1	4.2	4.2	1.3	3.0

a Western.

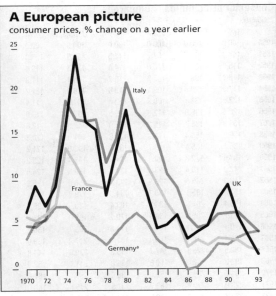

A European picture
consumer prices, % change on a year earlier

Italy
France
UK
Germanyª

1970 72 74 76 78 80 82 84 86 88 90 93

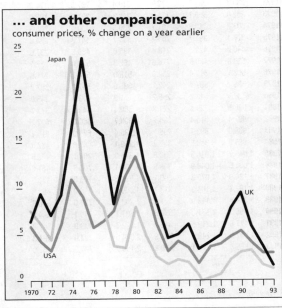

... and other comparisons
consumer prices, % change on a year earlier

Japan
UK
USA

1970 72 74 76 78 80 82 84 86 88 90 93

Consumer price indices compared
1950=100

	UK	France	Germany[a]	Italy	Japan	USA
1950	100.0	100.0	100.0	100.0	100.0	100.0
1951	107.3	117.7	107.7	112.5	116.5	108.0
1952	115.0	131.8	110.0	114.6	122.3	110.4
1953	116.7	129.3	107.9	116.2	130.4	111.3
1954	117.9	129.8	108.1	119.6	138.9	111.7
1955	122.6	131.1	109.9	122.4	137.5	111.4
1956	128.6	136.8	112.8	126.5	137.5	113.0
1957	133.3	135.7	115.2	128.0	142.0	117.0
1958	136.3	156.4	117.6	131.8	141.6	120.3
1959	136.3	165.4	118.7	131.1	143.0	121.2
1960	137.6	172.3	120.5	134.2	148.4	123.2
1961	142.3	176.4	123.3	137.1	156.5	124.5
1962	148.3	185.6	126.9	143.4	166.8	125.9
1963	151.3	195.1	130.7	154.3	179.8	127.4
1964	156.4	201.3	133.8	163.4	186.5	129.1
1965	163.7	206.8	138.1	170.7	198.9	131.1
1966	170.1	212.1	143.1	174.8	208.7	135.2
1967	174.4	218.1	145.4	181.3	217.2	139.0
1968	182.5	228.1	147.7	183.8	229.0	144.8
1969	192.3	242.0	150.5	188.8	241.1	152.6
1970	204.7	256.3	155.6	198.0	259.4	161.6
1971	223.9	270.4	163.7	207.5	275.5	168.6
1972	239.7	287.2	172.7	219.4	287.9	174.2
1973	262.0	308.1	184.8	243.1	321.6	185.0
1974	303.8	350.3	197.7	289.5	400.1	205.3
1975	377.4	391.7	209.4	338.7	447.3	224.0
1976	440.2	429.3	218.4	395.6	488.9	237.0
1977	509.8	469.6	226.5	462.9	528.0	252.4
1978	552.1	512.4	232.6	518.9	548.1	271.6
1979	626.1	567.7	242.1	595.6	567.8	302.2
1980	738.5	643.2	255.2	721.9	613.2	343.0
1981	826.5	729.4	271.3	850.4	643.3	378.7
1982	897.4	815.4	285.7	990.7	660.0	402.2
1983	938.9	893.7	295.1	1,136.4	671.9	415.1
1984	985.9	959.9	302.2	1,259.1	687.3	432.9
1985	1,045.7	1,015.5	308.8	1,375.0	701.1	448.5
1986	1,081.6	1,040.9	308.5	1,456.1	705.3	457.0
1987	1,126.9	1,075.3	309.1	1,524.5	705.3	473.9
1988	1,182.1	1,104.3	313.1	1,600.7	710.2	492.9
1989	1,274.4	1,143.0	321.9	1,700.0	726.6	516.6
1990	1,395.3	1,181.8	330.6	1,807.1	749.1	544.5
1991	1,477.8	1,219.6	342.2	1,922.7	773.8	567.3
1992	1,532.5	1,248.9	355.9	2,024.6	787.0	584.3
1993	1,556.8	1,275.1	370.8	2,109.7	797.2	601.9

a Western.

Consumer price inflation since 1800
1800 = 100

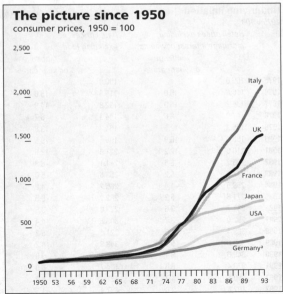

The picture since 1950
consumer prices, 1950 = 100

Producer prices
1975 = 100

	Output – all manufactured products: home sales		Input – materials and fuels purchased by manuf. industry	
		% change on year earlier		% change on year earlier
1975	100.0	23.1	100.0	10.3
1976	116.7	16.5	125.9	25.8
1977	138.6	18.9	143.2	13.8
1978	151.2	9.0	143.5	0.1
1979	168.9	11.8	167.3	16.7
1980	195.9	15.9	196.7	17.5
1981	216.7	10.7	222.9	13.3
1982	235.5	8.6	236.7	6.3
1983	250.5	6.5	249.7	5.5
1984	265.5	6.0	274.1	9.7
1985	281.9	6.2	274.1	0.0
1986	286.0	1.4	229.9	-16.2
1987	295.9	3.4	234.2	1.9
1988	306.5	3.7	239.7	2.4
1989	321.2	4.8	253.0	5.5
1990	341.3	6.2	251.3	-0.7
1991	359.7	5.4	245.7	-2.1
1992	371.0	3.1	244.7	-0.5
1993	385.3	4.0	255.8	4.5

Underlying inflation
1975 = 100

	Retail prices excluding mortgage interest payments		Retail prices excluding food	
		% change on year earlier		% change on year earlier
1975	100.0		100.0	
1976	116.6	16.6	115.6	15.6
1977	135.2	15.9	132.8	14.9
1978	147.0	8.6	144.3	8.7
1979	165.3	12.5	164.2	13.8
1980	193.1	16.9	196.5	19.6
1981	216.6	12.2	221.6	12.8
1982	235.2	8.5	241.1	8.8
1983	247.3	5.2	253.0	5.0
1984	258.5	4.4	265.2	4.8
1985	271.6	5.2	283.2	6.8
1986	281.7	3.6	293.0	3.5
1987	292.0	3.7	305.8	4.4
1988	305.4	4.6	321.5	5.2
1989	323.5	5.9	348.0	8.2
1990	349.6	8.1	381.9	9.8
1991	373.4	6.8	404.7	6.0
1992	390.8	4.7	421.1	4.0
1993	402.6	3.0	427.4	1.5

Part IV

GOVERNMENT FINANCE

Revenue and spending

Raising it

£bn

	Personal taxes	Corporate taxes	Customs & excise	Social security	Total receipts
1885	0.02	…	0.05	…	0.09
1890	0.01	…	0.05	…	0.10
1895	0.02	…	0.05	…	0.11
1900	0.03	…	0.07	…	0.14
1905	0.03	…	0.07	…	0.15
1910	0.06	…	0.07	…	0.20
1915	0.13	0.14	0.12	…	0.34
1920	0.39	0.22	0.33	…	1.43
1925	0.33	0.01	0.24	…	0.81
1930	0.32	0.00	0.25	…	0.86
1935	0.29	0.00	0.30	…	0.85
1940	0.55	0.07	0.51	…	1.28
1945	1.43	0.47	1.21	…	3.27
1950	1.42	0.26	1.58	0.44	5.02
1955	1.96	0.20	1.99	0.59	6.30
1960	2.29	0.26	2.37	0.91	8.10
1965	3.37	0.47	3.43	1.68	12.22
1970	5.49	1.67	5.13	2.66	21.21
1975	14.32	2.32	9.08	6.85	42.96
1980	24.31	4.84	22.56	13.94	91.71
1985	35.17	9.05	38.61	24.19	147.14
1990	53.74	22.06	54.79	32.50	191.79
1995	57.36	15.29	66.10	36.54	206.54

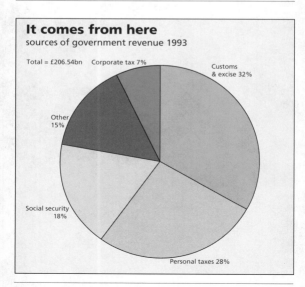

It comes from here
sources of government revenue 1993

Total = £206.54bn

Corporate tax 7%

Customs & excise 32%

Other 15%

Social security 18%

Personal taxes 28%

REVENUE AND SPENDING **67**

Spending it
£bn

	Defence	Education	Health & social services	Debt interest	Total spending
1885	...	...	...	...	...
1890	0.03	0.03	...	0.02	0.13
1895	0.04	0.04	...	0.02	0.16
1900	0.13	0.05	...	0.02	0.28
1905	0.06	0.07	...	0.02	0.24
1910	0.07	0.09	...	0.02	0.27
1915	0.72	0.09	...	0.06	0.96
1920	0.52	0.10	0.26	0.32	1.59
1925	0.13	0.10	0.24	0.30	1.07
1930	0.12	0.11	0.32	0.29	1.15
1935	0.14	0.12	0.35	0.21	1.12
1940	...	...	...	...	...
1945	...	...	...	0.53	4.59
1950	0.86	0.37	1.21	0.55	4.50
1955	1.54	0.55	1.69	0.77	6.26
1960	1.63	0.92	2.49	1.02	8.34
1965	2.11	1.59	3.91	1.35	12.38
1970	2.46	2.53	6.33	2.03	20.91
1975	5.17	6.63	15.43	4.13	51.48
1980	11.44	12.75	37.07	10.87	104.20
1985	18.26	17.40	64.39	17.47	157.38
1990	21.82	26.53	92.33	16.40	190.68
1995	23.44	33.71	123.27	17.72	252.70

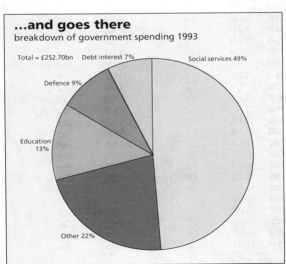

...and goes there
breakdown of government spending 1993

Total = £252.70bn

Debt interest 7%
Social services 49%
Defence 9%
Education 13%
Other 22%

Reserves, rates and money supply

Official reserves
End year

	$bn		$bn		$bn
1945	2.48	1962	2.81	1979	22.54
1946	2.70	1963	0.95	1980	27.48
1947	2.08	1964	0.83	1981	23.35
1948	1.86	1965	1.07	1982	17.00
1949	1.69	1966	1.11	1983	17.82
1950	3.30	1967	1.12	1984	15.69
1951	2.34	1968	1.01	1985	15.54
1952	1.85	1969	1.05	1986	21.92
1953	2.52	1970	1.18	1987	44.33
1954	2.76	1971	2.53	1988	51.69
1955	2.12	1972	2.17	1989	38.65
1956	2.13	1973	2.24	1990	38.46
1957	2.27	1974	6.79	1991	44.13
1958	3.07	1975	5.43	1992	41.65
1959	2.74	1976	4.13	1993	42.93
1960	3.23	1977	20.56	1994[a]	43.37
1961	3.32	1978	15.69		

Money supply
Amount outstanding, end period

	M0 £bn	% increase on year earlier	M4 £bn	% increase on year earlier
1970	4.099		26.644	
1971	4.289	4.6	30.973	16.2
1972	4.845	13.0	38.161	23.2
1973	5.339	10.2	46.556	22.0
1974	6.158	15.3	51.669	11.0
1975	6.873	11.6	57.938	12.1
1976	7.649	11.3	64.524	11.4
1977	8.652	13.1	74.092	14.8
1978	9.837	13.7	85.098	14.9
1979	11.014	12.0	97.317	14.4
1980	11.650	5.8	114.128	17.3
1981	11.925	2.4	137.812	20.8
1982	12.301	3.2	154.909	12.4
1983	13.038	6.0	175.462	13.3
1984	13.746	5.4	199.177	13.5
1985	14.278	3.9	225.109	13.0
1986	15.027	5.2	261.235	16.0
1987	15.663	4.2	303.007	16.0
1988	16.869	7.7	355.424	17.3
1989	17.826	5.7	422.337	18.8
1990	18.299	2.7	473.561	12.1
1991	18.854	3.0	501.624	5.9
1992	19.360	2.7	519.069	3.5
1993	20.496	5.9	548.758	5.7
1994[a]	21.643	7.2	562.303	4.8

a End September.

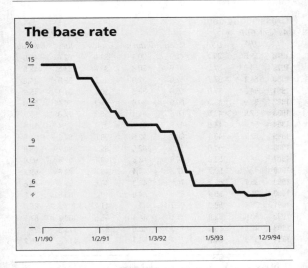

The base rate
%

Table along x-axis: 1/1/90, 1/2/91, 1/3/92, 1/5/93, 12/9/94

Interest rates
End year

	Base rate	3-month	5-year	20-year
			Government bonds	
1971	4.50	4.75	6.69	8.90
1972	7.50	9.06	7.55	8.90
1973	13.00	16.31	10.41	10.71
1974	12.00	12.83	12.51	14.77
1975	11.00	11.19	10.57	14.39
1976	14.00	14.63	12.06	14.43
1977	7.50	6.75	10.08	12.73
1978	12.50	12.63	11.32	12.47
1979	17.00	17.06	11.73	12.99
1980	14.00	14.88	13.84	13.79
1981	14.50	15.75	14.65	14.74
1982	10.25	10.63	12.79	12.88
1983	9.00	9.41	11.19	10.81
1984	9.75	10.13	11.29	10.69
1985	11.50	11.94	11.13	10.62
1986	11.00	11.13	10.01	9.87
1987	8.50	9.00	9.36	9.48
1988	13.00	13.19	9.66	9.36
1989	15.00	15.16	10.73	9.58
1990	14.00	14.00	12.08	11.08
1991	10.50	11.00	10.18	9.92
1992	7.00	7.25	8.96	9.15
1993	5.50	5.31	6.65	7.87
1994[a]	5.25	5.13	7.51	7.83

For definitions of money supply and reserves, see page 12.

Public debt

Gross public debt
As % of GDP

	UK	USA	Japan	Germany[a]	France	Italy	Canada
1978	58.6	39.2	41.9	30.1	31.0	62.4	46.6
1979	54.9	37.2	47.0	30.8	31.4	61.5	43.8
1980	54.1	37.7	52.0	32.8	30.9	59.0	44.6
1981	54.3	37.0	56.8	36.5	30.1	61.1	45.2
1982	52.9	41.0	60.9	39.6	34.2	66.4	50.3
1983	52.9	43.6	66.6	41.1	35.3	72.0	55.7
1984	54.4	44.9	67.9	41.7	37.1	77.4	59.4
1985	52.7	48.1	68.7	42.5	38.6	84.3	64.9
1986	51.1	51.0	72.3	42.5	39.3	88.2	68.8
1987	48.6	52.0	74.9	43.8	40.7	92.6	69.6
1988	42.2	52.7	72.9	44.4	40.6	94.8	69.2
1989	36.7	53.2	70.6	43.2	40.6	97.9	69.8
1990	34.6	55.4	69.8	44.0	40.2	100.5	72.5
1991	35.4	58.9	67.7	41.7	41.2	103.8	80.0
1992	40.6	62.0	71.1	44.4	45.5	108.3	87.5
1993	46.5	63.9	74.7	48.5	52.5	113.9	92.3
1994[b]	50.5	64.2	79.4	53.7	57.2	118.3	95.2

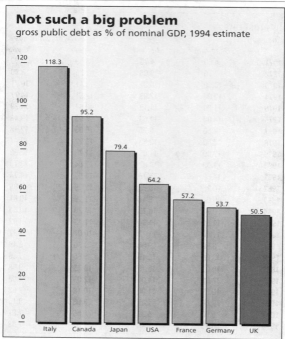

Not such a big problem
gross public debt as % of nominal GDP, 1994 estimate

	Italy	Canada	Japan	USA	France	Germany	UK
	118.3	95.2	79.4	64.2	57.2	53.7	50.5

a Western Germany up to 1990.

The interest burden
General government net debt interest payments as % of total expenditure

	UK	USA	Japan	Germany[a]	France	Italy	Canada
1978	6.2	3.7	2.0	1.9	1.4	10.5	4.2
1979	6.7	3.6	2.7	2.3	1.8	10.5	4.6
1980	7.1	3.7	3.3	2.7	1.8	11.1	4.9
1981	7.5	4.7	4.0	3.2	2.5	11.9	5.9
1982	7.2	4.9	4.4	4.0	2.4	13.8	6.5
1983	6.9	5.1	5.0	4.8	3.4	14.3	6.5
1984	7.4	6.1	5.5	4.9	3.6	15.2	7.9
1985	7.6	6.2	5.5	4.9	3.9	14.5	8.9
1986	7.4	5.9	5.1	5.0	4.1	15.3	9.4
1987	7.5	5.9	3.9	5.1	4.2	14.7	9.7
1988	7.0	6.0	3.3	5.1	4.2	15.2	10.1
1989	6.4	6.1	2.8	4.9	4.5	16.4	11.1
1990	5.8	6.3	1.7	4.6	4.8	17.1	11.7
1991	5.2	6.7	1.0	4.6	5.0	18.1	10.8
1992	4.8	6.2	0.9	6.1	5.5	20.4	10.1
1993	5.0	5.7	0.8	6.4	5.7	20.4	10.3
1994[b]	5.7	6.2	1.0	7.7	6.0	18.0	10.3

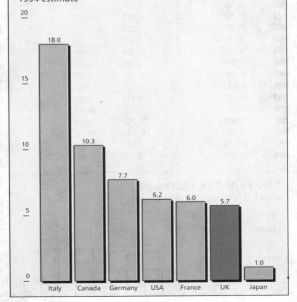

Interesting comparisons
general government net debt as % of total expenditure,
1994 estimate

b Forecasts.

Taxes

The tax take
£m

	Income tax	Surtax	Corporation tax	Capital gains tax	Estate duty
1908	34	...	...	...	18
1918	258	36	...	...	31
1928	327	56	...	...	81
1938	336	63	...	...	77
1948	1,360	100	...	...	178
1958	2,318	168	...	...	187
1968	4,349	225	1,344	47	382
1969	4,907	255	1,697	128	365
1970	5,731	248	1,583	139	357
1971	6,432	348	1,554	155	451
1972	6,477	341	1,533	208	459
1973	7,137	307	2,262	324	412
1974	10,271	186	2,859	382	339
1975	15,041	109	1,996	387	212
1976	17,014	62	2,655	323	124
1977	17,420	30	3,343	340	87
1978	18,748	15	3,940	353	46
1979	20,599	11	4,646	431	32
1980	24,295	5	4,645	508	27
1981	28,720	4	4,930	526	17
1982	30,361	2	5,677	632	12
1983	31,108	2	8,184	671	9
1984	32,507	1	8,341	730	6
1985	35,353	...	10,708	908	6
1986	38,499	...	13,495	1,064	7
1987	41,402	...	15,734	1,379	...
1988	43,433	...	18,537	2,323	...
1989	48,801	...	21,495	1,854	...
1990	55,287	...	21,495	1,852	...
1991	57,493	...	18,263	1,140	...
1992	56,797	...	15,783	982	...
1993	58,442	...	14,887	710	...
1994	65,000	...	18,800	900	...

The real tax increase
total tax revenue £m, 1994 prices

| 100,000 |
| 80,000 |
| 60,000 |
| 40,000 |
| 20,000 |
| 0 |

1908 1918 1928 1938 1948 1958 1968 1969 1970 1971 1972 1973 1974 1975 19

Inheritance & capital transfer tax	Stamp duty	Development land tax	Other taxes	Total
...	8	...	36	96
...	12	...	287	624
...	30	...	3	407
...	21	...	24	521
...	57	...	360	2,055
...	66	...	275	3,012
...	124	...	75	6,546
...	119	...	21	7,492
...	117	...	5	8,180
...	166	...	4	9,110
...	228	...	2	9,248
...	190	...	2	10,634
...	198	...	1	14,236
118	281	...	1	18,143
259	272	1	...	20,711
311	376	7	...	21,914
323	433	13	183	24,055
401	620	26	1,435	28,201
425	641	27	3,410	32,983
480	797	38	4,770	40,282
499	873	65	5,669	43,790
599	1,138	68	6,017	45,796
658	911	81	7,177	50,412
881	1,226	62	6,375	55,520
988	1,860	55	1,188	57,156
1,078	2,440	28	2,296	64,357
1,071	2,255	15	1,371	69,005
1,232	2,117	10	1,050	76,559
1,262	1,703	4	860	82,464
1,299	1,697	1	-216	79,676
1,211	1,264	1	69	76,107
1,333	1,737	1	359	77,469
1,400	1,900	...	500	88,500

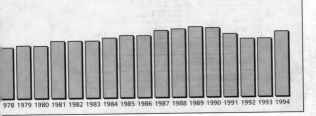

978 1979 1980 1981 1982 1983 1984 1985 1986 1987 1988 1989 1990 1991 1992 1993 1994

Tax comparisons

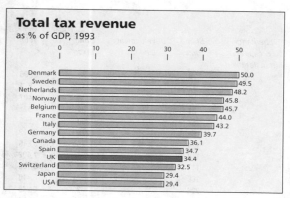

Total tax revenue
as % of GDP, 1993

Denmark	50.0
Sweden	49.5
Netherlands	48.2
Norway	45.8
Belgium	45.7
France	44.0
Italy	43.2
Germany	39.7
Canada	36.1
Spain	34.7
UK	34.4
Switzerland	32.5
Japan	29.4
USA	29.4

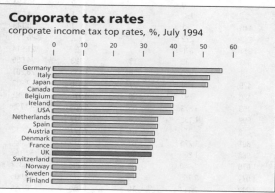

Corporate tax rates
corporate income tax top rates, %, July 1994

Germany
Italy
Japan
Canada
Belgium
Ireland
USA
Netherlands
Spain
Austria
Denmark
France
UK
Switzerland
Norway
Sweden
Finland

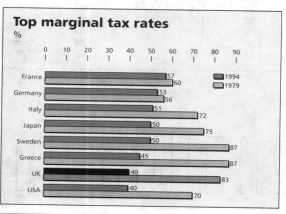

Top marginal tax rates
%

1994
1979

	1994	1979
France	57	60
Germany	53	56
Italy	51	72
Japan	50	75
Sweden	50	87
Greece	45	87
UK	40	83
USA	40	70

= Part V =
LABOUR

Employment

Breakdown of workforce
'000

	Total	Agriculture, forestry & fishing	Mining & quarrying	Manufacturing	Construction
1900	18,020	2,420	1,020	5,990	1,090
1905	18,400	…	…	…	…
1910	19,280	2,400	1,290	6,550	1,030
1915	20,890	…	…	…	…
1920	20,297	1,741	1,325	7,208	927
1925	18,588	1,576	1,205	6,227	924
1930	19,115	1,460	1,034	6,066	1,035
1935	20,037	1,370	870	6,387	1,141
1940	23,100	…	…	…	…
1945	24,200	…	…	…	…
1950	23,257	806	857	8,520	1,325
1955	24,298	692	867	9,222	1,385
1960	24,183	743	740	8,418	1,426
1965	25,204	605	597	8,561	1,621
1970	24,753	466	410	8,342	1,339
1975	25,050	397	352	7,490	1,314
1980	25,327	361	a	6,940	1,252
1985	24,539	341	a	5,365	1,022
1990	26,881	277	a	4,993	1,060
1993	24,924	258	a	3,890	812

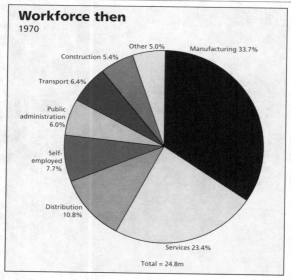

Workforce then
1970

Manufacturing 33.7%
Services 23.4%
Distribution 10.8%
Self-employed 7.7%
Public administration 6.0%
Transport 6.4%
Construction 5.4%
Other 5.0%

Total = 24.8m

a Included with gas, electricity and water under new heading of energy and water supply.

Gas, electricity & water	Transport & commun- ication	Distributive trades	Services	Public administration & defence	Self- employed
100	1,450	1,990	3,590	880	...
...	...	...	...	...	...
120	1,580	2,460	3,890	840	...
...	...	...	...	...	...
185	1,641	2,352	3,521	637	...
199	1,558	2,320	3,630	599	...
230	1,595	2,724	3,980	664	...
263	1,579	2,965	4,411	718	...
...	...	...	...	...	...
...	...	...	...	...	...
360	1,769	2,130	3,573	1,402	1,802
384	1,708	2,378	3,755	1,331	1,787
380	1,652	2,737	4,490	1,287	1,766
419	1,648	2,909	5,327	1,374	1,696
391	1,572	2,675	5,802	1,481	1,902
353	1,518	2,763	6,861	1,657	1,993
726	1,483	3,090	7,451	1,669	2,013
589	1,345	3,001	8,229	1,613	2,610
441	1,361	3,499	9,014	1,942	3,259
350	1,256	3,283	8,841	1,810	2,989

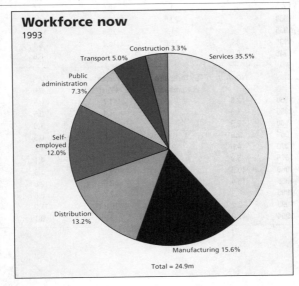

Workforce now
1993

Construction 3.3%
Transport 5.0%
Public administration 7.3%
Self-employed 12.0%
Distribution 13.2%
Manufacturing 15.6%
Services 35.5%

Total = 24.9m

Unemployment

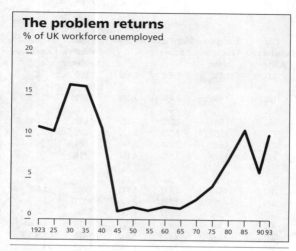

The problem returns
% of UK workforce unemployed

Regional trends

% of workforce unemployed

	North	North East	North West	Midlands
1923	...	11.5	14.2	9.9
1925	...	14.6	10.9	8.5
1930	...	20.8	23.9	14.9
1935	...	21.8	20.4	11.1
1939	18.7	11.8	15.4	8.1
1945	0.5	0.5	0.5	0.6

	North	Yorkshire & Humberside	North West	West Midlands
1950	2.6	...	1.7	0.6
1955	1.8	...	1.4	0.5
1960	2.9	...	1.9	1.0
1965	2.6	1.1	1.6	0.9
1970	4.6	2.8	2.7	1.9
1975	5.9	4.0	5.3	4.1
1980	10.9	7.8	9.3	7.8
1985	15.4	12.0	13.7	12.8
1990	8.9	6.8	7.7	6.0
1993	12.2	10.4	10.8	11.0
1994a	11.0	9.2	9.2	9.1

a October.

National trends
% of workforce unemployed

	Total	Wales	Scotland	N. Ireland
1923	11.2	6.3	13.8	16.4
1925	10.7	16.9	14.7	22.8
1930	16.3	26.7	18.7	22.6
1935	16.1	33.3	23.2	25.3
1939	11.1	22.0	16.1	26.2
1945	1.0	4.0	2.0	5.6
1950	1.5	4.0	3.0	6.5
1955	1.1	1.8	2.4	6.8
1960	1.6	2.7	3.6	6.7
1965	1.4	2.6	3.0	6.1
1970	2.5	3.8	4.2	6.8
1975	4.1	5.6	5.2	7.9
1980	7.3	10.3	10.0	13.7
1985	10.9	13.6	12.9	16.0
1990	5.8	6.6	8.0	13.3
1993	10.3	10.3	9.7	14.0
1994ª	8.9	9.0	8.8	12.7

South East	South West
9.2	10.4
5.5	8.0
8.0	10.5
8.5	12.3
8.6	7.2
0.7	0.7

East Midlands	East Anglia	South East	South West
0.7	...	1.1	1.4
0.6	...	0.7	1.1
1.1	...	1.0	1.7
0.9	1.3	0.9	1.6
2.2	2.1	1.6	2.8
3.6	3.4	2.8	4.7
6.4	5.7	4.8	6.7
9.8	8.1	8.1	9.3
5.1	3.7	4.0	4.4
9.6	8.4	9.1	9.8
8.4	6.8	8.7	8.0

Earnings

Pay norms
Average weekly earnings in manufacturing, £

	Men	% increase on previous year	Women	% increase on previous year
1947	6.71	6.0	3.50	6.7
1948	6.93	3.3	3.67	4.9
1949	7.40	6.8	3.95	7.6
1950	7.83	5.8	4.14	4.8
1951	8.60	9.8	4.50	8.7
1952	9.24	7.4	4.77	6.0
1953	9.83	6.4	5.15	8.0
1954	10.61	7.9	5.43	5.4
1955	11.55	8.9	5.78	6.4
1956	12.28	6.3	6.17	6.7
1957	13.06	6.4	6.49	5.2
1958	13.27	1.6	6.70	3.2
1959	14.21	7.1	7.07	5.5
1960	15.11	6.3	7.41	4.8
1961	15.89	5.2	7.71	4.0
1962	16.34	2.8	8.03	4.2
1963	17.29	5.8	8.41	4.7
1964	18.67	8.0	8.95	6.4
1965	20.16	8.0	9.60	7.3
1966	20.78	3.1	10.06	4.8
1967	21.89	5.3	10.54	4.8
1968	23.62	7.9	11.31	7.3
1969	25.54	8.1	11.87	5.0
1970	28.91	13.2	14.34	20.8
1971	31.37	8.5	15.80	10.2
1972	36.20	15.4	19.40	22.8
1973	41.23	13.9	22.68	16.9
1974	48.77	18.3	27.05	19.3
1975	59.32	21.6	34.23	26.5
1976	67.35	13.5	40.71	18.9
1977	73.04	8.4	44.46	9.2
1978	84.17	15.2	50.10	12.7
1979	97.59	15.9	58.46	16.7
1980	110.85	13.6	68.42	17.0
1981	122.36	10.4	75.73	10.7
1982	133.31	8.9	83.20	9.9
1983	146.19	9.7	90.32	8.6
1984	157.50	7.7	96.30	6.6
1985	172.60	9.6	104.50	8.5
1986	183.40	6.3	111.60	6.8
1987	195.90	6.8	119.60	7.2
1988	212.30	8.4	127.90	6.9
1989	230.60	8.6	138.20	8.1
1990	251.40	9.0	152.80	10.6
1991	261.80	4.1	162.10	6.1
1992	279.70	6.8	174.40	7.6
1993	287.90	2.9	182.40	4.6

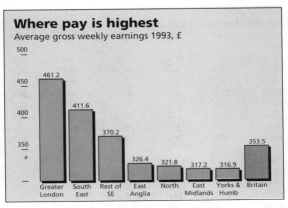

Where pay is highest
Average gross weekly earnings 1993, £

- Greater London 461.2
- South East 411.6
- Rest of SE 370.2
- East Anglia 326.4
- North 321.8
- East Midlands 317.2
- Yorks & Humb 316.9
- Britain 353.5

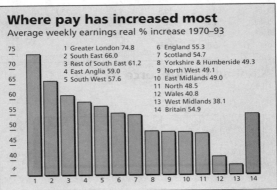

Where pay has increased most
Average weekly earnings real % increase 1970–93

1 Greater London 74.8
2 South East 66.0
3 Rest of South East 61.2
4 East Anglia 59.0
5 South West 57.6
6 England 55.3
7 Scotland 54.7
8 Yorkshire & Humberside 49.3
9 North West 49.1
10 East Midlands 49.0
11 North 48.5
12 Wales 40.8
13 West Midlands 38.1
14 Britain 54.9

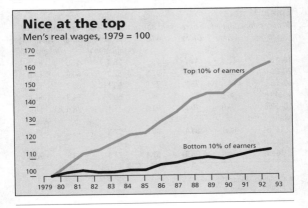

Nice at the top
Men's real wages, 1979 = 100

Top 10% of earners

Bottom 10% of earners

Sex, age and race

Middle-aged peak

% of resident population in relevant age group in civilian labour force

	1984	1986	1990	1991	1992
Men					
16–19	73.5	73.2	75.6	73.4	70.6
20–24	85.0	86.2	86.8	85.6	84.4
25–34	93.7	93.7	94.3	93.9	93.2
35–44	95.4	94.8	94.7	94.7	94.0
45–54	93.0	91.8	91.5	91.0	91.0
55–59	82.5	81.1	81.0	80.3	78.0
60–64	57.3	53.8	54.4	54.1	52.9
16+	74.5	73.8	74.3	73.7	73.0
Women					
16–19	69.4	70.3	71.5	70.7	67.3
20–24	70.2	70.7	75.1	72.7	71.8
25–34	61.1	63.5	70.0	69.7	69.4
35–44	70.9	72.1	76.5	76.7	77.0
45–54	69.5	70.5	72.8	72.7	74.5
55–59	51.8	51.8	54.9	54.5	54.7
60–64	21.8	19.1	22.7	24.1	23.4
16+	49.0	49.6	52.9	52.6	52.6

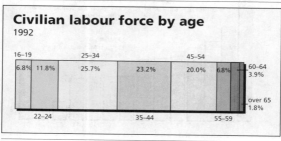

Civilian labour force by age
1992

16–19 6.8% | 22–24 11.8% | 25–34 25.7% | 35–44 23.2% | 45–54 20.0% | 55–59 6.8% | 60–64 3.9% | over 65 1.8%

Ethnic factors

% of resident population in relevant age group in civilian labour force

	White	Black[a]	Indian	Pakistani/ Bangladeshi	Other[b]	All ethnic groups
16–19	62.0	41.7	25.1	35.4	47.0	60.1
20–29	82.1	75.2	72.5	52.8	60.0	81.0
30–39	84.5	75.2	77.6	52.1	68.7	83.5
40–49	86.7	87.3	86.3	50.2	84.3	86.4
50–59/64	69.0	70.3	61.3	41.1	75.5	68.7
Males aged						
16–64	86.1	80.4	80.8	72.3	76.0	85.6
Females aged						
16–59	71.9	66.0	61.4	24.8	58.6	70.8

a Caribbean, African.
b Includes Chinese.

Women at work

Now equal in numbers
Employed in the workforce, '000

	Male	Female	Women as % of total workforce
1923	8,493	2,993	26.1
1925	8,717	3,175	26.7
1930	8,932	3,474	28.0
1935	10,055	3,527	26.0
1945	8,602	5,398	38.6
1950	13,937	7,118	33.8
1955	14,224	7,689	35.1
1960	14,719	8,098	35.5
1965	15,243	8,677	36.3
1970	14,604	8,842	37.7
1970	13,952	8,450	37.7
1975	13,443	9,170	40.6
1980	12,929	9,456	42.2
1985	11,858	9,560	44.6
1990	11,878	10,841	47.7
1991	11,341	10,670	48.5
1992	10,970	10,552	49.0
1993	10,883	10,656	49.5

But room for more at the top
% of women in top positions

	1992	1993	1994
Chairmen	0.4	0.3	0.1
Chief Executive/ Managing Directors	0.5	0.7	0.6
Finance Directors	0.9	1.3	1.5
Finance Controllers/ Chief Accountants	3.0	6.1	10.8
Investor Relations Officers	11.2	12.9	13.7
Company Secretaries	5.3	6.6	7.0
Other senior positions	1.3	1.3	2.0
Total	2.1	2.6	2.8

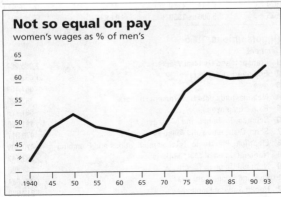

Not so equal on pay
women's wages as % of men's

Unions

The rise and fall of union appeal
Total union members, '000s

Year	Members	Year	Members	Year	Members	Year	Members
1892	1,576	1926	5,219	1960	9,835		
1893	1,559	1927	4,919	1961	9,916		
1894	1,530	1928	4,806	1962	10,014		
1895	1,504	1929	4,858	1963	10,067		
1896	1,608	1930	4,842	1964	10,218		
1897	1,731	1931	4,624	1965	10,325		
1898	1,752	1932	4,444	1966	10,259		
1899	1,911	1933	4,392	1967	10,194		
1900	2,022	1934	4,590	1968	10,200		
1901	2,025	1935	4,867	1969	10,471		
1902	2,013	1936	5,295	1970	11,187		
1903	1,994	1937	5,842	1971	11,135		
1904	1,967	1938	6,053	1972	11,359		
1905	1,997	1939	6,298	1973	11,456		
1906	2,210	1940	6,613	1974	11,764		
1907	2,513	1941	7,165	1975	12,193		
1908	2,485	1942	7,867	1976	12,386		
1909	2,477	1943	8,174	1977	12,846		
1910	2,565	1944	8,087	1978	13,112		
1911	3,139	1945	7,875	1979	13,477		
1912	3,416	1946	8,803	1980	12,952		
1913	4,135	1947	9,145	1981	12,311		
1914	4,145	1948	9,362	1982	11,744		
1915	4,359	1949	9,318	1983	11,300		
1916	4,644	1950	9,289	1984	11,064		
1917	5,499	1951	9,535	1985	10,819		
1918	6,533	1952	9,588	1986	10,598		
1919	7,926	1953	9,527	1987	10,480		
1920	8,348	1954	9,566	1988	10,387		
1921	6,633	1955	9,741	1989	10,043		
1922	5,625	1956	9,778	1990	9,810		
1923	5,429	1957	9,829	1991	9,489		
1924	5,544	1958	9,639	1992	8,929		
1925	5,506	1959	9,623				

Biggest unions, 1980
Members

1	Transport and General Workers	2,086,261
2	Engineering Workers	1,032,760
3	GMB	967,153
4	National and Local Government Officers	753,226
5	Public Employees	691,770
6	Science, Technical and Managerial	491,000
7	Shop, Distributive and Allied Workers	470,017
8	Electrical, Electronic, Telecommunications and Plumbing	420,000
9	National Union of Mineworkers	253,142
10	National Union of Teachers	248,896
11	Civil and Public Services	223,884
12	Health Service Employees	212,930

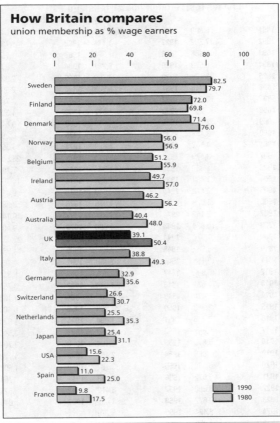

How Britain compares
union membership as % wage earners

Country	1990	1980
Sweden	82.5	79.7
Finland	72.0	69.8
Denmark	71.4	76.0
Norway	56.0	56.9
Belgium	51.2	55.9
Ireland	49.7	57.0
Austria	46.2	56.2
Australia	40.4	48.0
UK	39.1	50.4
Italy	38.8	49.3
Germany	32.9	35.6
Switzerland	26.6	30.7
Netherlands	25.5	35.3
Japan	25.4	31.1
USA	15.6	22.3
Spain	11.0	25.0
France	9.8	17.5

Biggest unions, 1994
Members

1	UNISON	1,486,984
2	Transport and General Workers	1,036,586
3	Amalgamated Engineering and Electrical	884,463
4	GMB	830,743
5	Manufacturing Science Finance	552,000
6	Shop, Distributive and Allied Workers	316,491
7	Graphical, Paper and Media	269,881
8	Communication Workers	175,266
9	National Union of Teachers	162,192
10	Construction, Allied Trades and Technicians	157,201
11	Banking, Insurance and Finance	153,582
12	Schoolmasters Union of Women Teachers	127,355

Strikes

Working days lost through industrial disputes[a]
'000s

Year	Days	Year	Days	Year	Days
1891	6,809	1926	162,233	1961	3,046
1892	17,382	1927	1,174	1962	5,798
1893	30,468	1928	1,388	1963	1,755
1894	9,529	1929	8,287	1964	2,277
1895	5,725	1930	4,399	1965	2,925
1896	3,746	1931	6,983	1966	2,398
1897	10,346	1932	6,488	1967	2,787
1898	15,289	1933	1,072	1968	4,690
1899	2,516	1934	959	1969	6,846
1900	3,153	1935	1,955	1970	10,980
1901	4,142	1936	1,829	1971	13,551
1902	3,479	1937	3,413	1972	23,909
1903	2,339	1938	1,334	1973	7,197
1904	1,484	1939	1,356	1974	14,750
1905	2,470	1940	940	1975	6,012
1906	3,029	1941	1,079	1976	3,284
1907	2,162	1942	1,527	1977	10,142
1908	10,834	1943	1,808	1978	9,405
1909	2,774	1944	3,714	1979	29,474
1910	9,867	1945	2,835	1980	11,964
1911	10,155	1946	2,158	1981	4,266
1912	40,890	1947	2,433	1982	5,313
1913	11,631	1948	1,944	1983	3,754
1914	9,878	1949	1,807	1984	27,135
1915	2,953	1950	1,389	1985	6,402
1916	2,446	1951	1,694	1986	1,920
1917	5,647	1952	1,792	1987	3,546
1918	5,875	1953	2,184	1988	3,702
1919	34,969	1954	2,457	1989	4,128
1920	26,568	1955	3,781	1990	1,903
1921	85,872	1956	2,083	1991	761
1922	19,850	1957	8,412	1992	528
1923	10,672	1958	3,462	1993	649
1924	8,424	1959	5,270		
1925	7,952	1960	3,024		

How Britain compares
Working days lost per 100,000 employees 1988–92

Country	Days	Country	Days
Greece	5,860	Portugal	70
Spain	660	USA	70
Canada	330	Norway	70
Italy	270	Belgium	40
Australia	210	France	40
New Zealand	190	Denmark	30
Finland	180	Germany	20
Ireland	160	Netherlands	10
UK	100	Austria	10
Sweden	100		

a 1891–1909 is Great Britain and Ireland; 1910 onwards is Great Britain and N. Ireland.

Part VI
BUSINESS
AND
FINANCE

Leading companies

The big thirty
By market capitalisation, £bn

1971

#	Company	£bn	#	Company	£bn
1	Shell	0.95	16	Prudential Assurance	0.15
2	British Petroleum	0.79	17	Guest Keen Nettlefolds	0.14
3	ICI	0.54	18	Nat. Westminster Bank	0.14
4	British American Tobacco	0.34	19	Commercial Union	0.14
5	Marks and Spencer	0.31	20	F.W. Woolworth UK	0.14
6	General Electric	0.25	21	Allied Breweries	0.13
7	RTZ	0.23	22	Barclays Bank	0.13
8	Great Universal Stores	0.23	23	Bass Charrington	0.13
9	Distillers	0.22	24	Plessey	0.12
10	Burmah Oil	0.20	25	Boots	0.12
11	Unilever	0.20	26	Glaxo	0.11
12	Imperial	0.19	27	Lloyds Bank	0.10
13	Courtaulds	0.16	28	Reed International	0.09
14	Beecham	0.15	29	Midland Bank	0.09
15	Royal Insurance	0.15	30	Thorn Electrical	0.09

1976

#	Company	£bn	#	Company	£bn
1	British Petroleum	4.55	16	Royal Insurance	0.92
2	Shell	4.23	17	Boots	0.91
3	ICI	3.34	18	Commercial Union	0.87
4	British American Tobacco	1.84	19	Courtaulds	0.82
5	Unilever	1.59	20	Midland Bank	0.78
6	General Electric	1.56	21	Allied Breweries	0.74
7	De Beers	1.34	22	Prudential Assurance	0.70
8	Marks and Spencer	1.26	23	Guest Keen Nettlefolds	0.68
9	Imperial	1.16	24	Glaxo Holdings	0.68
10	Barclays Bank	1.16	25	Lloyds Bank	0.61
11	Distillers	1.05	26	Standard Chartered Bank	0.59
12	Great Universal Stores	1.03	27	Thorn Electrical	0.58
13	Beecham	1.01	28	Land Securities	0.57
14	RTZ	0.94	29	F.W. Woolworth	0.56
15	Nat. Westminster Bank	0.93	30	Bass Charrington	0.54

1981

#	Company	£bn	#	Company	£bn
1	British Petroleum	16.52	16	Unilever	1.99
2	Shell	12.41	17	Grand Metropolitan	1.87
3	General Electric	7.96	18	Distillers	1.64
4	ICI	4.59	19	Bass	1.58
5	Marks and Spencer	3.62	20	Plessey	1.57
6	De Beers	3.58	21	Prudential Corporation	1.56
7	Barclays Bank	2.92	22	J. Sainsbury	1.46
8	Great Universal Stores	2.82	23	Lloyds Bank	1.37
9	Beecham	2.72	24	Commercial Union	1.36
10	RTZ	2.44	25	Standard Chartered Bank	1.35
11	Land Securities	2.38	26	Thorn-EMI	1.34
12	BAT Industries	2.25	27	Midland Bank	1.30
13	Nat. Westminster Bank	2.17	28	Burmah Oil	1.28
14	Racal Electronics	2.08	29	Royal Insurance	1.26
15	Boots	2.04	30	Imperial Group	1.23

1986

1	British Telecom	16.63	16	Unilever	3.65
2	British Petroleum	14.73	17	Nat. Westminster Bank	3.61
3	Shell	10.58	18	Prudential Corporation	3.41
4	Glaxo	8.23	19	Bass	3.10
5	ICI	7.23	20	Great Universal Stores	2.94
6	BTR	7.18	21	Imperial Group	2.79
7	Marks and Spencer	6.78	22	Boots	2.75
8	BAT Industries	6.72	23	Royal Insurance	2.71
9	General Electric	6.33	24	Allied-Lyons	2.70
10	Barclays Bank	4.72	25	Distillers	2.60
11	Grand Metropolitan	4.47	26	Lloyds Bank	2.51
12	Cable & Wireless	4.25	27	Burton	2.39
13	Hanson Trust	4.14	28	Sears	2.38
14	Beecham	3.93	29	Asda-MFI	2.36
15	J. Sainsbury	3.75	30	RTZ	2.33

1991

1	British Petroleum	34.54	16	J. Sainsbury	8.94
2	British Telecom	33.64	17	General Electric	8.85
3	Shell	29.28	18	RTZ	8.57
4	Glaxo	24.44	19	Nat. Westminster Bank	8.22
5	British Gas	18.50	20	SmithKline Beecham	8.21
6	Hanson Trust	17.12	21	De Beers	7.43
7	BAT Industries	16.53	22	Allied-Lyons	7.23
8	Guinness	13.18	23	LLoyds Bank	7.21
9	Grand Metropolitan	12.86	24	Bass	7.17
10	ICI	11.77	25	Wellcome	7.15
11	Marks and Spencer	11.64	26	Prudential	7.02
12	Barclays	11.08	27	Tesco	6.92
13	BTR	10.77	28	Boots	6.07
14	Unilever	10.49	29	Reuters	5.84
15	Cable & Wireless	9.14	30	Abbey National	5.81

1994

1	Shell	37.18	16	Unilever	12.60
2	British Telecom	35.17	17	General Electric	11.76
3	British Petroleum	34.58	18	Nat. Westminster Bank	11.45
4	Glaxo	26.64	19	Lloyds Bank	10.78
5	HSBC Holdings	21.19	20	Reuters	11.83
6	BAT Industries	20.89	21	J. Sainsbury	11.20
7	BTR	20.35	22	Zeneca	10.80
8	Hanson Trust	19.98	23	ICI	9.18
9	Marks and Spencer	18.03	24	Allied-Lyons	9.14
10	British Gas	17.85	25	De Beers	9.09
11	Cable & Wireless	14.42	26	Great Universal Stores	8.93
12	Barclays Bank	13.82	27	Prudential	8.90
13	Guinness	13.70	28	National Power	8.79
14	RTZ	13.69	29	Vodafone	8.67
15	Grand Metropolitan	13.31	30	SmithKline Beecham	8.59

Banking and insurance

Leading banks
Assets, £bn

1970			*1980*		
1	Barclays	6.60	1	Barclays	37.10
2	National Westminster	5.39	2	National Westminster	34.57
3	Midland	3.69	3	Midland	25.34
4	Lloyds	3.19	4	Lloyds	19.87
5	Standard & Chartered	2.36	5	Standard Chartered	15.42
6	Australia & New Zealand Banking Group	1.62	6	Royal Bank of Scotland	6.15
7	National & Commercial Banking Group	1.23	7	Grindlays Holdings	3.83
8	Bank of London & South America	0.89	8	Bank of Scotland	3.30
9	National & Grindlays	0.87	9	Kleinwort, Benson, Lonsdale	2.71
10	Bank of Scotland	0.59	10	Schroder Wagg	1.84

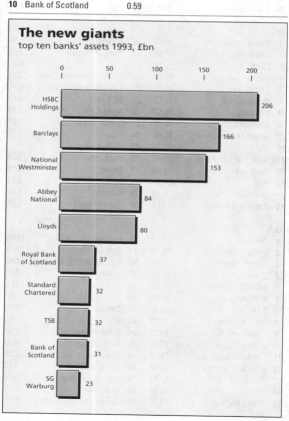

The new giants
top ten banks' assets 1993, £bn

HSBC Holdings	206
Barclays	166
National Westminster	153
Abbey National	84
Lloyds	80
Royal Bank of Scotland	37
Standard Chartered	32
TSB	32
Bank of Scotland	31
SG Warburg	23

Leading insurance companies
Premium income, £bn

Life			Non-Life		
1970			**1970**		
1	Prudential Corporation	2.00	1	Royal	0.37
2	Legal & General	1.01	2	Commercial Union	0.34
3	Standard Life	0.75	3	General Accident	0.19
4	Norwich Union	0.57	4	Guardian Royal	0.18
5	Guardian Royal Exchange	0.56	5	Sun Alliance	0.15
6	Pearl	0.52	6	Phoenix	0.09
7	Commercial Union	0.52	7	Eagle Star	0.08
8	Co-operative	0.48	8	Norwich Union	0.06
9	Sun Life	0.39	9	Prudential	0.05
10	Eagle Star	0.37	10	Mercantile & General	0.03
11	Scottish Widows	0.35	11	Co-operative	0.02
12	Royal	0.28	12	National Employers' Mutual	0.02
13	Liverpool Victoria	0.28	13	Vehicle & General	0.02
14	General Accident	0.27	14	Legal & General	0.02
15	Friends' Provident	0.26	15	Friends' Provident	0.02
1980			**1980**		
1	Prudential Corporation	4.76	1	Royal Insurance	1.22
2	Legal & General	3.07	2	Commercial Union	1.10
3	Commercial Union	2.28	3	General Accident	0.75
4	Standard Life	1.99	4	Guardian Royal Exchange	0.62
5	Norwich Union	1.49	5	Sun Alliance	0.52
6	Guardian Royal Exchange	1.30	6	Prudential Corporation	0.39
7	Scottish Widows	1.09	7	Eagle Star	0.36
8	Eagle Star	1.05	8	Phoenix	0.34
9	Pearl	1.02	9	Norwich Union	0.15
10	Royal Insurance	0.92	10	Legal & General	0.13
11	Sun Life	0.89	11	Co-operative	0.11
12	Co-operative	0.79	12	Cornhill	0.09
13	Equity & Law	0.72	13	National Employers' Mutual	0.08
14	Friends' Provident	0.67	14	Provincial	0.07
15	Hambro	0.65	15	Excess Insurance	0.07
1993			**1993**		
1	Prudential Corporation	7.44	1	General Accident	3.83
2	Standard Life	3.87	2	Commercial Union	3.57
3	Norwich Union	2.51	3	Royal Insurance	3.34
4	Legal & General	2.01	4	Sun Alliance	3.13
5	Commercial Union	2.01	5	Guardian Royal Exchange	2.24
6	Scottish Widows	1.79	6	Eagle Star	1.91
7	Sun Life	1.76	7	Norwich Union	1.40
8	Equitable Life	1.72	8	Prudential Corporation	1.05
9	Lloyds Abbey Life	1.38	9	Cornhill	0.62
10	Sun Alliance	1.30	10	Co-Operative	0.44
11	Allied Dunbar	1.28	11	London & Edinburgh	0.44
12	Friends' Provident	1.20	12	Nat. Farmers' Union Mutual	0.36
13	Scottish Amicable	1.11	13	Provincial	0.34
14	Royal Insurance	1.08	14	Legal & General	0.29
15	Co-operative	0.93	15	Gan Minster	0.18

Agriculture

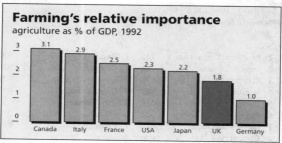

Farming's relative importance
agriculture as % of GDP, 1992

	Canada	Italy	France	USA	Japan	UK	Germany
	3.1	2.9	2.5	2.3	2.2	1.8	1.0

Agricultural output[a]
GDP constant factor cost, 1970 = 100

a Includes hunting, forestry and fishing.

1970 71 72 73 74 75 76 77 78 79 80 81 82 83 84 85 86 87 88 89 90 91 92 93

Crops
'000 tonnes harvested

	Wheat	Barley	Oats
1985	12,046	9,740	614
1986	13,911	10,014	503
1987	11,940	9,229	454
1988	11,751	8,778	548
1989	14,033	8,073	529
1990	14,033	7,911	530
1991	14,363	7,627	523
1992	14,092	7,366	504

Livestock
'000 on agricultural holdings

	Cattle	Pigs	Poultry
1985	12,911	7,865	119,456
1986	12,533	7,937	120,740
1987	12,170	7,943	128,801
1988	11,884	7,982	130,998
1989	11,975	7,509	120,351
1990	12,059	7,449	124,615
1991	11,866	7,596	127,228
1992	11,788	7,608	123,992

Manufacturing

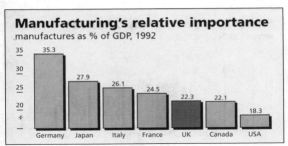

Manufacturing's relative importance
manufactures as % of GDP, 1992

Germany	Japan	Italy	France	UK	Canada	USA
35.3	27.9	26.1	24.5	22.3	22.1	18.3

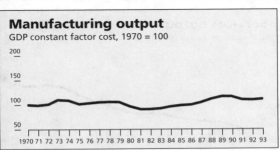

Manufacturing output
GDP constant factor cost, 1970 = 100

Leading sub-sectors
1993, £bn

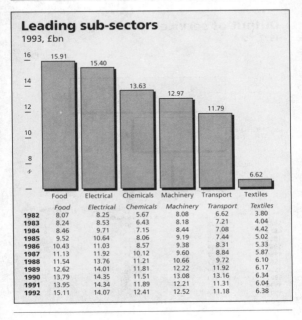

	Food	Electrical	Chemicals	Machinery	Transport	Textiles
	Food	*Electrical*	*Chemicals*	*Machinery*	*Transport*	*Textiles*
	15.91	15.40	13.63	12.97	11.79	6.62
1982	8.07	8.25	5.67	8.08	6.62	3.80
1983	8.24	8.53	6.43	8.18	7.21	4.04
1984	8.46	9.71	7.15	8.44	7.08	4.42
1985	9.52	10.64	8.06	9.19	7.44	5.02
1986	10.43	11.03	8.57	9.38	8.31	5.33
1987	11.13	11.92	10.12	9.60	8.84	5.87
1988	11.54	13.76	11.21	10.66	9.72	6.10
1989	12.62	14.01	11.81	12.22	11.92	6.17
1990	13.79	14.35	11.51	13.08	13.16	6.34
1991	13.95	14.34	11.89	12.21	11.31	6.04
1992	15.11	14.07	12.41	12.52	11.18	6.38

Services

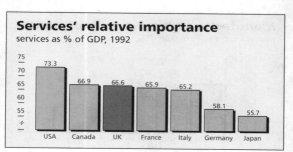

Services' relative importance
services as % of GDP, 1992

USA	Canada	UK	France	Italy	Germany	Japan
73.3	66.9	66.6	65.9	65.2	58.1	55.7

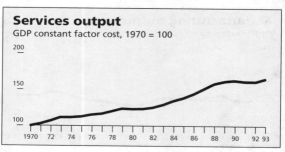

Services output
GDP constant factor cost, 1970 = 100

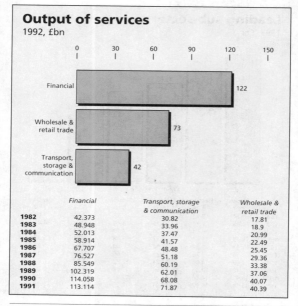

Output of services
1992, £bn

Financial	122
Wholesale & retail trade	73
Transport, storage & communication	42

	Financial	Transport, storage & communication	Wholesale & retail trade
1982	42.373	30.82	17.81
1983	48.948	33.96	18.9
1984	52.013	37.47	20.99
1985	58.914	41.57	22.49
1986	67.707	48.48	25.45
1987	76.527	51.18	29.36
1988	85.549	60.19	33.38
1989	102.319	62.01	37.06
1990	114.058	68.08	40.07
1991	113.114	71.87	40.39

Financing business

How money is raised

Money raised by UK and Irish listed companies, £m

	Equities	Convertibles	Debentures & loans	Preference	Eurobonds	Total
1981	2,493	253	43	120	...	2,909
1982	1,776	73	891	280	100	3,120
1983	2,569	99	461	1,382	70	4,581
1984	6,899	173	490	919	520	9,001
1985	4,775	795	597	440	7,239	13,846
1986	14,019	320	1,243	561	7,107	23,250
1987	18,648	982	1,275	141	5,611	26,657
1988	9,935	2,166	1,207	427	6,124	19,858
1989	12,626	1,309	2,421	780	9,446	26,581
1990	12,035	667	814	364	13,975	27,854
1991	18,312	1,502	1,023	925	13,370	35,131
1992	7,119	1,828	1,151	779	13,357	24,234
1993	17,712	3,251	1,981	1,549	24,642	49,135

Issues

	No. of issues	Money raised £m	Of which new companies No. of issues	Of which new companies Money raised £m
1981	2,267	2,909	63	631
1982	1,890	3,120	59	1,169
1983	2,519	4,581	79	1,592
1984	3,094	9,001	87	5,950
1985	3,242	13,846	80	1,462
1986	4,111	23,250	136	8,874
1987	4,883	26,657	155	5,002
1988	4,072	19,858	129	3,790
1989	3,956	26,581	110	7,578
1990	3,205	27,854	120	7,095
1991	3,319	35,131	101	7,474
1992	2,876	24,234	82	2,937
1993	2,655	49,135	180	5,966

The value of privatisation

	No. of issues	Money raised £m		No. of issues	Money raised £m
1981	2	374	1988	1	2,500
1982	2	620	1989	10	5,239
1983	2	297	1990	12	5,183
1984	4	4,654	1991	4	5,035
1985	1	363	1992	...	...
1986	2	6,930	1993	1	362
1987	3	3,488			

Stockmarkets

Indices compared

end year	London	Tokyo	New York	Frankfurt
1980	647.4	7063.13	963.98	480.92
1981	684.3	7681.84	875.00	490.39
1982	834.3	8016.67	1046.55	552.77
1983	1000.0	9893.82	1258.64	773.95
1984	1232.2	11542.60	1211.57	820.91
1985	1412.6	13083.18	1546.67	1366.23
1986	1679.0	18820.64	1895.95	1432.25
1987	1712.7	21564.00	1938.83	1000.00
1988	1793.1	30159.00	2168.57	1327.87
1989	2422.7	38915.87	2753.20	1790.37
1990	2143.5	23848.71	2633.66	1398.23
1991	2493.1	22983.77	3168.83	1577.98
1992	2846.5	16924.95	3301.11	1545.05
1993	3418.4	17417.24	3754.09	2266.68
1994[a]	3150.5	20449.39	3764.50	2146.64

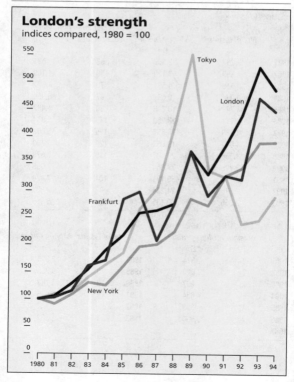

a 1994 is end July.

Value traded
$bn

	UK	USA	Japan	Germany
1984	48.86	786.20	286.18	29.76
1985	68.42	997.19	329.97	71.57
1986	132.91	1,796.00	1,145.62	135.70
1987	389.83	2,423.07	2,047.22	373.43
1988	579.17	1,719.73	2,597.64	350.27
1989	320.27	2,015.54	2,800.70	628.63
1990	278.74	1,815.48	1,602.39	501.81
1991	315.28	2,254.98	995.94	379.38
1992	383.00	2,678.52	635.26	446.02
1993	423.53	3,507.22	954.34	302.99

Market capitalisation
$bn

	UK	USA	Japan	Germany
1984	242.70	1,862.95	667.05	78.40
1985	328.00	2,324.65	978.66	183.77
1986	439.50	2,636.60	1,841.79	257.68
1987	680.72	2,588.89	2,802.95	213.17
1988	771.21	2,793.82	3,906.68	251.78
1989	826.60	3,505.69	4,392.60	365.18
1990	848.87	3,089.65	2,917.68	355.07
1991	987.95	4,099.48	3,130.86	393.45
1992	927.13	4,497.83	2,399.00	348.14
1993	1,151.65	5,223.77	2,999.76	463.48

Number of companies listed

	UK	USA	Japan	Germany
1984	2,171	7,977	1,802	449
1985	2,116	8,022	1,829	472
1986	2,106	8,403	1,866	492
1987	2,135	7,181	1,912	507
1988	2,054	6,680	1,967	609
1989	2,015	6,727	2,019	628
1990	1,701	6,599	2,071	413
1991	1,623	6,742	2,107	428
1992	1,874	7,014	2,118	665
1993	1,646	7,607	2,155	426

Confidence and failure

Business confidence

	CSO longer leading indicator, trend=100	Gallup consumer confidence survey	CBI optimism balance,
1965	95.55	…	-18.15
1966	95.83	…	-28.97
1967	103.73	…	-5.04
1968	100.89	…	18.52
1969	97.15	…	7.12
1970	95.82	…	0.08
1971	102.08	…	4.24
1972	105.18	…	31.05
1973	98.62	…	18.74
1974	92.95	-17.07	-44.69
1975	100.77	-25.19	-33.85
1976	101.35	-15.73	13.69
1977	103.02	-7.17	3.67
1978	103.60	6.95	0.67
1979	97.08	-2.92	-18.58
1980	92.13	-18.12	-50.83
1981	99.15	-20.54	-7.08
1982	101.03	-10.77	-9.17
1983	105.59	-2.02	16.75
1984	101.84	-5.00	9.17
1985	96.02	-10.16	3.42
1986	98.96	-6.64	0.17
1987	105.18	4.51	22.33
1988	104.66	1.92	9.83
1989	95.10	-17.25	-15.83
1990	93.21	-25.37	-33.17
1991	98.37	-17.02	-20.67
1992	96.88	-15.92	-9.42
1993	102.18	-12.58	14.58
1994[a]	102.60	-10.90	28.00

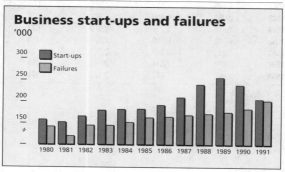

Business start-ups and failures
'000

a Third quarter.
For an explanation of confidence indices, see page 11.

Tourism

No. of visitors and receipts

	No. of foreign visitors to UK, '000s	Tourism receipts, £m	Tourist receipts, 1993 prices £m
1948	504	33	549
1949	563	43	690
1950	618	61	950
1951	712	75	1,089
1952	733	80	1,083
1953	819	88	1,174
1954	902	95	1,254
1955	1,037	111	1,409
1956	1,107	121	1,464
1957	1,180	129	1,506
1958	1,259	134	1,530
1959	1,395	143	1,633
1960	1,669	169	1,912
1961	1,824	176	1,925
1962	1,955	183	1,921
1963	2,159	188	1,935
1964	2,595	190	1,891
1965	2,895	193	1,836
1966	3,270	219	2,005
1967	3,557	236	2,107
1968	4,045	282	2,406
1969	5,057	359	2,906
1970	5,949	432	3,286
1971	6,410	500	3,476
1972	6,808	576	3,740
1973	7,439	726	4,315
1974	7,814	898	4,601
1975	8,787	1,218	5,025
1976	10,105	1,768	6,253
1977	11,518	2,352	7,182
1978	11,734	2,507	7,069
1979	11,563	2,797	6,955
1980	11,465	2,961	6,242
1981	10,578	2,970	5,594
1982	10,724	3,188	5,530
1983	11,556	4,003	6,638
1984	12,735	4,614	7,286
1985	13,481	5,442	8,102
1986	12,860	5,553	7,993
1987	14,412	6,260	8,648
1988	14,547	6,184	8,145
1989	16,036	6,945	8,484
1990	16,696	7,748	8,645
1991	15,811	7,386	7,781
1992	17,119	7,891	8,016
1993[a]	19,158	9,259	9,259

a Provisional figures.

How Britain compares

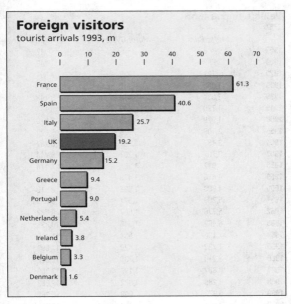

Foreign visitors
tourist arrivals 1993, m

France	61.3
Spain	40.6
Italy	25.7
UK	19.2
Germany	15.2
Greece	9.4
Portugal	9.0
Netherlands	5.4
Ireland	3.8
Belgium	3.3
Denmark	1.6

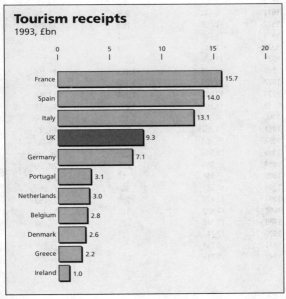

Tourism receipts
1993, £bn

France	15.7
Spain	14.0
Italy	13.1
UK	9.3
Germany	7.1
Portugal	3.1
Netherlands	3.0
Belgium	2.8
Denmark	2.6
Greece	2.2
Ireland	1.0

Roads and vehicles

Vehicle registration
'000s

	Motor Cars	Motor Cycles	All Vehicles
1903	8		17
1909	53	36	143
1920	187	228	591
1930	1,056	712	2,272
1939	2,034	418	3,148
1946	1,770	449	3,107
1950	1,979	643	3,970
1955	3,109	1,076	5,822
1956	3,437	1,137	6,287
1957	3,707	1,261	6,743
1958	4,047	1,300	7,175
1959	4,416	1,479	7,809
1960	4,900	1,583	8,512
1961	5,296	1,577	8,989
1962	5,776	1,567	9,532
1963	6,462	1,546	10,336
1964	7,190	1,534	11,176
1965	7,732	1,420	11,697
1966	8,210	1,239	12,022
1967	8,882	1,190	12,760
1968	9,285	1,082	13,082
1969	9,672	993	13,362
1970	9,971	923	13,548
1971	10,443	899	14,030
1972	11,006	866	14,584
1973	11,738	887	15,427
1974	11,917	918	15,642
1975	12,526	1,077	16,511
1976	13,184	1,175	17,318
1977	13,220	1,190	17,345
1978	13,626	1,194	17,758
1979	14,162	1,292	18,616
1980	14,660	1,372	19,199
1981	14,867	1,371	19,347
1982	15,264	1,370	19,762
1983	15,543	1,290	20,209
1984	16,055	1,225	20,765
1985	16,454	1,148	21,159
1986	16,981	1,065	21,699
1987	17,421	978	22,152
1988	18,432	912	23,301
1989	19,248	875	24,196
1990	19,742	833	24,672
1991	19,737	750	24,511
1992	20,116	688	24,851

A history of Britain's roads
Miles of road

	Total	of which motorways are
1909	282,380	
1951	297,466	
1959	309,406	13
1970	322,484	1,057
1980	339,633	2,556
1990	358,034	3,070
1992	362,327	3,147

Road accidents
'000

	Accidents	Deaths		Accidents	Deaths
1926	124	4,886	**1960**	272	6,970
1928	148	6,138	**1962**	264	6,709
1930	157	7,305	**1964**	292	7,820
1932	184	6,667	**1966**	292	7,985
1934	205	7,343	**1968**	264	6,810
1936	199	6,561	**1970**	267	7,499
1938	196	6,648	**1972**	265	7,763
1940	…	8,609	**1974**	244	6,876
1942	…	6,926	**1976**	259	6,570
1944	…	6,416	**1978**	265	6,813
1946	…	5,062	**1980**	252	6,010
1948	…	4,513	**1982**	256	5,934
1950	167	5,012	**1984**	253	5,599
1952	172	4,706	**1986**	248	5,382
1954	196	5,010	**1988**	247	5,052
1956	216	5,367	**1990**	258	5,217
1958	237	5,970	**1992**	233	4,229

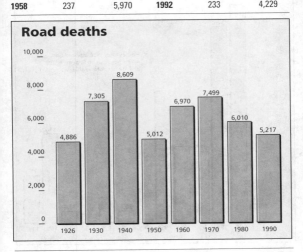

Road deaths

Rail

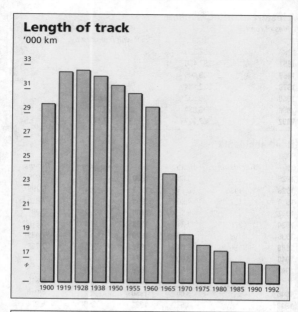

Length of track
'000 km

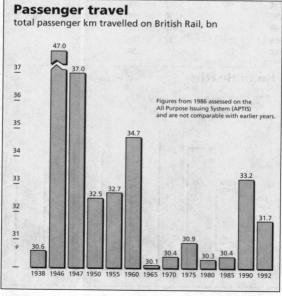

Passenger travel
total passenger km travelled on British Rail, bn

Figures from 1986 assessed on the
All Purpose Issuing System (APTIS)
and are not comparable with earlier years.

Government subsidies to British Rail

£m, real 1992 prices

Year	£m
1968	638
1970	576
1971	506
1972	940
1973	1,065
1974	2,028
1975	2,140
1976	1,842
1977	1,770
1978	1,585
1979	1,652
1980	1,509
1981/82	1,593
1982/83	1,635
1983/84	1,606
1984/85	1,485
1985/86	1,437
1986/87	1,220
1987/88	1,226
1988/89	786
1989/90	752
1990/91	815
1991/92	1,107

Rail buffs: who trains most

Rail km travelled per year per person

	1970	1975	1980	1985	1990
Japan	2,770	2,869	2,697	2,648	2,995
Switzerland	1,293	1,576	1,424	1,855	1,937
Eastern Germany	1,055	1,068	1,314	1,382	1,449
Ex-Soviet Union	1,092	1,218	1,250	1,333	1,445
Ex-Czechoslovakia	1,186	1,013	980	968	1,213
Austria	804	924	1,060	926	1,167
France	808	968	1,021	1,124	1,128
Hungary	1,548	1,519	1,400	1,127	1,042
Denmark	812	593	781	976	973
Italy	650	649	709	683	798
Netherlands	614	659	636	621	736
Western Germany	627	615	666	721	720
Belgium	829	817	711	710	702
Sweden	622	732	842	838	700
Portugal	442	550	614	606	608
Finland	434	637	628	612	602
Great Britain	539	622	533	636	575
Norway	516	499	489	482	471
Ex-Yugoslavia	540	…	448	519	462
Spain	444	506	400	416	436
Ireland	236	315	294	281	285
Greece	227	221	207	201	198
USA	83	74	79	75	84

Air

Busiest airports
Terminal passengers, '000

1975			1980		
1	Heathrow	21,295	1	Heathrow	27,484
2	Gatwick	5,342	2	Gatwick	9,703
3	Manchester	2,580	3	Manchester	4,316
4	Luton	1,869	4	Glasgow	2,339
5	Glasgow	1,763	5	Luton	2,088
6	Jersey	1,418	6	Birmingham	1,563
7	Belfast	1,184	7	Belfast	1,478
8	Birmingham	1,082	8	Aberdeen	1,448
9	Edinburgh	874	9	Jersey	1,353
10	Aberdeen	645	10	Edinburgh	1,162
11	Newcastle	605	11	Newcastle	917
12	East Midlands	545	12	East Midlands	668
13	Guernsey	525	13	Guernsey	534
14	Liverpool	437	14	Prestwick	394
15	Prestwick	395	15	Liverpool	380
Total all reporting airports		41,846	Total all reporting airports		57,822

1985			1990		
1	Heathrow	31,310	1	Heathrow	42,635
2	Gatwick	14,885	2	Gatwick	21,043
3	Manchester	6,054	3	Manchester	10,146
4	Glasgow	2,695	4	Glasgow	4,286
5	Aberdeen	1,697	5	Birmingham	3,492
6	Belfast	1,646	6	Luton	2,679
7	Birmingham	1,634	7	Edinburgh	2,492
8	Luton	1,586	8	Belfast	2,294
9	Edinburgh	1,574	9	Aberdeen	1,947
10	Jersey	1,552	10	Jersey	1,867
11	Newcastle	1,028	11	Newcastle	1,555
12	East Midlands	925	12	East Midlands	1,280
13	Guernsey	656	13	Stansted	1,156
14	Stansted	515	14	Guernsey	862
15	Leeds/Bradford	463	15	Leeds/Bradford	834
Total all reporting airports		70,434	Total all reporting airports		102,418

1993					
1	Heathrow	47,601	12	Jersey	1,569
2	Gatwick	20,054	13	East Midlands	1,372
3	Manchester	12,832	14	Cardiff, Wales	767
4	Glasgow	5,014	15	Guernsey	732
5	Birmingham	4,032	16	Leeds/Bradford	713
6	Edinburgh	2,709	17	Isle of Man	491
7	Stansted	2,670	18	Liverpool	460
8	Aberdeen	2,290	19	Sumburgh	423
9	Belfast	2,180	20	Southampton	418
10	Newcastle	2,076	21	Tees-side	318
11	Luton	1,844	Total all reporting airports		112,278

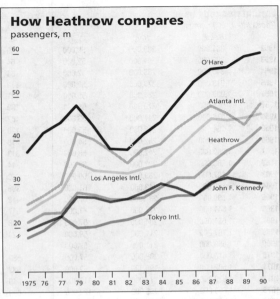

How Heathrow compares
passengers, m

O'Hare
Atlanta Intl.
Heathrow
Los Angeles Intl.
John F. Kennedy
Tokyo Intl.

1975 76 77 78 79 80 81 82 83 84 85 86 87 88 89 90

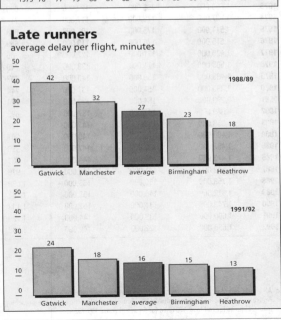

Late runners
average delay per flight, minutes

1988/89

Gatwick	Manchester	*average*	Birmingham	Heathrow
42	32	27	23	18

1991/92

Gatwick	Manchester	*average*	Birmingham	Heathrow
24	18	16	15	13

Freight: rail decline

Freight methods used
Goods lifted, '000 tonnes

	Road[a]	Rail[b]	Water[c]	Air[d]
1952	861,000	289,000	50,000	40
1953	889,000	294,000	52,000	64
1954	940,000	288,000	52,000	84
1955	1,013,000	279,000	50,000	113
1956	1,009,000	281,000	55,000	121
1957	985,000	279,000	55,000	139
1958	1,078,000	247,000	53,000	167
1959	1,164,000	238,000	53,000	226
1960	1,211,000	252,000	54,000	279
1961	1,260,000	242,000	56,000	313
1962	1,268,000	232,000	58,000	344
1963	1,407,000	239,000	60,000	360
1964	1,560,000	243,000	61,000	399
1965	1,590,000	232,000	62,000	418
1966	1,641,000	217,000	61,000	517
1967	1,651,000	204,000	57,000	488
1968	1,707,000	211,000	59,000	524
1969	1,658,000	211,000	59,000	585
1970	1,610,000	209,000	57,000	580
1971	1,582,000	198,000	52,000	532
1972	1,629,000	177,000	117,000	649
1973	1,660,000	196,000	122,000	699
1974	1,537,000	176,000	117,000	717
1975	1,511,000	175,000	108,000	638
1976	1,515,000	176,000	113,000	659
1977	1,429,000	171,000	122,000	705
1978	1,503,000	171,000	133,000	748
1979	1,499,000	169,000	140,000	797
1980	1,395,000	154,000	137,000	744
1981	1,299,000	154,000	129,000	724
1982	1,389,000	142,000	137,000	693
1983	1,358,000	145,000	143,000	726
1984	1,400,000	79,000	140,000	861
1985	1,452,000	122,000	142,000	850
1986	1,473,000	140,000	144,000	881
1987	1,542,000	141,000	142,000	976
1988	1,758,000	150,000	156,000	1,088
1989	1,812,000	146,000	155,000	1,151
1990	1,749,000	141,000	152,000	1,193
1991	1,600,000	135,000	144,000	1,120
1992	1,555,000	122,000	140,000	1,239

a All goods vehicles, including those up to 3.5 tonnes gross vehicle weight.
b Figures up to 1962 include free-hauled (i.e. departmental) traffic on revenue-earning trains. Figures for rail from 1991 are for financial years 1991/92 etc.

Freight methods used
Goods lifted, % of total carried

	Road	Rail	Water & Air
1952	71.7	24.1	4.2
1953	72.0	23.8	4.2
1954	73.4	22.5	4.1
1955	75.5	20.8	3.7
1956	75.0	20.9	4.1
1957	74.7	21.2	4.1
1958	78.2	17.9	3.9
1959	80.0	16.4	3.6
1960	79.8	16.6	3.6
1961	80.9	15.5	3.6
1962	81.4	14.9	3.7
1963	82.5	14.0	3.5
1964	83.7	13.0	3.3
1965	84.4	12.3	3.3
1966	85.5	11.3	3.2
1967	86.3	10.7	3.0
1968	86.3	10.7	3.0
1969	86.0	10.9	3.1
1970	85.8	11.1	3.1
1971	86.3	10.8	2.9
1972	84.7	9.2	6.1
1973	83.9	9.9	6.2
1974	84.0	9.6	6.4
1975	84.2	9.8	6.0
1976	83.9	9.8	6.3
1977	83.0	9.9	7.1
1978	83.1	9.5	7.4
1979	82.9	9.3	7.8
1980	82.7	9.1	8.2
1981	82.1	9.7	8.2
1982	83.2	8.5	8.3
1983	82.5	8.8	8.7
1984	86.4	4.9	8.7
1985	84.6	7.1	8.3
1986	83.8	8.0	8.2
1987	84.4	7.7	7.9
1988	85.1	7.3	7.6
1989	85.7	6.9	7.4
1990	85.6	6.9	7.5
1991	85.1	7.2	7.7
1992	85.5	6.7	7.8

c Figures from 1972 onwards are not comparable with earlier years. From 1972, water includes all UK coastwise and one-port freight movements by sea and inland waterway traffic. Earlier years include only GB coastwise traffic and internal traffic on BWB waterways.
d Goods uplifted plus good landed. Excludes mail.

Sea

Largest ports
Total cargo traffic, 1992, '000 tonnes

1	London	44,524	11	Dover	13,111
2	Tees & Hartlepool	43,392	12	Barry	9,489
3	Sullom Voe	41,430	13	Port Talbot	9,403
4	Grimsby-Immingham	39,083	14	Hull	8,609
5	Milford Haven	35,591	15	Orkney	8,520
6	Southampton	29,803	16	Manchester	7,484
7	Liverpool	27,810	17	Swansea	5,714
8	Forth	23,270	18	Bristol	4,897
9	Felixstowe	16,923	19	Glensanda	4,736
10	Medway	14,335	20	Harwich	4,685

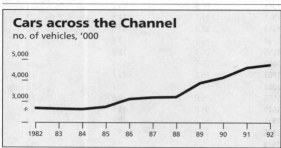

Cars across the Channel
no. of vehicles, '000

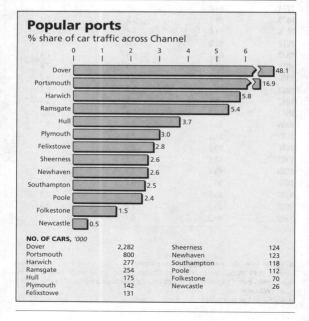

Popular ports
% share of car traffic across Channel

Dover	48.1
Portsmouth	16.9
Harwich	5.8
Ramsgate	5.4
Hull	3.7
Plymouth	3.0
Felixstowe	2.8
Sheerness	2.6
Newhaven	2.6
Southampton	2.5
Poole	2.4
Folkestone	1.5
Newcastle	0.5

NO. OF CARS, '000

Dover	2,282	Sheerness	124
Portsmouth	800	Newhaven	123
Harwich	277	Southampton	118
Ramsgate	254	Poole	112
Hull	175	Folkestone	70
Plymouth	142	Newcastle	26
Felixstowe	131		

Household size and spending

Households by size
UK

	Total, m	Average size[a]	No. of persons					
			1	2	3	4	5	6 or more
1951	14.5	3.2	11	27	25	19	10	8
1961	16.2	3.1	14	30	23	18	9	7
1971	18.2	2.9	18	32	19	17	8	6
1981	19.5	2.7	22	32	17	18	7	4
1991	21.9	2.5	27	34	16	16	5	2

Regional variations in households

	1985		1992	
	Average size[a]	% lone parents	Average size[a]	% lone parents
UK	2.62	…	2.50	…
England	2.60	8.9	2.46	10.0
Wales	2.68	8.9	2.58	10.0
Scotland	2.64	…	2.47	…
Northern Ireland	3.07	…	2.86	…
North	2.61	9.6	2.50	10.5
Yorkshire & Humberside	2.59	8.9	2.45	10.1
North West	2.64	9.9	2.51	11.0
West Midlands	2.66	9.0	2.52	10.1
East Midlands	2.62	8.4	2.48	9.6
East Anglia	2.61	7.4	2.46	8.3
South East	2.57	9.0	2.42	10.1
South West	2.56	7.7	2.43	8.6

Spending on housing
% of average weekly spending, 1993

UK	16.2
England	16.7
Wales	15.7
Scotland	13.4
Northern Ireland	9.4
North	15.0
Yorkshire & Humberside	14.7
North West	15.7
West Midlands	15.3
East Midlands	16.1
East Anglia	16.9
South East	18.2
Greater London	19.1
Rest of South East	17.8
South West	16.1

a Number of people.

The changing household

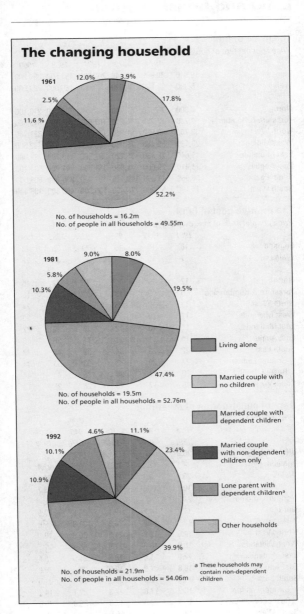

1961

3.9%
12.0%
17.8%
2.5%
11.6%
52.2%

No. of households = 16.2m
No. of people in all households = 49.55m

1981

9.0%
8.0%
5.8%
19.5%
10.3%
47.4%

No. of households = 19.5m
No. of people in all households = 52.76m

1992

4.6%
11.1%
10.1%
23.4%
10.9%
39.9%

No. of households = 21.9m
No. of people in all households = 54.06m

Living alone

Married couple with no children

Married couple with dependent children

Married couple with non-dependent children only

Lone parent with dependent children[a]

Other households

a These households may contain non-dependent children

Land and housing stock

The price of land
Prices per hectare of housing land, £

	1969	1974	1979	1984	1989	1990
England	19,510	48,899	73,149	202,900	451,600	354,900
Wales	8,390	21,820	31,020	...	180,000	231,500
North	6,300	26,530	61,240	...	284,800	216,100
Yorkshire & Humberside	9,730	28,280	41,210	107,900	250,900	343,800
North West	13,760	40,960	51,880	111,600	382,000	321,100
West Midlands	23,130	55,480	79,960	165,000	457,500	492,600
East Midlands	11,640	28,630	35,720	92,300	413,700	377,000
East Anglia	11,410	29,000	44,860	131,500	541,900	524,100
South East	36,960	117,398	119,145	397,800	895,000	636,500
South West	14,190	55,290	78,490	190,300	460,800	186,400

The relative cost of land
Price per plot as % of new dwelling price

	1981	1983	1985	1987	1989	1990
England	16	19	19	29	25	23
Wales	7	10[a]	11[a]	12[a]	19	22
North	12	15[a]	11[a]	19[a]	22	15
Yorkshire & Humberside	9	12	13	12	15	16
North West	13	13	15	17	25	21
West Midlands	17	20	23	26	21	25
East Midlands	11	13	12	18	26	27
East Anglia	14	11	21	17	36	45
South East	22	23	34	39	45	39
Greater London	27	29	33	53	63	33
Rest of South East	20	21	34	35	41	44
South West	15	17	23	26	25	13

Date of construction of dwellings
1992, %

	Pre 1891	1891 –1919	1919 –1944	1945 –1970	Post 1970
UK	26.3[b]		18.8	54.9[c]	
England	14.1	12.1	19.9	31.5	22.4
Wales	20.5	16.3	12.8	28.9	21.4
Scotland	10.4	14.6	16.1	35.1	23.7
Northern Ireland	21.2[b]		11.3	67.6[c]	
North	11.2	14.5	19.1	34.8	20.5
Yorkshire & Humberside	12.9	14.8	20.9	31.9	19.6
North West	14.5	13.9	21.5	30.3	19.8
West Midlands	10.9	10.9	21.6	35.4	21.2
East Midlands	12.8	11.6	18.3	31.9	25.4
East Anglia	18.8	7.5	12.8	30.0	30.9
South East	14.4	12.4	21.3	30.4	21.5
Greater London	18.3	17.6	27.3	22.1	14.7
Rest of South East	11.8	9.0	17.3	35.8	26.0
South West	19.3	9.5	15.0	30.3	25.9

Housing stock
No. of houses at censuses, '000s

	England & Wales	Scotland	Northern Ireland
1851	3,432	…	267
1861	3,924	…	269
1871	4,520	…	267
1881	5,218	799	273
1891	5,824	869	274
1901	6,710	986	291
1911	7,550	1,102	291
1921	7,979	1,109	…
1926	…	…	285
1931	9,400	1,197	…
1936/37	…	…	322
1951	12,389	1,442	346
1961	14,646	1,627	387
1966	15,449	1,691	419
1971	16,455	1,717	455
1981	19,110	1,970	501
1991	20,976	2,158	572

	Apr 1966	Apr 1971	Dec 1976	Dec 1981	Dec 1986	Dec 1991
UK	17,865	19,288	20,599	21,581	22,566	23,622
England	14,885	16,065	17,168	18,021	18,852	19,725
Wales	886	959	1,029	1,089	1,128	1,179
Scotland	1,697	1,809	1,921	1,970	2,050	2,142
Northern Ireland	397	455	481	500	535	576
North	1,094	1,099	1,169	1,214	1,249	1,286
Yorkshire & Humberside	1,633	1,742	1,829	1,900	1,959	2,025
North West	2,239	2,304	2,396	2,466	2,527	2,594
West Midlands	1,594	1,735	1,840	1,941	2,018	2,093
East Midlands	1,114	1,283	1,393	1,484	1,557	1,644
East Anglia	545	611	692	755	810	875
South East	5,414	5,835	6,236	6,531	6,891	7,245
Greater London	…	2,555	2,640	2,676	2,780	2,889
Rest of South East	…	…	3,596	3,855	4,111	4,356
South West	1,252	1,456	1,613	1,727	1,844	1,964

a Estimate.
b Pre 1919.
c Post 1944.

Housebuilding

Public sector decline

No. of house completions in Great Britain, '000s (%)

	Private enterprise	Housing Associations	Local authorities, new towns & govt. departments	Total
1948	32.8 (14.4)	1.8 (0.8)	193.0 (84.8)	227.6
1949	25.8 (13.1)	1.4 (0.7)	170.4 (86.2)	197.6
1950	27.4 (13.8)	1.6 (0.8)	169.2 (85.4)	198.2
1951	22.6 (11.6)	1.8 (0.9)	170.5 (87.5)	194.9
1952	34.3 (14.3)	2.2 (0.9)	203.4 (84.8)	239.9
1953	62.9 (19.7)	7.9 (2.5)	247.9 (77.8)	318.7
1954	90.6 (26.0)	14.9 (4.3)	242.3 (69.7)	347.8
1955	113.5 (35.7)	4.6 (1.4)	199.4 (62.8)	317.5
1956	124.2 (41.3)	2.7 (0.9)	173.8 (57.8)	300.7
1957	126.5 (42.0)	2.0 (0.7)	172.6 (57.3)	301.1
1958	128.1 (46.8)	1.2 (0.4)	144.3 (52.7)	273.6
1959	150.7 (54.5)	1.1 (0.4)	124.8 (45.1)	276.6
1960	168.6 (56.6)	1.8 (0.6)	127.4 (42.8)	297.8
1961	177.5 (60.0)	1.6 (0.5)	116.9 (39.5)	296.0
1962	174.8 (57.2)	1.6 (0.5)	129.0 (42.2)	305.4
1963	174.9 (58.5)	2.0 (0.7)	122.1 (40.8)	299.0
1964	218.1 (58.4)	2.9 (0.8)	152.7 (40.9)	373.7
1965	213.8 (55.9)	4.0 (1.0)	164.5 (43.0)	382.3
1966	205.4 (53.3)	4.6 (1.2)	175.6 (45.5)	385.6
1967	200.4 (49.6)	5.0 (1.2)	198.9 (49.2)	404.3
1968	222.0 (53.7)	6.3 (1.5)	185.4 (44.8)	413.7
1969	181.7 (49.5)	7.3 (2.0)	177.8 (48.5)	366.8
1970	170.3 (48.6)	8.5 (2.4)	171.6 (49.0)	350.4
1971	191.6 (54.6)	10.7 (3.1)	148.3 (42.3)	350.6
1972	196.5 (61.5)	7.7 (2.4)	115.2 (36.1)	319.4
1973	186.6 (63.4)	8.9 (3.0)	98.6 (33.5)	294.1
1974	140.9 (52.3)	9.9 (3.7)	118.7 (44.0)	269.5
1975	150.8 (48.2)	14.7 (4.7)	147.6 (47.1)	313.1
1976	152.2 (48.3)	15.8 (5.0)	147.2 (46.7)	315.2
1977	140.8 (46.4)	25.1 (8.3)	137.4 (45.3)	303.3
1978	149.0 (53.3)	22.8 (8.1)	108.0 (38.6)	279.8
1979	140.5 (57.5)	17.8 (7.3)	86.2 (35.3)	244.5
1980	128.4 (54.5)	21.1 (9.0)	86.0 (36.5)	235.5
1981	115.0 (57.6)	19.3 (9.7)	65.5 (32.8)	199.8
1982	125.4 (71.3)	13.1 (7.5)	37.3 (21.2)	175.8
1983	148.1 (78.2)	16.1 (6.8)	35.1 (14.9)	235.3
1984	159.4 (75.9)	16.6 (7.9)	34.1 (16.2)	210.1
1985	156.5 (79.5)	13.1 (6.7)	27.2 (13.8)	196.8
1986	170.4 (82.8)	12.5 (6.1)	22.9 (11.1)	205.8
1987	183.7 (84.9)	12.5 (5.8)	20.1 (9.3)	216.4
1988	199.5 (86.0)	12.8 (5.5)	19.7 (8.5)	232.0
1989	179.6 (85.1)	13.9 (6.6)	17.6 (8.3)	211.1
1990	159.0 (82.7)	16.8 (8.7)	16.5 (8.6)	192.3
1991	151.7 (83.5)	19.7 (10.8)	10.3 (5.7)	181.7
1992	140.0 (82.2)	25.7 (15.1)	4.6 (2.7)	170.3
1993	137.5 (78.9)	34.4 (19.7)	2.3 (1.3)	174.2

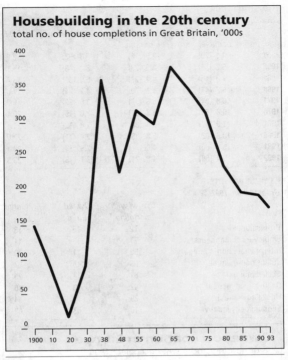

Housebuilding in the 20th century
total no. of house completions in Great Britain, '000s

Regional variations
New dwellings per '000 pop.

	1968	1970	1975	1980	1985	1990	1992
UK	...	...	5.8	4.3	3.5	3.4	3.0
England	7.7	6.3	5.6	4.3	3.4	3.4	3.0
Wales	7.1	5.7	6.2	3.7	2.9	3.6	3.4
Scotland	8.1	8.6	6.5	4.0	3.6	3.9	3.2
Northern Ireland	...	...	5.8	4.2	5.6	5.0	4.8
North	7.9	5.9	5.6	3.7	2.9	3.0	2.6
Yorkshire & Humberside	7.5	5.8	5.0	4.2	2.7	2.6	2.7
North West	6.9	6.6	5.0	3.8	2.7	2.8	2.7
West Midlands	8.6	6.3	5.0	4.2	3.1	3.1	2.8
East Midlands	8.4	6.8	7.0	4.7	3.5	3.6	3.5
East Anglia	10.3	8.1	8.9	6.5	5.7	6.0	4.6
South East	7.1	6.1	5.5	4.3	3.4	3.4	3.0
Greater London	...	...	...	3.3	1.3	2.6	2.2
Rest of South East	...	...	...	5.0	4.7	4.0	3.3
South West	8.8	6.6	6.2	4.8	5.3	4.2	3.4

Home ownership

Housing stock
Dwellings in Great Britain, m (%)

	Owner-occupied	Public sector rented	Other	Total
1951	4.1 (29)	2.5 (18)	7.3 (53)	13.9
1956	5.2 (34)	3.5 (23)	6.4 (43)	15.1
1961	7.0 (43)	4.4 (27)	5.0 (30)	16.4
1966	8.3 (47)	5.1 (29)	4.2 (24)	17.6
1971	9.6 (51)	5.8 (30)	3.6 (19)	19.0
1976	10.8 (54)	6.3 (31)	3.0 (15)	20.1
1981	11.9 (57)	6.4 (30)	2.8 (13)	21.1
1986	13.8 (63)	5.8 (26)	2.4 (11)	22.0
1991	15.3 (66)	4.9 (21)	2.9 (13)	23.1
1992	15.4 (66)	4.8 (21)	3.1 (13)	23.3

Class divisions
Great Britain, 1992, %

	Owned with mortgage	Owned outright	Rented[a]
Professional	72	15	13
Employers & managers	77	13	11
Intermediate non-managers	69	11	20
Junior non-manual	58	15	27
Skilled manual	61	14	25
Semi-skilled manual	42	13	46
Unskilled manual	29	17	54
Economically inactive	10	43	47

Owner-occupation in Europe
% of housing stock owner-occupied, 1990

Ireland
Greece[1]
Spain
Italy
UK
Luxembourg[2]
Belgium[2]
Portugal
France
Denmark
Netherlands
Germany[3]

1 1988.
2 1991.
3 West Germany only 1987.

Owner-occupation by region
% of total

	1969	1976	1981	1986	1989	1993
UK	...	54	57	62	67	68
England	51	56	59	64	68	67
Wales	54	59	63	67	71	72
Scotland	30	34	36	43	49	55
Northern Ireland	...	51	54	61	64	66
North	41	46	49	55	59	61
Yorkshire & Humberside	48	54	57	62	66	66
North West	54	58	61	65	68	67
West Midlands	49	55	59	63	67	67
East Midlands	50	57	61	66	70	70
East Anglia	51	56	60	66	70	68
Greater London	46	47	50	56	61	57
Rest of South East	57	61	65	71	74	73
South West	57	62	65	70	73	72

Sales of local authority dwellings[b]

	Stock at April 1979, '000s	Sales 1979 –1992	Stock at end-1992	Total sales as % of stock at April 1979
UK	6,679	1,823	4,856	27.3
England	5,256	1,473	3,783	28.0
Wales	308	92	216	30.0
Scotland	903	205	698	22.7
Northern Ireland	213	53	160	25.0
North	465	114	351	24.5
Yorkshire & Humberside	603	136	467	22.6
North West	690	150	540	21.7
West Midlands	629	157	472	25.0
East Midlands	430	121	309	28.1
East Anglia	200	63	137	31.3
Greater London	911	247	664	27.1
Rest of South East	938	364	574	38.8
South West	388	120	268	30.8

a Includes renting from housing association and those renting with a job or business.
b Includes dwellings transferred to housing associations and private developers.

House prices

National variations
£

	UK	Wales	Scotland	N. Ireland
1970	4,975	4,434	5,002	4,387
1971	5,632	4,803	5,407	4,650
1972	7,734	5,935	6,233	4,934
1973	9,942	8,382	8,595	6,181
1974	10,990	9,401	9,775	8,710
1975	11,787	10,083	11,139	10,023
1976	12,704	11,129	12,974	12,860
1977	13,650	11,673	14,236	15,722
1978	15,594	13,373	16,147	18,395
1979	19,925	17,061	19,371	21,824
1980	23,596	19,363	21,754	23,656
1981	24,188	20,155	23,014	19,890
1982	23,644	19,662	22,522	20,177
1983	26,469	22,533	23,822	20,878
1984	29,106	23,665	25,865	21,455
1985	31,103	25,005	26,941	23,012
1986	36,276	27,354	28,242	25,743
1987	40,391	29,704	29,591	27,773
1988	49,355	34,244	31,479	29,875
1989	54,846	42,981	35,394	30,280
1990	59,785	46,464	41,744	31,849
1991	62,455	48,989	48,772	35,352
1992	60,821	49,685	49,224	37,775
1993	61,223	52,070	49,553	38,878

Regional variations
£

	North	Yorkshire & Humberside	North-West	West Midlands	East Midlands
1970	3,942	3,634	4,184	4,490	3,966
1975	9,601	9,085	9,771	10,866	9,989
1976	10,453	9,995	10,500	11,621	10,646
1977	11,773	10,772	11,523	12,528	11,367
1978	13,044	12,099	13,410	14,342	12,810
1979	15,443	15,003	16,902	18,493	15,836
1980	17,710	17,689	20,092	21,663	18,928
1981	18,602	19,202	20,554	21,755	19,465
1982	18,071	18,180	20,744	20,992	19,487
1983	20,034	20,870	22,827	23,133	22,034
1984	22,604	22,356	24,410	24,989	24,377
1985	22,786	23,338	25,126	25,855	25,539
1986	24,333	25,607	27,503	28,437	28,483
1987	27,275	27,747	29,527	32,657	31,808
1988	30,193	32,685	34,074	41,700	40,521
1989	37,374	41,817	42,126	49,815	49,421
1990	43,655	47,231	50,005	54,694	52,620
1991	46,005	52,343	53,178	58,659	55,740
1992	48,347	52,278	56,377	57,827	54,599
1993	49,337	54,346	54,890	58,315	53,370

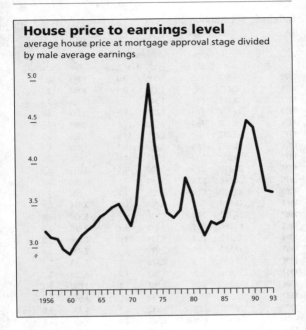

House price to earnings level
average house price at mortgage approval stage divided by male average earnings

East Anglia	Greater London	South East	South West
4,515	6,882	6,223	4,879
11,528	14,918	14,664	12,096
11,850	15,566	15,548	13,003
12,176	16,745	16,466	13,555
13,968	19,160	18,915	15,503
18,461	25,793	24,675	20,494
22,808	30,968	29,832	25,293
23,060	30,757	29,975	25,365
23,358	30,712	29,676	25,514
25,814	34,632	33,753	27,996
28,296	39,346	37,334	30,612
31,661	44,301	40,487	32,948
36,061	54,863	48,544	38,536
42,681	66,024	57,387	44,728
57,295	77,697	72,561	58,457
64,610	82,383	81,635	67,004
61,427	83,821	80,525	65,378
61,141	85,742	79,042	65,346
56,770	78,254	74,347	61,460
58,039	78,399	74,605	60,791

Housing purchase loans

Balances outstanding end year
UK

	Building Societies		Local Authorities		Insurance companies and Pension Funds	
	£m	% of total	£m	% of total	£m	% of total
1970	8,810	76.5	1,035	9.0	1,171	10.2
1971	10,410	78.1	1,142	8.6	1,188	8.9
1972	12,625	78.4	1,341	8.3	1,184	7.3
1973	14,624	77.1	1,696	8.9	1,317	6.9
1974	16,114	75.4	2,253	10.5	1,484	6.9
1975	18,882	75.5	2,872	11.5	1,533	6.1
1976	22,500	78.0	2,939	10.2	1,572	5.4
1977	26,600	80.3	2,943	8.9	1,580	4.8
1978	31,715	82.3	2,900	7.5	1,623	4.2
1979	36,986	82.1	3,193	7.1	1,854	4.1
1980	42,696	81.4	3,809	7.3	2,030	3.9
1981	49,019	78.7	4,080	6.6	2,118	3.4
1982	57,152	74.8	4,635	6.1	2,124	2.8
1983	68,056	74.6	4,329	4.7	2,250	2.5
1984	82,586	76.2	4,134	3.8	2,506	2.3
1985	97,213	76.3	3,632	2.9	2,707	2.1
1986	116,640	75.6	3,126	2.0	3,215	2.1
1987	131,557	71.6	2,693	1.5	4,203	2.3
1988	155,277	69.3	2,364	1.1	4,686	2.1
1989	152,542	59.1	2,134	0.8	4,542	1.8
1990	176,682	59.9	1,812	0.6	4,752	1.6
1991	197,609	61.6	1,366	0.4	3,604	1.1
1992	211,329	62.3	1,029	0.3	3,508	1.0
1993	221,142	62.2	734	0.2	2,481	0.7

Mortgage[a] arrears and possessions
UK, '000s

	No. of Mortgages	Loans in arrears at end period		Properties taken into possession in period
		By 6–12 months	By over 12 months	
1971	4,506	17.6	…	2.8
1976	5,322	16.0	…	5.0
1981	6,336	21.5	…	4.9
1982	6,518	27.4	5.5	6.9
1983	6,846	29.4	7.5	8.4
1984	7,313	48.3	9.5	12.4
1985	7,717	57.1	13.1	19.3
1986	8,138	52.1	13.0	24.1
1987	8,283	55.5	15.0	26.4
1988	8,564	42.8	10.3	18.5
1989	9,125	66.8	13.8	15.8
1990	9,415	123.1	36.1	43.9
1991	9,815	183.6	91.7	75.5
1992	9,922	205.0	147.0	68.5
1993	9,998	191.6	158.0	31.8

Banks		Other specialist Mortgage lenders		Other public sector		Total
£m	% of total	£m	% of total	£m	% of total	£m
415	3.6	...	...	79	0.7	11,510
505	3.8	...	...	91	0.7	13,336
850	5.3	...	...	113	0.7	16,113
1,160	6.1	...	...	159	0.8	18,956
1,250	5.8	...	...	272	1.3	21,373
1,310	5.2	...	...	405	1.6	25,002
1,380	4.8	...	...	465	1.6	28,856
1,520	4.6	...	...	483	1.5	33,126
1,805	4.7	...	...	500	1.3	38,533
2,430	5.4	...	...	572	1.3	45,001
2,880	5.5	...	...	1,026	2.0	52,557
5,673	9.1	...	...	1,379	2.2	62,567
10,751	14.1	...	...	1,737	2.3	76,399
14,845	16.3	...	...	1,778	1.9	91,524
16,888	15.6	480	0.4	1,737	1.6	108,331
21,111	16.6	971	0.8	1,798	1.4	127,432
25,916	16.8	3,539	2.3	1,852	1.2	154,288
35,948	19.6	7,495	4.1	1,901	1.0	183,797
45,335	20.2	14,227	6.4	2,045	0.9	223,934
79,190	30.7	17,416	6.8	2,179	0.8	258,003
85,677	29	24,038	8.1	2,077	0.7	295,038
90,371	28.2	26,222	8.2	1,641	0.5	320,813
96,470	28.5	25,115	7.4	1,516	0.4	338,967
107,245	30.2	22,303	6.3	1,457	0.4	355,362

County court actions for mortgage possessions[b]

Actions, '000s

	1987	1989	1991	1993
England	74.0	86.2	176.4	109.7
Wales	5.1	5.1	10.2	6.4
North	4.7	4.5	6.9	4.6
Yorkshire & Humberside	7.8	7.4	14.1	8.4
North West	13.0	11.3	21.4	14.1
West Midlands	9.9	8.5	17.7	10.3
East Midlands	6.4	6.2	13.5	7.7
East Anglia	2.3	3.2	6.2	3.9
South East	24.5	37.9	79.9	48.9
Greater London	9.0	15.9	35.3	21.3
Rest of South East	15.6	22.0	44.6	27.7
South West	5.3	7.2	16.7	11.7

a Council of Mortgage Lenders estimates covering members of the Council, who account for 95% of all mortgages outstanding.
b Local authority and private.

Building societies

Numbers

	No. of societies	No. of branches	No. of shareholders '000s	No. of depositors '000s	No. of borrowers '000s
1930	1,026	...	1,449	428	720
1940	952	...	2,088	771	1,503
1950	819	...	2,256	654	1,508
1960	726	...	3,910	571	2,349
1970	481	2,016	10,265	618	3,655
1980	273	5,684	30,636	915	5,383
1985	167	6,926	39,996	2,149	6,657
1990	117	6,051	36,948	4,299	6,724
1991	110	5,921	37,925	4,698	6,998
1992	105	5,765	37,533	3,879	7,055
1993	101	5,654	37,809	5,486	7,229

Assets, loans and balances

	Share balances £m	Deposit & loan balances, £m	Mortgage balances £m	Total assets £m	Advances during yr. Number '000s	Advances during yr. Amount £m
1930	303	45	316	371	159	89
1940	552	142	678	756	43	21
1950	962	205	1,060	1,256	302	270
1960	2,721	222	2,647	3,166	387	560
1970	9,788	382	8,752	10,819	624	1,954
1980	48,915	1,762	42,437	53,793	936	9,503
1985	102,332	10,752	96,765	120,763	1,682	26,531
1990	160,538	40,695	175,745	216,848	1,397	43,081
1991	177,519	49,517	196,946	243,980	1,492	42,948
1992	187,108	57,068	210,995	262,515	1,187	34,989
1993	194,975	64,861	224,168	281,152	1,011	33,183

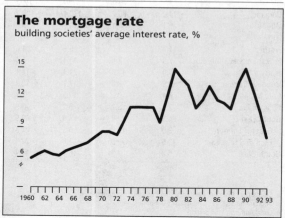

The mortgage rate
building societies' average interest rate, %

Part IX
HEALTH

Living longer

Expectation of life at varying ages
Further number of years which a person can expect to live, UK

Males

	1901	1931	1951	1961	1971	1981	1991	2001
at birth	48.0	58.4	66.2	67.9	68.8	70.8	73.2	74.5
at age 1 year	55.0	62.1	67.5	68.6	69.2	70.7	72.8	74.0
at age 10 years	51.4	55.6	59.1	60.0	60.5	62.0	64.0	65.2
at age 20 years	42.7	46.7	49.5	50.4	50.9	52.3	54.2	55.4
at age 40 years	26.8	29.5	30.9	31.5	31.9	33.2	35.1	36.2
at age 60 years	13.4	14.4	14.8	15.0	15.3	16.3	17.6	18.7
at age 80 years	4.9	4.8	4.8	5.2	5.5	5.7	6.3	7.0

Females

	1901	1931	1951	1961	1971	1981	1991	2001
at birth	51.6	62.4	71.2	73.8	75.0	76.8	78.8	79.9
at age 1 year	57.4	65.1	72.1	74.2	75.2	76.6	78.3	79.3
at age 10 years	53.9	58.6	63.6	65.6	66.5	67.8	69.5	70.5
at age 20 years	45.2	49.6	53.9	55.7	56.7	57.9	59.6	60.6
at age 40 years	29.1	32.4	35.1	36.5	37.3	38.5	40.0	41.0
at age 60 years	14.9	16.4	17.9	19.0	19.8	20.8	21.9	22.7
at age 80 years	5.4	5.4	5.8	6.3	6.9	7.5	8.3	8.8

Expectation of life at birth
Number of years which a person can expect to live

	1961	1971	1981	1990
Males				
UK	67.9	68.8	70.8	73.0
England & Wales	68.1	69.0	71.0	73.2
Scotland	66.3	67.3	69.0	71.1
Northern Ireland	67.6	67.6	69.3	71.8
Females				
UK	73.8	75.0	76.8	78.5
England & Wales	74.0	75.2	77.0	78.7
Scotland	72.0	73.7	75.2	76.7
Northern Ireland	72.4	73.7	75.7	77.6

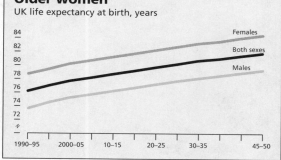

Older women
UK life expectancy at birth, years

Females

Both sexes

Males

84 — 82 — 80 — 78 — 76 — 74 — 72 —

1990–95   2000–05   10–15   20–25   30–35   45–50

A hundred up
Number of centenarians

	No. 1991 census	Per million population
England and Wales	6,619	86
Wales	373	85
North	346	72
Yorkshire & Humberside	563	78
North West	726	76
West Midlands	520	68
East Midlands	474	79
East Anglia	322	95
South East	2,463	92
South West	832	117

Octogenarian boom
Growth in proportion of over 80-year olds in total population

	1960	2000	2040
UK	1.92	4.08	5.94
Australia	1.24	2.99	5.95
Belgium	1.94	3.65	8.33
Canada	1.25	3.53	7.95
Finland	0.93	3.34	6.79
Japan	0.72	3.6	8.69
New Zealand	1.51	2.79	5.03
Spain	1.41	3.43	6.47
Switzerland	1.55	3.93	6.61
USA	1.40	3.49	7.63

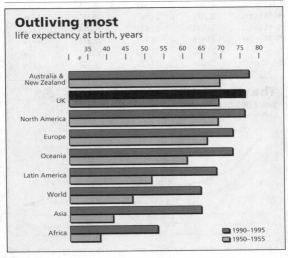

Outliving most
life expectancy at birth, years

1990–1995
1950–1955

Dying older

Death rates, UK

Males

	1900-02	1910-12	1920-22	1930-32
All ages[a]	340,664	303,703	284,876	284,249
Per 1,000 pop.	18.4	14.9	13.5	12.9
1 year	87,242	63,885	48,044	28,840
1–4 years	37,834	29,452	19,008	11,276
5–9 years	8,429	7,091	6,052	4,580
10–14 years	4,696	4,095	3,953	2,890
15–19 years	7,047	5,873	5,906	5,076
20–24 years	8,766	6,817	6,572	6,495
25–34 years	19,154	16,141	13,663	12,327
35–44 years	24,739	21,813	19,702	16,326
45–54 years	30,488	28,981	29,256	29,376
55–64 years	37,610	37,721	40,583	47,989
65–74 years	39,765	45,140	49,398	63,804
75–84 years	28,320	29,397	34,937	45,247
85 and over	6,563	7,283	7,801	10,022

Females

	1900-02	1910-12	1920-22	1930-32
All ages	322,058	289,608	274,772	275,336
Per 1,000 pop.	16.3	13.3	11.9	11.5
1 year	68,770	49,865	335,356	21,072
1–4 years	36,164	27,817	17,323	9,995
5–9 years	8,757	7,113	5,808	3,990
10–14 years	5,034	4,355	4,133	2,734
15–19 years	6,818	5,683	5,729	4,721
20–24 years	8,264	6,531	6753	5,931
25–34 years	18,702	15,676	14,878	12,699
35–44 years	21,887	19,647	18,121	15,373
45–54 years	25,679	24,481	24,347	24,695
55–64 years	34,521	32,813	34,026	39,471
65–74 years	42,456	46,453	48,573	59,520
75–84 years	34,907	37,353	45,521	56,250
85 and over	10,099	11,828	14,203	18,886

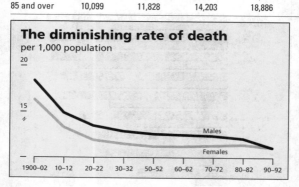

The diminishing rate of death

per 1,000 population

Males

Females

1900–02 10–12 20–22 30–32 50–52 60–62 70–72 80–82 90–92

a In some years the totals include a small number of persons whose age was not stated.

1940-42	1950-52	1960-62	1970-72	1980-82	1990-92
314,643	307,312	318,850	335,166	330,495	312,521
...	12.6	12.5	12.4	12.1	11.1
24,624	14,105	12,234	9,158	4,829	3,315
6,949	2,585	1,733	1,485	774	623
3,400	1,317	971	1,019	527	372
2,474	919	871	802	652	396
4,653	1,498	1,718	1,778	1,999	1,349
4,246	2,289	1,857	2,104	1,943	2,059
11,506	5,862	3,842	3,590	3,736	4,334
17,296	11,074	8,753	7,733	6,568	6,979
30,082	27,637	26,422	24,608	19,728	15,412
57,076	53,691	63,009	64,898	54,159	40,424
79,652	86,435	87,542	105,058	105,155	87,849
59,733	79,768	83,291	82,905	98,488	106,376
12,900	20,131	26,605	30,027	31,936	43,032
296,646	291,597	304,871	322,968	330,269	328,218
...	11.2	11.2	11.3	11.4	11.1
17,936	10,293	8,887	6,666	3,561	2,431
5,952	2,098	1,334	1,183	585	485
2,743	880	627	654	355	259
2,068	625	522	459	425	255
4,180	1,115	684	718	733	520
5,028	1,717	811	900	772	714
11,261	5,018	2,504	2,110	2,099	1,989
14,255	8,989	6,513	5,345	4,360	4,340
23,629	18,875	16,720	15,594	12,206	9,707
42,651	37,075	36,078	36,177	32,052	25,105
70,907	75,220	73,118	75,599	72,618	61,951
71,377	92,848	105,956	109,539	117,760	115,467
24,658	36,844	51,117	68,024	82,743	104,994

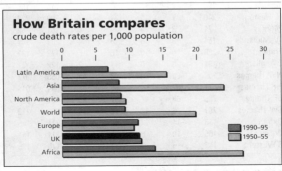

How Britain compares
crude death rates per 1,000 population

Latin America
Asia
North America
World
Europe
UK
Africa

1990–95
1950–55

Death: the causes

Mostly natural

	1935	1950	1960
Total deaths	**561,234**	**590,136**	**603,328**
from natural causes	**536,275**	**568,119**	**576,747**
of which:			
Tuberculosis (all forms)	33,485	20,405	4,058
Whooping cough	2,110	485	48
Meningococcal infection	...	327	118
Measles	1,825	271	33
Cancer – malignant disease	71,997	97,465	112,222
Diabetes mellitus	5,471	4,342	4,202
Mental disorders	...	...	...
Nervous system diseases	...	...	...
Cerebrovascular disease	50,922	75,154	88,262
Heart disease	119,453	169,202	173,579
Respiratory disease	75,208	55,796	57,397
Ulcer of stomach/duodenum	5,272	5,820	5,386
Liver disease & cirrhosis	...	...	...
from accidents & violence	**26,139**	**22,017**	**26,581**
of which:			
Motor vehicle accidents	6,859	4,842	7,496
Suicide	5,794	4,788	5,583

Aids

Cases by exposure category, cumulative totals to December 31st 1993

	Sexual intercourse		Injecting drug		Other & undeter-	Cases cumul-	
	Males	Females	use	Blood[b]	mined	ative	Deaths
UK	6,985	403	438	484	219	8,529	5,653
England	6,625	374	272	430	189	7,890	5,203
Wales	85	5	3	19	6	118	95
Scotland	243	20	162	31	23	479	323
N Ireland	32	4	1	4	1	42	32
North	90	7	3	36	3	139	98
Yorkshire	150	9	13	34	8	214	150
N Western	240	7	15	31	7	300	222
Mersey	71	3	4	19	4	101	82
W. Midlands	154	13	6	26	4	203	147
Trent	136	5	10	16	5	172	132
E Anglian	91	8	10	11	2	122	71
NW Thames	2,802	86	79	42	44	3,053	1,977
NE Thames	1,411	107	54	65	47	1,684	1,014
SE Thames	786	66	47	57	25	981	680
SW Thames	251	36	12	12	18	329	219
Oxford	136	11	12	46	6	211	145
Wessex	165	10	6	21	9	211	141
S Western	142	6	1	14	7	170	125

a Blood/blood factor and tissue recipients.
b Data for Scotland and Northern Ireland are for 1991.

1970	1980	1985	1990	1992ᵇ
655,382	**661,519**	**670,656**	**641,799**	**631,495**
629,067	**637,030**	**648,082**	**617,296**	**608,608**
1,950	1,059	896	651	664
22	6	4	8	1
163	81	111	189	178
51	34	12	2	3
131,158	146,308	158,017	161,718	164,545
5,581	5,477	8,077	8,486	8,639
1,608	3,928	12,989	14,439	14,128
7,134	7,367	12,390	12,711	12,692
91,691	82,800	83,665	76,409	75,970
213,451	225,839	221,162	198,3501	194,105
87,367	80,746	49,614	41,286	40,618
4,280	5,019	5,427	4,815	4,762
1,671	2,696	3,074	3,623	3,592
26,315	**24,489**	**22,574**	**21,282**	**19,932**
7,884	6,863	5,720	5,701	4,822
4,386	4,917	5,105	4,643	4,606

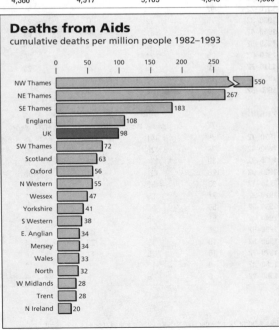

Deaths from Aids
cumulative deaths per million people 1982–1993

NW Thames	550
NE Thames	267
SE Thames	183
England	108
UK	98
SW Thames	72
Scotland	63
Oxford	56
N Western	55
Wessex	47
Yorkshire	41
S Western	38
E. Anglian	34
Mersey	34
Wales	33
North	32
W Midlands	28
Trent	28
N Ireland	20

Infant mortality

Overall

	UK	England & Wales	Scotland	N. Ireland
1870–72	150	156	126	96
1880–82	137	141	118	101
1890–92	145	149	125	107
1900–02	142	146	124	113
1910–22	110	110	109	101
1920–22	82	80	94	86
1930–32	67	65	84	75
1940–42	59	55	77	80
1950–52	30	29	37	40
1960–62	22	22	26	27
1970–72	18	18	19	22
1980–82	12	11	12	13
1990–92	7	7	7	7

Male

	UK	England & Wales	Scotland	N. Ireland
1870–72	163	169	135	105
1880–82	150	154	129	110
1890–92	159	164	136	115
1900–02	156	160	136	123
1910–12	121	121	120	110
1920–22	92	90	106	95
1930–32	75	72	94	83
1940–42	66	62	87	89
1950–52	34	33	42	45
1960–62	25	24	30	30
1970–72	20	20	22	24
1980–82	13	13	13	15
1990–92	8	8	8	8

Female

	UK	England & Wales	Scotland	N. Ireland
1870–72	136	141	115	86
1880–82	124	128	108	92
1890–92	130	134	114	99
1900–02	128	131	111	103
1910–12	98	98	97	92
1920–22	71	69	82	77
1930–32	58	55	73	66
1940–42	51	48	66	70
1950–52	26	25	32	36
1960–62	19	19	22	24
1970–72	16	15	17	20
1980–82	10	10	10	12
1990–92	6	6	6	6

Infant mortality is the number of deaths under one year per 1,000 live births.

Regional differences
1991

Yorkshire & Humberside	8.6
North	8.5
East Midlands	7.8
North-West	7.5
Greater London	7.0
South-West	6.4
South-East	6.3
East Anglia	6.1

Class matters
Infant deaths by father's occupation, 1986–90, England & Wales

Unskilled manual	13.1
Semi-skilled manual	10.5
Skilled manual	8.4
Armed forces	7.8
Intermediate & junior non-managerial	7.5
Employers & managers	6.6
Professional	6.6

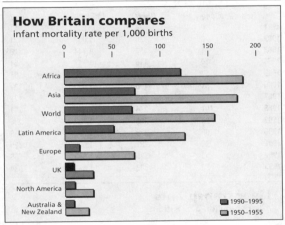

How Britain compares
infant mortality rate per 1,000 births

Africa, Asia, World, Latin America, Europe, UK, North America, Australia & New Zealand

■ 1990–1995
□ 1950–1955

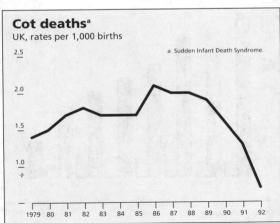

Cot deaths[a]
UK, rates per 1,000 births

a Sudden Infant Death Syndrome.

1979 80 81 82 83 84 85 86 87 88 89 90 91 92

Diseases and transplants

Notifications of infectious diseases, UK

	1955	1960	1965	1970
Scarlet fever	38,850	36,326	28,982	14,402
Measles	...	...	502,066[a]	307,318[a]
Whooping cough	88,061	66,628	14,498	19,788
Dysentery	49,734	52,011	33,813	14,213
Food poisoning	...	...	5,001[a]	7,566[a]
Tuberculosis				
total	47,071	28,381	19,333	14,167
respiratory	41,293	24,837	16,231	11,377
other	5,778	3,544	3,102	2790

Organ transplants, UK

	Heart and lung	Heart	Kidney	Liver
1981	0	24	905	11
1982	0	36	1,033	21
1983	1	53	1,144	20
1984	10	116	1,443	51
1985	37	137	1,336	88
1986	51	176	1,493	127
1987	72	243	1,485	172
1988	101	274	1,575	241
1989	94	295	1,732	295
1990	95	329	1,730	359
1991	79	281	1,628	420
1992	53	325	1,640	506
1993	36	302	1,571	534

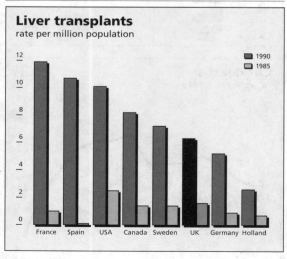

Liver transplants
rate per million population

legend: 1990, 1985

France, Spain, USA, Canada, Sweden, UK, Germany, Holland

a England and Wales only.
b Excludes Northern Ireland.

1975	1980	1985	1990	1992
10,235	12,936	7,451	9,505	5,978
148,643[b]	147,938	104,774	15,642	12,317
9,923	22,873	24,244	16,862	2,750
9,375	3,595	6,112	3,042	20,620
10,276[b]	12,021	21,364	55,988	67,579
12,612	10,486	6,647	5,897	6,441
9,649	7,789	5,292	4,476	4,706
2,963	2,697	1,404	1,469	1,711

Occupational hazards

Deaths due to occupationally related lung disease[b], Great Britain

	Asbestosis without mesothelioma	Mesothelioma	Pneumoconiosis	Total
1982	128	504	314	983
1983	121	573	317	1,059
1984	129	624	314	1,101
1985	140	615	324	1,111
1986	166	702	337	1,249
1987	144	808	279	1,272
1988	152	862	281	1,326
1989	157	899	317	1,406
1990	164	881	328	1,398
1991	163	1,017	287	1,491

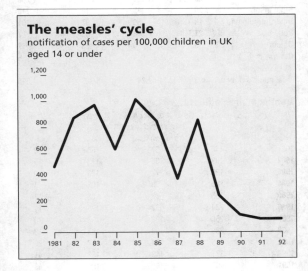

The measles' cycle

notification of cases per 100,000 children in UK aged 14 or under

Drugs

Addicts[a]
1992

	Heroin	Methadone	Dipipanone
UK	16,964	10,011	320
England	15,669	8,825	203
Wales	277	314	12
Scotland	997	860	102
Northern Ireland	21	12	3
North	159	89	6
Yorkshire & Humberside	1,234	428	16
North West	5,157	2,632	21
West Midlands	783	418	16
East Midlands	269	430	11
East Anglia	397	386	8
Greater London	5,184	2,527	35
Rest of South East	1,479	1,225	67
South West	1,007	690	23

New addicts
UK

	1973	1981	1986	1987
Heroin	508	1,660	4,855	4,082
Methadone	328	431	659	627
Cocaine	132	174	520	431
Morphine	226	355	343	250
Dipipanone	28	473	116	113
Dextromoraminde	28	59	97	101
Pethidine	27	45	33	37
Opium	0	0	23	17
Others	2	4	4	5
Total addicts notified	806	2,248	5,325	4,593

Deaths of drug addicts

UK	Total	Not primarily associated with drug misuse	Overdose	Other
1981	140	57	80	3
1982	183	65	113	5
1983	195	72	123	0
1984	145	38	103	4
1985	166	63	86	17
1986	233	97	125	11
1987	266	108	138	20
1988	289	108	163	18
1989	310	124	157	29
1990	371	143	187	41
1991	403	164	196	43
1992	506	201	284	21

	Cocaine	Morphine	Other	Total[b]
	1,951	321	320	24,703
	1,871	247	255	22,240
	39	14	28	579
	41	58	31	1,849
	0	2	6	35
	14	3	3	241
	68	25	18	1,557
	401	44	42	6,764
	98	30	23	1,160
	25	26	10	663
	28	10	13	705
	891	54	62	7,010
	182	36	55	2,572
	164	19	29	1,568

1988	1989	1990	1991	1992	1993
4,630	4,883	5,819	6,328	7,658	9,063
576	682	1,469	2,180	2,493	3,362
462	527	633	882	1,131	1,375
203	259	296	185	161	120
124	109	154	155	158	128
80	75	78	89	76	60
44	36	39	37	49	44
18	15	14	12	5	25
2	1	4	1	0	2
5,212	5,639	6,923	8,007	9,663	11561

Seizures of controlled drugs

UK	Total	By authority, %			
		Police			HM Customs & Excise[c]
		Total	Metropolitan	Other	
1985	30,466	88	28	60	12
1986	30,478	83	27	56	17
1987	30,690	84	28	56	16
1988	38,235	86	33	53	14
1989	52,131	86	33	53	14
1990	60,859	88	30	57	12
1991	69,805	89	29	61	11
1992	72,065	89	26	63	11

a Notified under the Misuse of Drugs Act to Home Office.
b Addicts may use more than one notifiable drug so total may be smaller than sum.
c In terms of weight customs seize well over 80%.

Smoking

Cigarette smokers
% of persons over 16 years who smoke cigarettes

	1974	1978	1982	1986	1990	1992
Great Britain	45	40	35	33	30	29
England	45	40	35	32	30	28
Wales	46	40	35	31	31	33
Scotland	48	45	42	36	34	34
Northern Ireland	...	...	...	...	32	30
North	46	41	41	35	32	30
Yorkshire & Humberside	43	39	35	34	29	28
North West	48	43	36	35	34	30
West Midlands	45	39	35	34	30	27
East Midlands	44	39	33	31	29	25
East Anglia	39	38	30	31	26	28
South East	46	39	34	32	30	28
South West	41	39	34	29	27	26

Serious habits
% of persons over 16 years who smoke more than 20 cigarettes a day

	1980		1986		1990	
	Males	Females	Males	Females	Males	Females
Great Britain	21	13	15	10	14	9
England	20	13	14	9	14	9
Wales	25	16	14	10	18	10
Scotland	27	16	19	15	15	13
North	26	17	16	11	16	9
Yorks & Humberside	20	14	14	11	13	8
North West	25	16	15	9	14	11
West Midlands	19	12	17	10	16	8
East Midlands	22	13	15	8	12	10
East Anglia	20	9	13	9	10	5
Greater London	21	13	14	10	16	10
Rest of South East	18	11	13	8	12	8
South West	15	11	13	7	11	6

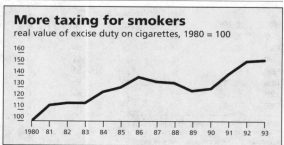

More taxing for smokers
real value of excise duty on cigarettes, 1980 = 100

Who smokes most

% of persons over 16 years who smoke cigarettes

1974		1992	
Wales	46	Scotland	34
Scotland	45	Wales	33
England	45	England	28
North West	48	North West	30
North	46	North	30
South East	46	South East	28
West Midlands	45	Yorkshire & Humberside	28
East Midlands	44	East Anglia	28
Yorkshire & Humberside	43	West Midlands	27
South West	41	South West	26
East Anglia	39	East Midlands	25

Class seriousness

% GB population over 16 years who smoke more than 20 cigarettes a day, 1990

	Males	Females
Professional	5	6
Employers and Managers	12	7
Intermediate and junior non-manual	8	7
Skilled manual	17	11
Semi-skilled manual	18	12
Unskilled manual	22	13
Total	14	9

How Britain compares

Tobacco consumption per year, kg per head of adult population

	1974–76	1990	2000
UK	2.6	1.9	1.6
Bulgaria	3.6	4.1	4.3
France	2.8	2.3	2.1
Germany	3.2	2.3	2.1
Greece	3.2	3.0	3.3
Ireland	3.2	2.4	2.1
Italy	2.2	1.9	2.0
Netherlands	3.8	3.0	2.7
Poland	3.4	3.5	3.7
Portugal	1.3	1.9	2.0
Spain	2.5	2.4	2.6
Sweden	1.9	1.5	1.3
Switzerland	3.7	2.9	2.3
USA	3.8	2.6	2.2
Canada	3.8	2.6	2.2
Japan	3.5	2.4	1.9

Health spending

Government spending on the NHS
Years ending 31 March, £m (figures in brackets are amount expressed in 1992/93 prices)

	Current expenditure	Capital expenditure	Total
1965/66	1,215 (11,275.2)	104 (965.1)	1,319
1966/67	1,333 (11,871.6)	114 (1.015.3)	1,447
1967/68	1,453 (12,625.3)	135 (1,173.0)	1,588
1968/69	1,565 (12,837.2)	144 (1,181.2)	1,709
1969/70	1,653 (12,955.9)	144 (1,128.6)	1,797
1970/71	1,941 (14,072.3)	170 (1,232.5)	2,111
1971/72	2,195 (14,619.3)	210 (1,398.7)	2,405
1972/73	2,491 (15,411.0)	255 (1,577.6)	2,746
1973/74	2,759 (15,423.8)	296 (1,654.7)	3,055
1974/75	3,793 (17,837.4)	302 (1,420.2)	4,095
1975/76	5,065 (19,055.4)	405 (1,523.7)	5,470
1976/77	5,826 (19,037.1)	423 (1,382.2)	6,249
1977/78	6,486 (18,888.1)	410 (1,194.0)	6,896
1978/79	7,369 (19,995.4)	466 (1,264.5)	7,835
1979/80	8,673 (19,889.3)	522 (1,197.1)	9,195
1980/81	11,256 (22,415.4)	688 (1,370.1)	11,944
1981/82	12,435 (22,106.7)	832 (1,479.1)	13,267
1982/83	13,528 (22,825.4)	857 (1,446.0)	14,385
1983/84	14,497 (23,221.9)	886 (1,419.2)	15,383
1984/85	15,322 (23,463.4)	990 (1,516.0)	16,312
1985/86	16,343 (23697.4)	1,091 (1,582.0)	17,434
1986/87	17,569 (24,554.3)	1,160 (1,621.2)	18,729
1987/88	19,373 (26,105.7)	1,212 (1,633.2)	20,585
1988/89	21,493 (27,124.4)	1,309 (1,652.0)	22,802
1989/90	22,726 (26,628.4)	2,071 (2,426.6)	24,797
1990/91	25,917 (27,772.5)	1,848 (1,980.3)	27,765
1991/92	29,932 (30,704.0)	1,791 (1,837.2)	31,723
1992/93	33,029 (33.029.0)	1,883 (1,883.0)	34,914

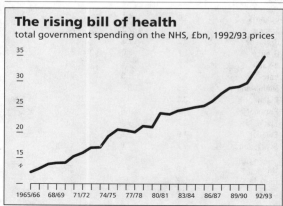

The rising bill of health
total government spending on the NHS, £bn, 1992/93 prices

How Britain compares

Spending on health as % of domestic spending

	1960	1970	1980	1991
UK	3.9	4.6	5.9	6.6
OECD average	3.9	5.1	7.0	8.1
Australia	4.8	5.6	7.1	8.6
Austria	4.4	5.5	7.7	8.5
Belgium	3.4	4.2	6.5	8.1
Canada	5.3	7.2	7.5	9.9
Denmark	3.6	5.9	6.7	7.0
Finland	3.8	5.7	6.4	8.9
France	4.3	5.9	7.5	9.1
Germany	4.9	6.0	8.4	9.1
Greece	2.6	3.7	4.0	4.8
Iceland	3.4	5.4	6.5	8.3
Ireland	3.8	5.1	8.1	8.0
Italy	3.6	5.2	6.6	8.3
Japan	3.0	4.6	6.5	6.8
Luxembourg	...	4.7	6.8	6.6
Netherlands	4.0	5.9	8.0	8.7
New Zealand	4.2	5.1	7.2	7.7
Norway	3.2	4.9	7.1	8.4
Portugal	...	3.0	5.1	6.2
Spain	1.6	3.6	5.4	6.5
Sweden	4.7	7.1	9.2	8.8
Switzerland	3.3	5.1	7.0	8.0
Turkey	...	...	3.7	4.1
USA	5.3	7.4	9.2	13.3

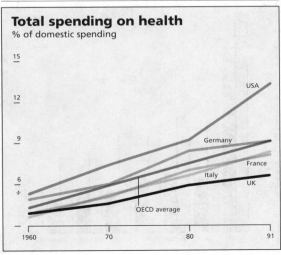

Total spending on health

% of domestic spending

Hospital services

Beds and treatment

	Hospital beds per 1,000 population			Cases treated per bed		Finished consultant episodes, 1993	
	1981	1986	1993	1981	1993	'000s	% in NHS trusts
England	7.5	6.7	4.8	16.4	33.8	7,829.4	38
Wales	8.2	7.7	6.2	16.4	27.9	503.7	4
Scotland	11.3	10.9	9.2	13.1	20.2	941.7	10
Northern Ireland	11.1	10.2	7.3	14.6	23.5	275.1	50
Northern	7.8	7.5	6.0	16.4	29.5	551.0	30
Yorkshire	8.0	7.1	5.0	16.1	34.7	645.3	49
North Western	7.6	7.1	5.5	18.1	33.6	745.0	27
Mersey	8.6	7.4	4.8	14.2	37.6	434.0	75
West Midlands	6.8	6.2	4.4	16.4	35.8	840.6	18
Trent	6.7	6.2	4.4	16.5	36.0	751.5	31
East Anglia	6.9	6.3	4.8	16.8	32.2	320.1	16
NW Thames	7.8	6.6	4.5	15.5	28.7	468.4	59
NE Thames	7.6	6.9	4.8	16.7	34.0	624.2	50
SE Thames	7.6	6.4	4.1	17.0	37.5	572.1	22
SW Thames	8.6	7.1	5.0	12.8	27.5	419.7	42
Oxford	5.7	4.9	3.6	20.4	39.0	363.5	21
Wessex	6.7	6.0	4.4	17.3	35.6	470.9	35
South Western	7.8	6.7	4.8	15.2	33.4	529.7	69

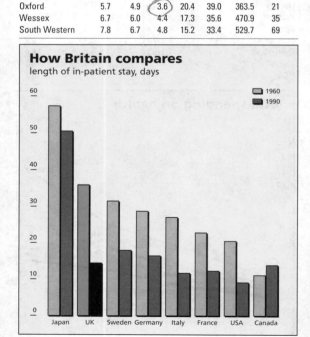

How Britain compares
length of in-patient stay, days

■ 1960
■ 1990

Japan UK Sweden Germany Italy France USA Canada

NHS waiting lists

In-patient waiting lists
At end September, '000s

	1976	1981	1986	1990	1991
General surgery	200.5[a]	169.1[a]	180.3[a]	173.3	169.0
Orthopaedics	109.8	145.1	160.5	154.1	151.5
Ear, nose or throat	121.7	115.4	132.2	125.5	125.3
Gynaecology	91.8	105.6	106.6	98.7	97.8
Oral surgery	26.5	35.5	56.3	52.5	49.7
Plastic surgery	44.7	49.2	46.1	51.3	41.7
Ophthalmology	41.2	43.4	64.6	91.2	99.5
Urology	22.0[b]	29.1[b]	42.7[b]	47.3	46.7
Other	42.5	44.2	41.3	47.9	49.0
All specialties	700.8	736.6	830.6	841.2	830.1

Regional differences
Waiting lists at end September 1993, '000s

	Ordinary admissions				Day case admissions			
	Total waiting '000s	Months waited, % under 6	6–12	over 12	Total waiting '000s	Months waited, % under 6	6–12	over 12
UK	788.1	...	...	...	415.2	...	...	...
England	666.9	65.4	26.5	8.1	365.1	77.1	18.3	4.6
Wales	40.3	...	85.5	14.5	13.4	...	...	...
Scotland	55.5	75.8	16.3	7.9	26.7	77.1	11.7	11.2
Northern Ireland	25.4	58.7	22.8	18.5	10.0	68.0	18.0	10.0
Northern	39.5	67.6	26.1	6.3	25.6	77.2	19.1	3.7
Yorkshire	53.5	64.7	24.9	10.4	26.0	77.3	17.3	5.4
North Western	62.6	66.4	24.1	9.5	34.4	78.1	16.4	5.5
Mersey	34.6	71.8	27.7	0.5	22.1	82.9	16.9	0.2
West Midlands	69.5	66.1	28.2	5.7	37.4	77.5	18.4	4.1
Trent	60.8	66.0	25.7	8.3	30.2	80.0	16.2	3.8
East Anglia	30.1	65.6	24.9	9.5	13.9	76.7	18.6	4.7
NW Thames	39.2	60.1	28.7	11.2	22.3	75.2	19.4	5.4
NE Thames	64.3	57.5	29.1	13.4	35.5	70.8	22.5	6.7
SE Thames	55.5	62.8	27.7	9.5	25.9	74.7	19.9	5.4
SW Thames	37.5	65.0	27.0	8.0	26.3	75.7	19.4	4.9
Oxford	30.5	68.3	25.3	6.4	15.2	80.5	15.9	3.6
Wessex	41.0	67.1	24.7	8.2	21.2	76.2	18.8	5.0
South Western	41.0	70.7	26.7	2.6	24.0	81.5	17.8	0.7

a Includes Northern Ireland figures for urology.
b Great Britain only.

Doctors and dentists

General medical practitioners

	1982		1992			
	No.[a]	Average list size	No.[a]	Average list size	GP fund-holders	Opticians[b]
UK	28,065	2102	32,020	1,870	6,606	c
England	22,786	2,155	25,968	1,922	6,098	6,601
Wales	1,431	2,013	1,676	1,743	157	530
Scotland	3,040	1,778	3,445	1,555	351	946
Northern Ireland	808	1,981	931	1,826	...	204
Northern	1,458	2,194	1,675	1,876	392	392
Yorkshire	1,742	2,120	1,988	1,878	587	597
North Western	1,870	2,197	2,051	1,988	329	669
Mersey	1,167	2,182	1,247	1,986	423	443
West Midlands	2,459	2,176	2,747	1,969	767	838
Trent	2109	2,251	2,473	1,930	731	745
East Anglia	918	2,078	1,142	1,793	278	360
NW Thames	1,855	2,147	1,974	2,027	458	945
NE Thames	1,849	2,171	2,041	2,043	229	928
SE Thames	1,785	2,147	1,580	1,969	360	829
SW Thames	1,428	2,198	1,996	1,960	374	791
Oxford	1,117	2,190	1,380	1,869	431	531
Wessex	1,361	2,055	1,644	1,785	325	549
South Western	1,668	2,003	2,030	1,741	414	550

GPs and dentists
UK, '000s

	No. of doctors[a] in practice	Average no. of patients per doctor	No. of dentists in practice	Average no. of persons per dentist
1961	23.6	2.25	11.9	4.4
1971	24.0	2.39	12.5	4.5
1976	25.4	2.29	13.6	4.1
1981	27.5	2.15	15.2	3.7
1986	30.2	1.99	17.3	3.3
1987	30.7	1.97	17.6	3.2
1988	31.2	1.94	18.0	3.2
1989	31.5	1.91	18.4	3.1
1990	31.6	1.90	18.6	3.1
1991	31.7	1.90	18.6	3.1
1992	32.0	1.87	18.6	3.1
1993	30.3[d]	1.90[d]	19.1	3.0

a Unrestricted principals.
b Includes optometrists and Ophthalmic Medical practitioners.
c May practise in more than one region.
d England and Wales.

General dental practitioners

	1982	1992		
	No.	No.	Average list size	No. registered as % of pop.
UK	15,708	18,607	1,829	59
England	13,258	15,411	1,864	59
Wales	678	831	2,012	58
Scotland	1,369	1,777	1,536	53
Northern Ireland	403	588	1,538	56
Northern	645	868	2,080	58
Yorkshire	898	1,101	2,044	61
North Western	1,003	1,258	1,972	62
Mersey	630	768	1,972	63
West Midlands	1,226	1,401	2,209	59
Trent	966	1,264	2,244	59
East Anglia	483	598	2,191	63
NW Thames	1,458	1,400	1,377	55
NE Thames	1,114	1,202	1,701	54
SE Thames	1,176	1,237	1,400	58
SW Thames	1,127	1,309	1,608	57
Oxford	670	825	1,764	56
Wessex	778	960	1,934	63
South Western	1,084	1,220	1,896	66

Primary health care nursing staff
Whole time equivalents, rate per 1,000 population

	Community psychiatric nurses		Midwives		Health visitors		District nurses	
	1981	1992	1981	1992	1981	1992	1981	1992
England	2	9	7	9	20	21	31	20
Wales	3	…	7	…	19	…	43	…
Scotland	…	7	3	5	29	33	45	40
Northern Ireland	…	9	4	10	29	32	41	38
Northern	2	12	7	8	20	22	33	29
Yorkshire	2	10	7	9	20	21	31	17
North Western	2	10	9	11	23	29	38	24
Mersey	4	10	9	9	20	20	31	21
West Midlands	1	8	8	9	20	21	31	20
Trent	2	8	10	10	19	21	30	20
East Anglia	3	8	10	9	17	17	29	16
NW Thames	2	8	5	6	21	20	26	17
NE Thames	2	9	7	6	18	20	27	19
SE Thames	1	6	6	8	19	21	34	18
SW Thames	5	9	6	8	22	18	33	19
Oxford	3	7	7	7	20	22	32	21
Wessex	3	9	6	8	20	21	29	21
South Western	3	10	4	10	20	20	30	19

Prescriptions

Numbers and costs
UK

	Prescriptions dispensed [a]	Average total cost per prescription	Average no. of prescriptions per person	Average prescription cost per person [b]
	m	*£*		*£*
1961	233.2	0.41	4.7	1.9
1971	304.5	0.77	5.6	4.3
1981	370.0	3.46	6.6	23.0
1986	397.5	5.11	7.0	36.0
1987	413.6	5.47	7.3	40.0
1988	427.7	5.91	7.5	44.1
1989	435.8	6.26	7.5	47.2
1990	446.6	6.68	7.8	52.1
1991	467.8	7.14	8.2	58.5
1992	488.2	7.64	8.6	65.5

Regional variations [c]

	No. of prescription items per person [d]				Average cost per person, £	No. exempt from charges, %
	1981	*1991*	*1991* [e]	*1992* [e]	*1992*	*1992*
United Kingdom	6.6	8.1	8.6	9.0	60.63	...
England	6.5	7.8	8.4	8.8	59.08	81.0
Wales	8.6	10.7	10.8	11.3	71.18	...
Scotland	6.2	8.2	9.0	9.4	65.67	86.3
Northern Ireland	8.1	9.9	9.9	10.4	72.01	91.3
Northern	7.0	8.9	9.3	9.6	64.23	82.4
Yorkshire	6.9	8.7	9.1	9.4	59.62	81.7
North Western	7.5	9.5	10.0	10.4	65.17	82.6
Mersey	7.2	9.3	9.8	10.2	66.95	84.0
West Midlands	6.6	8.2	8.7	9.1	58.54	82.1
Trent	6.6	8.3	8.8	9.1	58.86	81.1
East Anglia	6.4	7.6	8.0	8.4	58.22	78.7
NW Thames	5.6	6.1	7.3	7.7	54.56	78.3
NE Thames	6.2	7.0	7.9	8.3	58.33	81.9
SE Thames	6.3	7.2	8.0	8.4	56.74	81.2
SW Thames	5.9	6.5	7.2	7.6	55.98	77.9
Oxford	5.6	6.4	6.9	7.2	52.97	75.4
Wessex	6.9	7.6	8.0	8.3	58.05	79.2
South Western	6.5	7.7	8.2	8.5	58.99	80.7

a Items dispensed by community pharmacists and appliance contractors only.
b Based on number of people on NHS prescribing list.
c Figures relate to NHS prescriptions dispensed by community pharmacists, appliance contractors, dispensing doctors and prescriptions submitted by prescribing doctors for items personally administered.
d Rates per head are based on mid-year population estimates.
e New basis.

Part X
EDUCATION

School enrolment

Pupils in school
'000s

	1965/66	1970/71	1975/76	1980/81
UK	9,084	10,232	11,301	10,633
England	7,856[a]	8,361	9,258	8,720
Wales	[a]	512	576	545
Scotland	921	1,006	1,094	1,005
Northern Ireland	307	353	374	363

Age, % of all in age group				
2 to 4	9.5	13.7	23.7	40.4
5 to 10	99.1	98.8	100.0	100.7
11	100.3	100.2	100.1	101.4
12 to 14	100.2	100.5	100.0	100.5
15	61.0	70.6	99.5	97.7
16	27.7	35.6	50.6	29.0
17	14.8	20.3	20.7	17.8
18 and over	5.1	7.0	6.8	2.3

Age, % of all males in age group				
14	99.6	100.6	100.0	100.0
15	61.0	70.9	99.6	97.3
16	28.7	36.3	50.6	27.4
17	16.2	21.3	21.0	17.6

Age, % of all females in age group				
14	99.9	101.1	100.0	100.2
15	60.9	70.3	99.5	98.1
16	26.7	34.9	50.8	30.6
17	13.2	19.3	20.4	17.8

School sizes
% pupils on register in schools of size, 1992/3

	50 or under	51–100	101–200	201 or over
UK	7.3	10.8	26.0	39.6
England	5.0	10.0	27.0	41.3
Wales	14.1	13.8	29.6	30.6
Scotland	18.6	10.9	18.9	36.6
Northern Ireland	13.8	20.3	18.2	28.5
North	7.0	9.8	29.5	35.8
Yorkshire & Humberside	5.4	10.2	29.5	36.8
North West	2.4	5.1	26.6	50.2
West Midlands	4.8	8.3	23.1	46.2
East Midlands	8.0	13.7	28.2	33.4
East Anglia	9.6	17.9	25.4	30.9
Greater London	…	1.1	22.1	59.4
Rest of South East	4.2	10.7	29.7	38.7
South West	9.0	18.6	26.2	32.0

a England and Wales combined.

	1985/86	1989/90	1990/91	1991/92
	9,565	9,199	9,260	9,368
	7,830	7,557	7,617	7,712
	495	480	482	487
	894	821	821	826
	346	340	341	343
	42.6	43.3	44.1	45.0
	99.9	98.9	98.9	98.0
	102.5	99.6	99.0	98.8
	101.7	100.1	99.8	99.2
	97.3	100.3	99.5	98.3
	32.1	37.5	40.6	43.8
	18.8	23.6	25.5	28.2
	3.0	3.3	3.8	4.4
	100.6	100.6	99.8	99.6
	97.4	100.1	99.4	98.2
	30.9	35.7	38.4	41.9
	18.5	22.7	24.3	26.7
	100.5	100.4	100.0	99.7
	97.8	100.5	99.6	98.4
	33.4	39.5	42.8	45.8
	19.0	24.6	26.8	29.9

400 or under	401–800	801–1000	1001 or over	Total no. of schools, '000s
2.0	7.1	3.3	3.9	28.5
1.8	7.3	3.5	4.1	22.6
0.7	5.2	2.1	3.9	1.9
2.8	5.5	3.1	3.5	2.8
5.0	9.2	3.0	2.1	1.2
3.4	7.7	2.7	4.0	1.6
4.0	6.9	2.9	4.3	2.5
0.5	7.1	4.3	3.9	3.0
1.6	8.1	4.2	3.6	2.5
2.2	7.8	2.8	4.0	2.1
2.3	8.2	2.1	3.6	1.1
0.6	7.0	4.6	5.0	2.4
1.6	7.5	3.6	4.0	4.9
1.5	5.9	2.6	4.2	2.5

Pupil/teacher ratios

Pupils per teacher

England	1965/66	1970/71	1975/76	1980/81
Nursery	24.9	19.1	21.1	19.7
Primary	28.2	27.0	24.0	22.6
Secondary	18.3	17.9	17.0	16.6
Non-maintained	13.8	13.7	13.4	12.5
Special	11.2	10.2	8.6	7.6
All schools	21.9	21.4	19.4	18.2

Wales				
Nursery	20.7	19.9	19.4	19.0
Primary	25.0	25.0	22.8	21.7
Secondary	19.0	18.3	17.1	16.6
Non-maintained	13.3	13.8	12.3	12.1
Special	10.9	10.4	10.9	7.7
All schools	21.7	21.4	19.6	18.5

Scotland				
Nursery	...	36.6	24.5	25.3
Primary	...	27.9	22.4	20.3
Secondary	...	16.1	15.1	14.4
Non-maintained	...	17.3	16.3	15.1
Special	...	11.6	9.7	6.8
All schools	...	22.1	18.6	16.9

Northern Ireland				
Nursery	24.7	27.6	30.0	23.5
Primary	29.5	28.9	26.4	23.6
Secondary	19.8	18.6	17.2	15.2
Non-maintained	18.7	17.9	17.4	16.5
Special	11.4	10.7	9.8	8.4
All schools	24.7	23.5	21.3	18.9

Class sizes
Maintained schools only

	One teacher classes			
	Primary		Secondary	
	1981	*1993*	*1981*	*1993*
England	25.2	26.6	20.8	20.9
Wales	...	...	...	19.7
Scotland	...	...	...	...
North	24.1	26.3	20.5	20.7
Yorkshire & Humberside	24.7	26.4	21.3	20.9
North West	26.0	27.4	20.7	20.8
West Midlands	25.1	26.9	20.8	21.1
East Midlands	26.0	26.5	21.2	20.6
East Anglia	24.5	25.5	21.0	20.7
Greater London	23.1	26.5	19.6	21.2
Rest of South East	26.2	26.5	21.1	20.9
South West	26.1	26.7	21.7	21.2

1985/86	1989/90	1990/91	1991/92
19.6	19.3	18.9	18.9
22.1	21.8	22.0	22.0
15.9	15.0	15.3	15.5
11.3	10.9	10.8	10.6
6.8	5.9	5.8	5.8
17.4	17.0	17.2	17.2
20.2	20.8	20.6	20.4
22.1	22.3	22.3	22.3
16.1	15.3	15.4	15.6
10.7	10.5	9.8	9.7
7.0	6.5	6.3	6.3
18.2	18.1	18.2	18.2
...	26.3	25.7	26.2
20.4	19.7	19.5	19.5
13.5	12.4	12.2	12.4
12.2	10.8	10.6	10.4
5.4	4.7	4.5	4.5
...	15.3	15.2	15.3
23.5	24.0	24.7	24.5
23.4	23.2	22.9	22.6
14.9	14.9	14.7	15.1
15.8	12.2	11.0	10.6
8.1	7.1	6.9	6.9
18.5	18.3	18.1	18.3

All classes			
Primary		*Secondary*	
1981	1993	1981	1993
25.5	27.0	21.5	21.4
...	25.0	...	21.4
23.8	24.5	19.9	19.4
24.7	26.6	21.2	21.4
25.1	26.8	21.9	21.4
26.2	27.9	21.4	21.3
25.4	27.2	21.3	21.6
26.3	26.8	22.0	21.2
24.9	25.9	22.2	21.4
23.5	26.8	20.2	21.7
26.6	26.8	21.8	21.4
26.4	26.9	22.2	21.6

Independent schools

Facts and figures

	1985	1990	1992	1993
No. of Schools				
Boys'	640	477	447	424
Girls'	455	432	406	391
Mixed	1,367	1,558	1,594	1,617
Total	2,462	2,467	2,447	2,432
No. of full-time pupils by age and sex				
2 to 4	28,253	36,011	38,268	38,335
5 to 10	179,310	207,156	207,675	203,055
11 to 15	263,051	259,082	259,409	252,203
16 and over	73,720	81,372	78,247	79,313
Total boys[a]	301,449	319,699	318,423	312,945
Total girls[a]	257,608	283,304	285,177	281,162
Total[a]	559,057	603,003	603,600	594,107
Attending boys' schools				
Boys	180,850	146,239	135,622	128,521
Girls	5,071	2,337	2,170	2,091
Attending girls' schools				
Boys	2,143	2,540	2,544	2,305
Girls	151,192	151,958	146,252	140,815
Attending mixed schools				
Boys	118,456	170,920	180,257	182,119
Girls	101,345	129,009	136,755	138,256
Boarding schools				
Boys'	417	292	254	233
Girls'	225	200	177	165
Mixed	398	498	511	506
Total	1,040	990	942	904
No. of boarders				
Boys	81,498	73,810	67,768	63,517
Girls	44,422	44,101	41,450	38,785
Total	125,920	117,911	109,218	102,302
Teaching staff				
Full-time	40,067	46,232	47,926	48,005
Part-time	7,180	8,179	8,384	8,349
Total	47,247	54,411	56,310	56,354
Pupil/teacher ratio				
England	11.4	10.9	10.7	10.5
Wales	10.6	10.0	9.7	9.7
Scotland	11.2	10.7	10.7	11.3

a Includes part-time pupils aged 2–4.

The costs

ISIS registered independent schools and average fees per term, 1994

	No. of schools	Boarding fee, £	Weekly boarding fee, £	Average day fee, £	Average fee, £
Wales	30	2,777	2,345	1,346	1,686
Scotland	51	3,259	2,712	1,270	1,596
Ireland	14	1,683	2,177	672	814
North	194	3,009	2,583	1,202	1,367
West Midlands	147	3,329	2,572	1,399	1,802
East Midlands	166	3,370	2,608	1,426	1,836
East Anglia	95	2,983	2,733	1,389	1,649
Greater London	166	3,716	3,196	1,562	1,630
South East	285	3,294	2,972	1,604	2,097
South & West	193	3,378	2,674	1,410	2,004
All	1,341	3,261	2,733	1,400	1,743

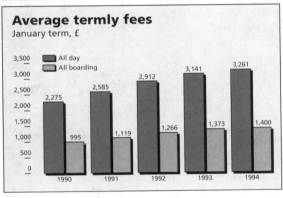

Average termly fees
January term, £

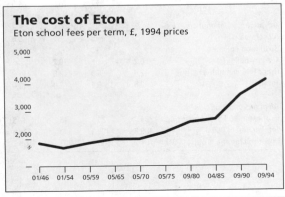

The cost of Eton
Eton school fees per term, £, 1994 prices

Sixteen plus

School leavers

16 year-olds staying on at school or going to further education, '000s
1981/82

	Staying on at school	Going to FE Full-time	Part-time	Participation in education, %
UK	...	...	...	...
England	244.4	135.2	66.5	56.4
Wales	15.1	8.3	4.4	58.1
Scotland	...	...	...	...
Northern Ireland	8.6	3.2	2.6	...
North	13.4	8.3	5.9	51.6
Yorkshire & Humberside	23.0	13.3	8.5	54.4
North West	29.9	21.5	12.7	57.9
West Midlands	24.4	19.1	6.9	57.2
East Midlands	16.7	12.3	6.1	54.6
East Anglia	8.5	4.8	2.1	49.5
Greater London	41.2	14.3	6.7	59.2
Rest of South East	64.7	27.9	11.9	58.1
South West	22.5	13.7	5.7	55.5

Staying on

% of estimated population in education, England

	16-year-olds		17-year-olds	
	1983/4	1993/4	1983/4	1993/4
A/AS level				
Grant maintained schools	a	4.5	a	4.1
Other maintained schools	13.1	14.6	11.9	13.3
Independent schools	3.7	6.0	3.3	5.5
Sixth form colleges	2.8	6.5	2.7	6.2
Tertiary colleges	0.5	b	0.5	b
Other FHE institutions	1.6	5.1	2.1	5.4
Total	21.7	36.7	20.5	34.5
Advanced vocational courses				
All schools	...	1.2	...	0.6
Sixth form colleges	...	0.3	...	0.4
Tertiary colleges	0.2	b	0.2	b
Other FHE institutions	2.4	6.9	2.8	11.0
Total	2.6	8.4	2.9	12.0
All pupils and students				
% of estimated pop. age group	64.3	80	46	67.5
Total number ('000s)	489.6	429.2	360	375.6
Pop. total for age group ('000s)	761.7	536.2	782.1	556.7

Staying on	Going to FE		Participation in
at school	Full-time	Part-time	education, %
300.1	166.7	49.6	76.7
243.0	144.1	36.2	76.3
14.6	9.4	1.6	75.0
31.4	5.9	8.6	76.8
11.2	7.1	3.3	88.1
13.9	8.8	3.2	69.1
22.6	13.9	4.8	71.1
28.8	20.3	6.0	72.6
25.9	15.9	5.0	74.5
19.6	12.5	3.1	73.8
10.9	6.1	1.4	74.7
33.9	17.9	3.3	78.9
64.9	31.6	6.1	81.5
23.3	17.1	3.4	81.3

(1992/93)

	16-year-olds		17-year-olds	
	1983/4	1993/4	1983/4	1993/4
GCSE				
Grant maintained schools	a	0.6	a	0.1
Other maintained schools	5.7	2.1	0.4	0.3
Independent schools	0.7	0.5	0.1	0.1
Sixth form colleges	1.3	1.6	0.2	0.2
Tertiary colleges	0.3	b	0.1	b
Other FHE institutions	2.0	2.1	1.0	0.8
Total	10.0	6.8	1.8	1.5
Intermediate vocational courses				
Grant maintained schools	a	1.0	a	0.1
Others	1.7	4.6	0.2	0.4
Independent schools	0.2	0.3	0.1	0.3
Sixth form colleges	0.2	0.9	b	0.3
Tertiary colleges	0.7	b	0.3	b
Other FHE institutions	10.2	13.4	5.3	8.1
Total	12.9	20.2	6.0	9.2

a Not applicable.
b Nil or negligible.
FE = further education.
FHE = further higher education.

Student numbers

New students

First year student enrolments on higher education courses in England, '000s
Full-time

	1989	1992	1993[a]	% change 89–93
Aged under 21				
Postgraduate	0.3	0.3	0.2	-33
First degree	107.1	148.9	153.0	43
Other HE	20.5	32.3	34.3	67
Total	127.9	181.5	187.5	47
Aged 21–24				
Postgraduate	15.2	23.2	26.2	72
First degree	13.1	27.2	29.7	127
Other HE	7.2	12.5	12.9	79
Total	35.4	62.9	68.8	94
Aged over 25				
Postgraduate	13.2	19.4	20.8	58
First degree	14.5	30.7	35.8	147
Other HE	10.9	18.3	17.9	64
Total	38.7	68.5	74.4	92
All ages				
Postgraduate	28.7	42.9	47.2	64
First degree	134.7	206.9	218.5	62
Other HE	38.7	63.1	65.1	68
Total	202.1	312.9	330.8	64

Student numbers
UK, '000s

	1970/71		1975/76	
	Males	Females	Males	Females
Full-time and sandwich students				
Universities				
Undergraduates	134	59	141	77
Postgraduates	33	10	37	13
Polytechnics and other H.Ed				
Undergraduates	107[c]	114[c]	123[c]	123[c]
Postgraduates	c	c	c	c
All full-time students	274	182	301	214
Part-time students				
Universities				
Undergraduates	3	2	2	2
Postgraduates	15	3	17	5
Open University	14	5	34	22
Polytechnics and other H.Ed				
Undergraduates	110[c]	12[c]	115[c]	21[c]
Postgraduates	c	c	c	c
All part-time students	142	23	168	50
All students	416	205	470	264

a Provisional.   b Nil or negligible.

	Part-time		
1989	1992	1993[b]	% change 89–93
0.1	[b]	0.1	–
1.2	1.5	1.5	25
27.8	18.8	15.8	-43
29.0	20.3	17.4	-40
3.3	4.0	4.3	30
2.9	4.9	5.0	72
30.2	27.0	24.5	-19
36.4	35.8	33.8	-7
22.0	36.5	39.7	80
9.1	18.9	19.1	110
63.8	74.5	80.7	26
95.0	129.9	139.5	47
25.4	40.5	44.2	74
13.2	25.3	25.5	93
121.8	120.3	120.9	-1
160.4	186.1	190.6	19

1980/81		1985/86		1991/92	
Males	Females	Males	Females	Males	Females
157	101	148	108	178	150
34	15	37	17	46	28
120	95	146	129	207	211
7	6	7	7	11	12
318	217	339	261	442	400
2	2	5	5	6	8
20	8	22	11	31	23
38	29	43	36	51	48
138	42	134	65	144	107
9	3	12	5	21	17
207	86	215	122	253	202
524	303	553	384	696	602

c Undergraduate and postgraduate figures combined.

Universities ranked

Entry requirements *Av. points*		Student/staff ratios	
Cambridge	29	London	9
Oxford	29	Belfast	10
Nottingham	26	York	10
London School of Economics	26	Buckingham	10
Imperial	25	Imperial College, London	10
St. Andrews	25	University College, London	10
Durham	25	Leeds	11
Bristol	25	King's College, London	11
Edinburgh	25	Birmingham	11
Manchester	24	Cambridge	11
Liverpool	24	Reading	12
York	24	Warwick	12
Sheffield	24	Loughborough	12
Birmingham	24	Manchester	12
Leeds	24	Glasgow	12
Glasgow	24	Nottingham	12
Warwick	24	Oxford	12
Southampton	23	Sheffield	12
Bath	23	Strathclyde	12
Lancaster	23	University of Central England	12
King's College, London	23	University of Wales, Cardiff	12
UMIST	23	Westminster	12
Exeter	23	Goldsmiths	12
East Anglia	23	Liverpool	12
		Edinburgh	12
		Durham	12
		Dundee	12
		Bath	12
		Southampton	12

Completion rates[b]	%	International students	%
Huddersfield	99	London School of Economics	54
Cambridge	99	Buckingham	50
Reading	99	Imperial College, London	37
Durham	98	Essex	30
Kingston	97	London	27
King's College, London	96	Wolverhampton	26
Lampeter	96	Queen Mary	25
Sussex	95	Kent	24
Bristol	95	UMIST	21
Oxford	95	Sussex	20
Sunderland	95	Hull	20
Aberdeen	95	Salford	20
Leeds	95	Reading	20
Wolverhampton	94	University College, London	19
		King's College, London	19

UMIST = University of Manchester Institute of Science and Technology.

Research/further study

	%
Lampeter	48
St. Andrews	45
Belfast	45
Bangor	45
Aberystwyth	45
Essex	43
Leicester	42
University of Wales, Cardiff	42
Oxford	41
Dundee	40
Cambridge	39
Hull	36
Durham	36
Aberdeen	36
Glasgow	36
London School of Economics	36

First class honours

	%
Imperial College, London	20
Oxford	17
Cambridge	17
King's College, London	13
St. Andrews	13
UMIST	13
Glasgow	13
Heriot-Watt	12
Aberdeen	12
Bristol	12
University College, London	12
Edinburgh	12
Bath	12
Strathclyde	12
Loughborough	11
Royal Holloway	11
Surrey	11

Permanent employment[c]

	%
Hertfordshire	80
Buckingham	80
Robert Gordon	77
Anglia	75
Manchester Metropolitan	75
Middlesex	75
Leeds Metropolitan	75
De Montfort	70
South Bank	70
University of Central England	70
Nottingham Trent	70
Westminster	70
Brighton	70
Aston	69
Portsmouth	68
Thames Valley	65
Goldsmiths	65
Huddersfield	62
Salford	62
Brunel	62

Unemployed graduates[c]

	%
Buckingham	4
De Montfort	5
Surrey	5
Oxford	5
St. Andrews	6
Salford	7
Brunel	7
Royal Holloway	7
Cambridge	7
Dundee	7
King's College, London	8
Brighton	8
Durham	8
Manchester Metropolitan	9
Warwick	9
Bournemouth	9
Middlesex	9
Aberdeen	9
Nottingham	9
Oxford Brookes	9
Napier	9

a A-level points required for entry.
b First degrees.
c 6 months after graduating.

Qualifications and jobs

Qualifications: the first degree
England, '000s

| | 1989 | | |
	Male	Female	Total
Medicine & dentistry	1.7	1.4	3.1
Studies allied to medicine	0.7	1.6	2.4
Biological sciences	2.2	2.6	4.8
Veterinary science etc.	0.5	0.5	0.9
Physical sciences	4.6	1.8	6.4
Mathematical sciences	4.2	1.4	5.5
Engineering & technology	10.6	1.0	11.7
Architecture & related studies	2.1	0.6	2.7
Social sciences	8.0	7.7	15.7
Business & financial sciences	4.2	3.5	7.6
Librarianship etc.	0.2	0.6	0.7
Languages & related studies	2.2	5.7	7.9
Humanities	2.2	2.3	4.6
Creative arts	2.9	4.0	6.9
Education	1.1	3.7	4.8
Multi-disciplinary studies	6.4	8.0	14.5
All Subjects	53.9	46.3	100.2

What graduates do
England, '000s

| | 1983 | | 1989 | |
	Male	Female	Male	Female
Permanent employment	23.6	15.7	26.4	21.9
Temporary employment	1.2	1.4	1.8	2.2
Overseas employment (home students)	0.8	0.9	1.0	1.3
Teacher training	3.3	5.3	2.6	4.0
Other further education & training	5.3	3.0	5.4	3.8
Overseas graduates leaving Britain	3.0	1.2	3.0	1.4
Not available for employment	0.6	0.9	2.0	2.2
Believed unemployed	5.2	3.6	2.6	2.0
Total of known destination	43.1	32.0	44.8	38.7
Unknown	7.1	5.1	8.1	6.4
Total	50.2	37.1	52.9	45.1

a Provisional.

1993[a]			% change 1989–93		
Male	Female	Total	Male	Female	Total
1.8	1.5	3.3	6	15	8
1.2	3.6	4.8	71	119	103
2.5	3.6	6.1	13	38	26
0.6	0.6	1.2	17	31	24
5.9	3.0	9.0	28	69	41
6.3	2.5	8.8	51	82	59
12.7	1.9	14.5	19	79	25
3.4	0.9	4.3	62	60	58
8.8	9.6	18.4	10	26	18
6.5	6.0	12.5	57	74	65
0.4	0.9	1.3	100	62	86
2.7	6.9	9.6	23	22	22
2.9	3.1	6.0	29	33	31
3.8	5.7	9.4	31	41	37
1.1	3.5	4.6	0	-4	-4
9.2	12.6	21.8	43	56	50
69.6	66.0	135.5	29	43	35

1993		% change 1983–93		
Male	Female	Male	Female	Total
25.0	26.5	6	69	31
4.0	4.2	233	190	215
1.2	1.6	50	78	65
3.6	6.1	9	15	13
8.7	6.7	64	123	87
5.3	3.3	77	175	105
2.2	2.6	266	187	320
8.3	5.3	60	48	55
58.3	56.4	35	76	53
9.5	8.1	34	59	44
67.7	64.5	35	74	52

How Britain compares

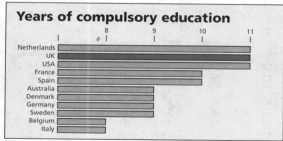

Years of compulsory education

Netherlands	
UK	
USA	
France	
Spain	
Australia	
Denmark	
Germany	
Sweden	
Belgium	
Italy	

Scale: 8, 9, 10, 11

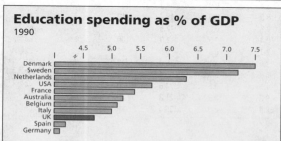

Education spending as % of GDP
1990

Denmark	
Sweden	
Netherlands	
USA	
France	
Australia	
Belgium	
Italy	
UK	
Spain	
Germany	

Scale: 4.5, 5.0, 5.5, 6.0, 6.5, 7.0, 7.5

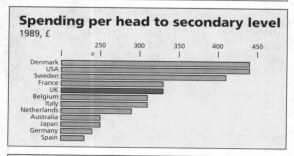

Spending per head to secondary level
1989, £

Denmark	
USA	
Sweden	
France	
UK	
Belgium	
Italy	
Netherlands	
Australia	
Japan	
Germany	
Spain	

Scale: 250, 300, 350, 400, 450

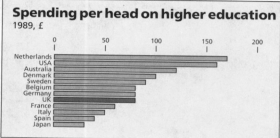

Spending per head on higher education
1989, £

Netherlands	
USA	
Australia	
Denmark	
Sweden	
Belgium	
Germany	
UK	
France	
Italy	
Spain	
Japan	

Scale: 0, 50, 100, 150, 200

Note: Germany data are for western Germany.

Part XI
CRIME AND PUNISHMENT

Regional variations in crime

Total crime
registered offences per 100,000 population

	1975	1980	1985	1990ᵇ	1992ᵇ
England	4,296	5,501	7,317	9,047	11,003
Wales	3,976	4,762	6,276	7,979	9,935
Scotlandᵇ	...	7,075	8,994	10,502	11,535
Northern Ireland	2,423	3,620	4,151	3,599	4,194
North	4,731	6,299	9,162	11,892	13,630
Yorkshire & Humberside	4,491	5,608	7,449	10,000	12,566
North West	4,819	6,209	8,924	10,056	11,827
West Midlands	3,543	5,176	7,122	8,304	10,464
East Midlands	4,057	5,179	6,542	8,844	11,379
East Anglia	3,312	4,013	5,021	6,697	8,553
South East	4,612	5,796	7,345	8,896	10,586
Greater London	...	...	...	...	12,795
Rest of South East	...	...	...	...	9,001
South West	3,220	3,922	5,375	7,374	9,436

Violence against the person
registered offences per 100,000 population

	1975	1980	1985	1990	1992
England	144	198	245	364	391
Wales	147	183	237	381	453
Scotlandᵇ	...	143	208	266	323
Northern Ireland	162	155	222	212	255
North	168	230	281	399	433
Yorkshire & Humberside	192	241	302	433	429
North West	138	202	240	311	363
West Midlands	130	217	280	387	414
East Midlands	202	258	311	465	507
East Anglia	115	161	180	301	322
South East	132	178	221	352	379
Greater London	...	...	...	...	511
Rest of South East	...	...	...	...	285
South West	106	146	189	304	314

Sexual offences
registered offences per 100,000 population

	1975	1980	1985	1990	1992
England	48	43	44	58	58
Wales	47	37	33	52	56
Scotlandᵇ	...	44	50	64	65
Northern Ireland	16	24	42	50	60
North	50	43	44	54	52
Yorkshire & Humberside	66	53	52	67	59
North West	45	41	37	47	47
West Midlands	48	46	45	51	53
East Midlands	66	60	50	67	66

clear-up rate, %

	1986	1987	1988	1989	1990	1991	1992
England	32	32	35	33	31	29	25
Wales	40	43	42	43	40	35	35
Scotland[b]	34	34	34	33	32	31	32
Northern Ireland	37	43	45	43	38	36	34
North	39	41	43	40	36	35	24
Yorkshire & Humberside	37	38	42	39	37	31	26
North West	34	34	38	37	38	39	36
West Midlands	33	37	43	40	37	32	28
East Midlands	38	39	40	38	36	30	28
East Anglia	38	38	39	40	38	36	32
South East	24	23	25	24	21	21	20
Greater London[c]	...	...	...	...	...	17	16
Rest of South East	...	...	...	...	...	25	24
South West	34	35	38	37	32	30	22

clear-up rate, %

	1986	1987	1988	1989	1990	1991	1992
England	71	74	75	76	76	77	75
Wales	83	87	85	89	88	88	88
Scotland[b]	82	79	78	81	82	81	78
Northern Ireland	57	71	68	58	62	62	64
North	78	79	80	80	78	79	76
Yorkshire & Humberside	73	81	79	80	84	82	84
North West	68	71	75	77	76	76	74
West Midlands	74	76	80	80	82	81	80
East Midlands	76	80	79	80	80	81	79
East Anglia	84	83	85	85	86	85	86
South East	62	65	66	68	67	69	69
Greater London[c]	...	...	...	...	...	63	61
Rest of South East	...	...	...	...	...	78	78
South West	80	85	83	88	85	85	76

clear-up rate, %

	1986	1987	1988	1989	1990	1991	1992
England	71	74	74	74	75	74	73
Wales	86	96	90	93	95	93	93
Scotland[b]	76	78	78	77	79	77	76
Northern Ireland	79	91	84	86	92	87	80
North	74	81	80	80	84	83	80
Yorkshire & Humberside	73	81	82	76	84	77	82
North West	72	77	78	79	81	80	80
West Midlands	70	72	78	78	75	76	75
East Midlands	77	78	79	77	81	80	74

For footnotes see over page.

Sexual offences (cont.)
registered offences per 100,000 population

	1975	1980	1985	1990	1992
East Anglia	40	39	37	55	57
South East	42	39	44	61	65
Greater London	...	...	...	...	80
Rest of South East	...	...	...	...	54
South West	46	36	40	54	50

Robbery
registered offences per 100,000 population

	1975	1980	1985	1990	1992
England	23	32	58	75	108
Wales	15	11	10	16	23
Scotland[b]	...	72	86	91	133
Northern Ireland	128	84	116	103	115
North	14	13	22	30	52
Yorkshire & Humberside	18	17	25	41	81
North West	27	28	59	71	113
West Midlands	17	29	50	68	110
East Midlands	23	19	26	40	67
East Anglia	9	7	12	21	31
South East	33	53	99	121	159
Greater London	...	...	...	...	320
Rest of South East	...	...	...	...	44
South West	8	10	15	33	47

Burglary
registered offences per 100,000 population

	1975	1980	1985	1990	1992
England	1,059	1,270	1,765	2,017	2,677
Wales	1,081	1,170	1,512	1,570	2,235
Scotland[b]	...	1,522	1,960	1,994	2,214
Northern Ireland	924	1,283	1,303	932	1,063
North	1,359	1,687	2,644	2,939	3,614
Yorkshire & Humberside	1,273	1,417	1,955	2,474	3,747
North West	1,408	1,609	2,615	2,459	2,928
West Midlands	906	1,341	1,987	2,006	3,031
East Midlands	1,012	1,168	1,317	1,754	2,626
East Anglia	660	715	1,022	1,372	1,941
South East	1,007	1,217	1,526	1,829	2,220
Greater London	...	...	...	...	2,604
Rest of South East	...	...	...	...	1,944
South West	653	757	1,099	1,538	2,278

clear-up rate, %

	1986	1987	1988	1989	1990	1991	1992
East Anglia	78	83	79	84	86	83	79
South East	64	66	65	66	64	64	66
Greater London[c]	...	...	...	...	...	54	58
Rest of South East	...	...	...	...	...	76	76
South West	81	79	81	82	85	88	74

clear-up rate, %

	1986	1987	1988	1989	1990	1991	1992
England	20	21	23	26	26	23	22
Wales	56	58	45	57	58	48	47
Scotland[b]	29	29	29	29	28	27	24
Northern Ireland	19	19	23	23	18	17	19
North	35	38	42	43	37	35	34
Yorkshire & Humberside	36	40	41	41	39	34	28
North West	23	23	28	32	31	29	27
West Midlands	27	33	40	40	43	33	26
East Midlands	37	38	47	45	39	33	34
East Anglia	42	44	43	50	48	45	41
South East	14	15	16	18	18	16	16
Greater London[c]	...	...	...	...	...	13	13
Rest of South East	...	...	...	...	...	31	31
South West	29	29	31	36	39	34	25

clear-up rate, %

	1986	1987	1988	1989	1990	1991	1992
England	26	27	29	27	25	23	19
Wales	31	32	32	34	33	26	28
Scotland[b]	19	19	18	17	16	15	14
Northern Ireland	26	30	29	27	22	22	19
North	33	37	39	35	34	30	19
Yorkshire & Humberside	32	31	36	34	30	24	17
North West	29	29	31	33	34	35	32
West Midlands	32	41	44	38	33	29	23
East Midlands	31	32	35	32	31	25	23
East Anglia	26	29	28	31	30	27	25
South East	16	15	15	14	13	14	14
Greater London[c]	...	...	...	...	...	11	11
Rest of South East	...	...	...	...	...	17	16
South West	23	23	24	25	21	20	13

a In England and Wales, offences of trafficking in controlled drugs were included only from January 1983.
b Figures for Scotland are not strictly comparable with others because of differences in the legal system, recording practices and classification.
c The Metropolitan Police use a different method for assessing the clear-up rate, hence the lower figure.

Rising crime[a]

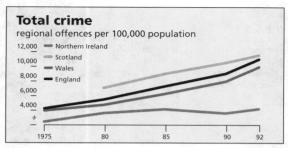

Total crime
regional offences per 100,000 population

- Northern Ireland
- Scotland
- Wales
- England

12,000
10,000
8,000
6,000
4,000

1975   80   85   90   92

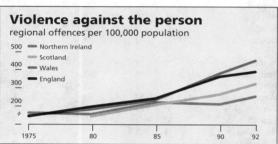

Violence against the person
regional offences per 100,000 population

- Northern Ireland
- Scotland
- Wales
- England

500
400
300
200

1975   80   85   90   92

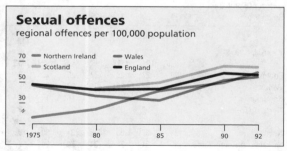

Sexual offences
regional offences per 100,000 population

- Northern Ireland
- Scotland
- Wales
- England

70
50
30

1975   80   85   90   92

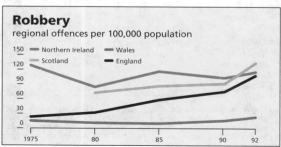

Robbery
regional offences per 100,000 population

- Northern Ireland
- Scotland
- Wales
- England

150
120
90
60
30
0

1975   80   85   90   92

Where crime is highest

Total crime
Offences per 100,000 population, 1992

1	North	13,630	8	South East	10,586
2	Greater London	12,795	9	West Midlands	10,464
3	Yorkshire & Humberside	12,566	10	Wales	9,935
4	North West	11,827	11	South West	9,436
5	Scotland	11,535	12	Rest of South East	9,001
6	East Midlands	11,379	13	Northern Ireland	4,194
7	England	11,003	14	East Anglia	8.553

Violence against the person
Offences per 100,000 population, 1992

1	Greater London	511	8	South East	379
2	East Midlands	507	9	North West	363
3	Wales	453	10	Scotland	323
4	North	433	11	East Anglia	322
5	Yorkshire & Humberside	429	12	South West	314
6	West Midlands	414	13	Rest of South East	285
7	England	391	14	Northern Ireland	255

Sexual offences
Offences per 100,000 population, 1992

1	Greater London	80	8	East Anglia	57
2	East Midlands	66	9	Wales	56
3	South East	65	10	Rest of South East	54
4	Scotland	65	11	West Midlands	53
5	Northern Ireland	60	12	North	52
6	Yorkshire & Humberside	59	13	South West	50
7	England	58	14	North West	47

Robbery
Offences per 100,000 population, 1992

1	Greater London	320	8	Yorkshire & Humberside	81
2	South East	159	9	East Midlands	67
3	Scotland	133	10	North	52
4	Northern Ireland	115	11	South West	47
5	North West	113	12	Rest of South East	44
6	West Midlands	110	13	East Anglia	31
7	England	108	14	Wales	23

Burglary
Offences per 100,000 population, 1992

1	Yorkshire & Humberside	3,747	8	South West	2,278
2	North	3,614	9	Wales	2,235
3	West Midlands	3,031	10	South East	2,220
4	North West	2,928	11	Scotland	2,214
5	England	2,677	12	Rest of South East	1,944
6	East Midlands	2,626	13	East Anglia	1,941
7	Greater London	2,604	14	Northern Ireland	1,063

a Figures for Scotland are not comparable with others because of the differences in the legal system, recording practices and classification.

Recent trends in crime

Rises and falls
Notifiable offences by police force area

	Total no. of offences	% accounted for			
		Violent crime[a]	Burglary	Vehicle crime	Criminal damage
Avon & Somerset	169,690	6	22	34	13
Bedfordshire	55,611	5	26	34	13
Cambridgeshire	61,312	6	22	27	12
Cheshire	77,427	5	26	27	16
Cleveland	79,385	4	23	28	19
Cumbria	42,521	5	23	25	18
Derbyshire	87,924	5	29	27	18
Devon & Cornwall	114,124	5	28	26	12
Dorset	53,153	4	17	25	13
Durham	66,032	5	20	28	18
Essex	108,779	5	24	26	16
Gloucestershire	63,177	5	27	30	10
Greater Manchester	345,138	5	27	30	18
Hampshire	142,470	5	22	26	16
Hertfordshire	54,268	5	23	33	17
Humberside	139,006	4	33	26	14
Kent	157,083	5	18	28	17
Lancashire	128,434	3	21	26	21
Leicestershire	98,949	6	26	29	15
Lincolnshire	49,951	6	25	19	18
London, City of	5,069	5	13	13	4
Merseyside	138,663	8	24	23	17
Metropolitan Police	883,741	9	18	24	20
Norfolk	59,754	5	27	26	13
Northamptonshire	58,892	5	29	30	15
Northumbria	210,444	4	29	24	25
North Yorkshire	59,273	4	28	25	14
Nottinghamshire	156,362	6	25	23	18
South Yorkshire	156,541	4	34	29	15
Staffordshire	96,005	7	30	27	16
Suffolk	41,574	6	20	19	16
Surrey	49,478	6	23	27	14
Sussex	106,262	4	23	24	18
Thames Valley	191,748	4	20	32	16
Warwickshire	43,970	4	27	31	14
West Mercia	82,848	5	21	28	17
West Midlands	323,267	6	29	29	16
West Yorkshire	297,108	5	31	28	15
Wiltshire	39,159	8	22	22	16
Dyfed-Powys	22,817	11	17	17	21
Gwent	40,873	7	18	26	18
North Wales	44,843	8	24	24	17
South Wales	162,020	4	23	32	21
England & Wales	5,365,379	6	24	27	17

a Offences of violence against the person, sexual offences and robbery.

% change on previous year

Total	Violence against the person	Sexual offences	Robbery	Burglary	Vehicle crime	Criminal damage
-8	20	83	20	-17	-14	11
-9	-8	23	-12	-10	-9	-7
-12	9	12	-12	-16	-14	-4
-7	6	46	-3	-11	-14	5
-2	-8	15	45	-6	-7	7
-9	-3	2	-11[b]	-17	-12	-1
-5	-5	2	15	3	-11	3
-8	2	23	3	2	-11	-20
...	10	21	-8	-13	3	21
-3	4	16	-7	-8	-3	-1
-6	6	-9	-21	-4	-12	2
3	22	248	5	-3	-2	24
-12	-2	-9	15	-12	-13	-6
-7	5	18	-14	-14	-8	2
-8	4	25	-32	-6	-5	-3
-1	...	-4	8	-1	9	-2
-4	12	21	-11	-10	-5	-2
-7	1	15	-15	-10	-11	4
-3	11	2	-5	0	-6	...
-5	-3	5	...	1	-16	12
-18	-14	-27[b]	-29[b]	-20	-36	-39
-5	2	11	11	-7	-7	1
-6	15	15	4	-14	-13	...
-11	11	15	-20	-14	-16	...
-3	-10	12	7	28	12	-30
-5	1	...	10	-5	-9	-3
4	12	16	51	-1	5	34
-6	-4	2	...	-4	-18	8
5	-2	10	17	8	2	10
-5	10	22	2	-6	-11	3
-6	-3	11	-23	-12	-15	-2
-9	23	27	-32	-16	-14	-4
-11	3	-8	-5	-19	-18	18
-4	11	9	2	...	-5	-6
-6	14	7	...	-10	-5	-6
1	1	6	6	-7	2	22
-4	-2	-9	16	-9	-4	4
-3	1	21	-7	-4	-6	3
-9	3	-16	3	-7	-12	1
-13	3	-40	...	-20	-12	-6
1	6	-10	-5[b]	-6	2	9
-10	13	77	-9	-15	-16	-4
-5	2	...	11	-4	-5	-9
-5	5	13	5	-8	-9	...

b Based on totals of less than 100 offences.

Driving offences

Overall offences
'000s

	England & Wales	Scotland	Northern Ireland
1935	432.8	35.4	19.6
1940	208.1	23.1	13.9
1945	148.4	16.6	18.8
1950	357.9	31.8	23.8
1955	407.9	38.7	27.7
1960	622.5	60.8	33.8
1965	856.7ᵃ	82.5	27.1
1970	991.1	84.5	21.8
1975	1,194.7ᵇ	173.4ᵇ	24.6
1980	1,294.1	236.9	28.7
1985	1,052.0	220.3	27.3
1990	704.6	296.2	27.2
1991	713.1	305.6	20.1
1992	723.1	306.4	20.8

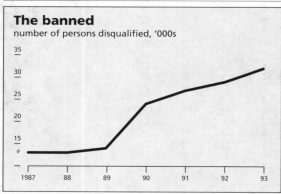

The banned
number of persons disqualified, '000s

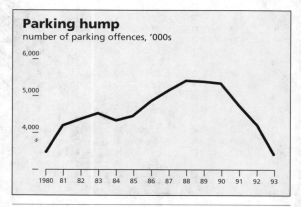

Parking hump
number of parking offences, '000s

Offences of driving after consuming alcohol or taking drugs

	Total proceedings	% found guilty	% attracting custodial sentence		average sentence, months	
	1992	1992	1987	1992	1987	1992
UK	125,690	87.2	2.9	3.9	3.0	3.0
England	103,371	86.3	3.0	4.2	2.9	3.0
Wales	6,837	87.0	2.3	3.2	3.4	3.5
Scotland	10,310	92.6	3.1	3.2	3.2	3.2
Northern Ireland	5,172	93.9	1.5	0.8	7.2	4.9
North	7,058	88.4	3.3	3.6	3.2	3.6
Yorkshire & Humberside	10,603	87.4	3.7	5.2	2.8	2.8
North West	16,007	87.8	3.7	4.8	2.9	3.1
West Midlands	13,023	86.6	3.2	4.3	3.0	3.2
East Midlands	7,473	86.4	3.6	6.5	2.9	2.7
East Anglia	3,330	90.4	2.3	3.1	2.5	2.8
South East	37,622	84.0	2.5	3.6	2.9	2.8
South West	8,255	88.0	2.9	3.6	2.7	2.9

Breath tests
England and Wales

	Total no. of tests, '000	No. positive or refused, '000	% positive or refused
1982	206.6	88.6	43
1983	241.2	98.4	41
1984	207.6	87.6	42
1985	250.3	95.7	38
1986	303.0	97.8	32
1987	399.8	111.4	28
1988	443.3	111.7	25
1989	540.9	108.0	20
1990	596.6	102.4	17
1991	562.5	90.3	16
1992	531.3	57.1	16

a 1964.
b 1974.

Prisons

Locking up more
Daily average prison population, '000s

	England & Wales	Scotland	N Ireland	Total
1935	11.3	1.7	0.3	13.3
1940	9.4	1.3	0.2	10.9
1945	14.7	1.9	0.4	17.0
1948	19.8	1.9	0.5	22.2
1949	19.9	1.8	0.4	22.1
1950	20.5	1.7	0.4	22.6
1951	21.8	1.8	0.4	24.0
1952	23.7	2.1	0.4	26.2
1953	23.6	2.1	0.4	26.1
1954	22.4	2.1	0.4	24.9
1955	21.1	2.1	0.4	23.6
1956	20.8	2.2	0.4	23.4
1957	22.6	2.4	0.4	25.4
1958	25.4	2.6	0.4	28.4
1959	26.6	2.9	0.4	29.9
1960	27.1	2.8	0.4	30.3
1961	29.0	3	0.4	32.4
1962	31.1	3.2	0.4	34.7
1963	30.9	3.5	0.4	34.8
1964	29.6	3.2	0.4	33.2
1965	30.4	3.4	0.5	34.3
1966	33.1	3.8	0.6	37.5
1967	35.0	4.2	0.7	39.9
1968	32.5	4.5	0.7	37.7
1969	34.7	4.8	0.7	40.2
1970	39.0	5	0.9	44.9
1971	39.8	5.3	1.1	46.2
1972	38.3	5.2	1.6	45.1
1973	36.8	4.8	2.1	43.7
1974	36.9	4.7	2.6	44.2
1975	39.8	4.9	2.7	47.4
1976	41.4	4.9	2.6	48.9
1977	41.6	4.9	2.6	49.1
1978	41.8	5.1	2.8	49.7
1979	42.2	4.6	2.7	49.5
1980	42.2	4.9	2.5	49.6
1981	43.3	4.5	2.5	50.3
1982	43.7	4.9	2.5	51.1
1983	43.8	5.1	2.4	51.3
1984	43.3	4.8	2.2	50.3
1985	46.3	5.3	2.1	53.7
1986	46.9	5.6	1.9	54.4
1987	49.0	5.3	1.9	56.2
1988	50.0	5.1	1.9	57.0
1989	48.6	4.4	1.8	54.8
1990	45.6	4.6	1.8	52.0
1991	45.9	4.7	1.8	52.4
1992	45.8	5.1	1.8	52.7

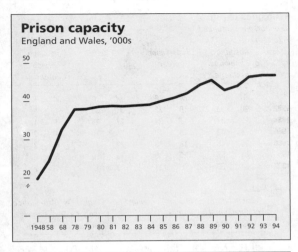

Prison capacity
England and Wales, '000s

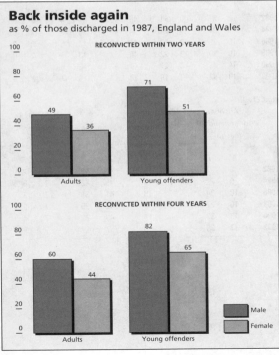

Back inside again
as % of those discharged in 1987, England and Wales

RECONVICTED WITHIN TWO YEARS

RECONVICTED WITHIN FOUR YEARS

Male
Female

Sentencing facts

Who goes to jail
% of persons sentenced
Age 14–17

	Absolute or conditional discharge		Supervision order		Fine		Community service order	
	M	F	M	F	M	F	M	F
1982	20	33	16	23	31	33	*	*
1984	22	37	17	21	27	28	3	1
1986	24	42	18	19	24	26	4	2
1988	25	48	18	18	22	21	5	2
1990	31	53	20	19	18	16	5	2
1992	34	56	20	21	13	11	5	2

Age 17–21

	Absolute or conditional discharge		Probation order		Fine		Community service order		Attendance centre order	
	M	F	M	F	M	F	M	F	M	F
1982	8	21	9	21	46	46	11	4	2	0
1984	9	24	10	21	44	44	13	5	2	0
1986	10	26	12	22	41	40	14	5	2	0
1988	10	29	12	22	40	37	13	6	2	0
1990	14	36	13	21	41	32	13	6	2	0
1992	19	42	13	19	33	27	15	7	3	0

Age 21+

	Absolute or conditional discharge		Probation order		Fine		Community service order	
	M	F	M	F	M	F	M	F
1982	8	21	6	16	47	48	6	2
1984	9	22	7	17	45	43	7	3
1986	10	24	7	19	41	38	7	3
1988	10	27	8	18	42	35	7	3
1990	13	32	8	18	43	32	7	4
1992	17	36	9	16	37	27	9	5

Attendance centre order		Care order		Young offenders institution		Otherwise dealt with		Total immediate custody		Total community sentence	
M	F	M	F	M	F	M	F	M	F	M	F
16	6	3	5	12	1	1	0	12	1	32	29
16	7	2	3	12	2	1	1	12	2	36	29
15	7	2	2	11	2	1	1	11	2	37	28
16	5	1	2	11	2	2	1	11	2	39	25
16	5	1	1	7	1	3	2	7	1	41	26
16	6	*	*	9	1	3	3	9	1	42	29

Young offenders institution		Imprisonment fully suspended		Imprisonment unsuspended		Otherwise dealt with		Total immediate custody		Total community sentence	
M	F	M	F	M	F	M	F	M	F	M	F
12	1	5	4	7	3	1	1	18	4	22	25
20	5	*	*	*	*	1	1	20	5	25	26
21	5	*	*	*	*	1	1	21	5	28	27
20	5	*	*	*	*	2	2	20	5	27	28
14	3	*	*	*	*	2	2	14	3	29	27
15	3	*	*	*	*	3	3	15	3	31	25

Imprisonment fully suspended		Imprisonment partly suspended		Imprisonment unsuspended		Otherwise dealt with		Total immediate custody		Total community sentence	
M	F	M	F	M	F	M	F	M	F	M	F
12	7	1	0	18	5	1	1	19	5	12	18
11	8	2	1	18	5	2	1	20	6	14	20
12	8	1	1	20	6	1	1	21	7	14	22
12	8	1	1	19	6	2	1	20	7	15	21
10	8	1	0	17	5	2	2	17	6	15	21
8	7	0	0	17	6	3	2	18	6	18	22

Custody numbers

Male prisoners

Annual average population in custody in England and Wales, '000s

	Convicted unsentenced	Young offenders	Adults	All males
1987	1.5	8.6	27.7	47.2
1988	1.6	8.2	28.8	48.2
1989	1.7	7.1	29.5	46.8
1990	1.7	6.1	28.2	44.0
1991	1.8	5.3	28.9	44.3
1992	1.9	5.3	28.9	44.2

Female prisoners

Annual average population in custody in England and Wales, '000s

	Convicted unsentenced	Young offenders	Adults	All females
1987	0.07	0.21	1.09	1.77
1988	0.08	0.19	1.09	1.79
1989	0.09	0.18	1.12	1.77
1990	0.08	0.14	1.07	1.60
1991	0.10	0.14	1.03	1.56
1992	0.11	0.13	1.06	1.58

Lifers

Annual population serving life sentences in England and Wales at 30 June

	Male	of which young offenders	Female	of which young offenders	Total
1985	1,884	115	54	6	1,938
1986	2,020	113	60	8	2,080
1987	2,167	105	65	8	2,232
1988	2,318	105	69	9	2,387
1989	2,478	109	80	5	2,558
1990	2,603	115	86	4	2,689
1991	2,708	122	92	5	2,800
1992	2,812	105	95	5	2,907

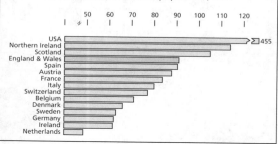

How Britain compares

rate of imprisonment per 100,000 population, 1992

USA
Northern Ireland
Scotland
England & Wales
Spain
Austria
France
Italy
Switzerland
Belgium
Denmark
Sweden
Germany
Ireland
Netherlands

Part XII
PEOPLE AND CULTURE

Marriage and divorce

Men getting married
'000s

	1938	1950	1960	1970
Bachelors	375.9	354.4	352.6	412.4
Divorced men	4.8	26.9	19.7	38.1
Widowers	28.4	26.7	21.3	20.5
Under 21	14.1	23.2	46.6	81.4
21–24	117.7	141.2	161.0	209.7
25–29	156.2	121.3	94.6	91.1
30–34	60.1	47.3	32.8	30.3
35–44	33.9	41.6	27.0	26.0
45–54	13.0	17.3	14.9	14.5
55 and over	12.4	14.9	15.9	17.9

Women getting married
'000s

	1938	1950	1960	1970
Spinsters	387.0	361.2	356.8	415.9
Divorced women	4.1	23.9	19.0	36.2
Widows	18.0	22.9	17.8	18.9
Under 21	67.6	99.9	141.9	186.0
21–24	151.3	148.2	139.9	171.6
25–29	110.2	77.6	48.0	51.2
30–34	38.1	29.6	19.4	18.3
35–44	25.0	30.3	20.8	18.6
45–54	9.6	13.5	13.1	13.2
55 and over	5.5	7.6	9.8	12.1

Divorce
Divorces per thousand women

	1961	1966	1971	1976	1981	1986	1991
under 25	2.4	4.1	7.5	14.5	22.3	30.7	27.7
25 to 29	4.3	7.6	13.0	20.4	26.7	28.6	31.3
30 to 34	3.8	6.1	10.5	18.3	20.2	22.0	25.1
35 to 44	2.7	3.9	6.7	12.6	14.9	15.8	17.2
45+	0.9	1.2	2.8	4.0	3.9	4.1	4.5

Divorces per thousand men

	1961	1966	1971	1976	1981	1986	1991
under 25	1.4	2.6	5.0	13.6	17.7	30.9	25.9
25 to 29	3.9	6.8	12.5	21.4	27.6	31.2	32.9
30 to 34	4.1	6.8	11.8	18.9	22.8	25.1	28.5
35 to 44	3.1	4.5	7.9	14.1	17.0	18.0	20.1
45+	1.1	1.5	3.1	4.5	4.8	5.2	5.6

Divorces by duration of marriage

up to 4	11.3	12.1	13.4	18.0	20.5	24.5	23.3
5 to 9	30.6	32.3	30.5	30.2	29.1	27.5	27.0
10 to 14	22.9	21.4	19.4	18.7	19.6	17.5	18.3
15 to 19	13.9	14.8	12.6	12.8	12.8	12.8	12.8
20+	21.2	19.4	24.2	20.3	18.0	17.5	18.6

1980	1990
314.8	276.5
87.7	88.2
15.9	10.7
52.6	15.9
141.8	92.3
98.8	122.8
48.1	57.0
39.4	50.0
19.4	22.0
18.3	15.5

1980	1990
319.1	279.4
83.4	85.6
16.0	10.4
127.5	45.6
133.3	119.0
65.8	103.2
34.1	42.8
30.7	39.0
15.0	16.8
12.0	8.9

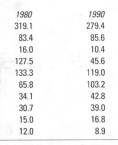

One more time
remarriages

AS % OF ALL MARRIAGES

1961: 14 1971: 20 1981: 34 1989: 36

OF THE DIVORCED
AS % OF ALL MARRIAGES

1961: 9 1971: 15 1981: 31 1989: 34

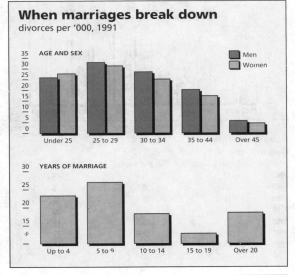

When marriages break down
divorces per '000, 1991

AGE AND SEX

Men
Women

Under 25 25 to 29 30 to 34 35 to 44 Over 45

YEARS OF MARRIAGE

Up to 4 5 to 9 10 to 14 15 to 19 Over 20

Family planning

Contraceptive use
Women aged 16–49, Great Britain, %

	1976[a]	1983[a]	1986	1989	1991
Users	68	75	71	69	70
Pill	29	28	23	22	23
IUD	6	6	7	5	5
Condom	14	13	13	15	16
Cap/diaphragm	2	1	2	1	1
Withdrawal	5	4	4	4	3
Safe period	1	1	1	1	1
Other	1	1	1	1	1
Sterilisation	13	22	23	23	25
Female	7	11	12	11	12
Male	6	10	11	12	13
Non-users	32	25	29	31	30
Sterile after another operation	2	2	3	5	3
Pregnant/wanting to get pregnant	7	7	7	7	9
Other	24	16	19	19	21

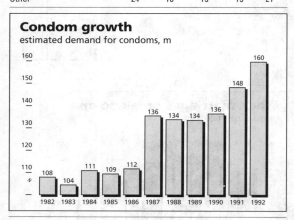

Condom growth
estimated demand for condoms, m

1982	1983	1984	1985	1986	1987	1988	1989	1990	1991	1992
108	104	111	109	112	136	134	134	136	148	160

Buying condoms
Condom sales in UK by distributor, m

	National Health Service	Over the counter	Vending machine
1986	22.3	80.4	9.1
1987	20.9	98.9	15.7
1988	16.6	96.6	20.6
1989	20.7	92.0	20.7
1990	23.2	93.5	19.9
1991	27.8	97.6	22.8
1992	37.4	96.3	25.8

a Figures for 1976 and 1983 refer to women aged 18–44.

Abortion
% of total, Great Britain

	1971	1981	1986	1991	1992
Single women					
Under 16	4.3	4.3	3.9	2.8	2.8
16 to 19	36.1	38.7	34.0	27.3	25.5
20 to 34	55.9	54.6	59.9	67.1	68.5
35 to 44	1.9	2.0	2.2	2.7	3.1
Total no., '000s	63.4	96.4	115.2	127.6	121.8
Married women					
16 to 19	1.4	2.0	1.5	1.2	1.0
20 to 34	63.9	66.8	66.8	69.7	69.6
35 to 44	31.9	29.8	30.8	28.2	28.5
45+	0.9	1.0	0.9	0.9	0.8
Total no., '000s	58.6	55.5	47.2	42.0	40.4
All women[b]					
Under 16	2.1	2.4	2.5	1.9	1.9
16 to 19	18.0	22.8	22.2	18.9	17.5
20 to 34	60.9	60.6	62.9	68.3	69.1
35 to 44	16.8	13.3	12.1	10.7	11.2
45+	0.8	0.4	0.3	0.3	0.3
Total no., '000s	133.1	136.9	171.5	181.9	182.8

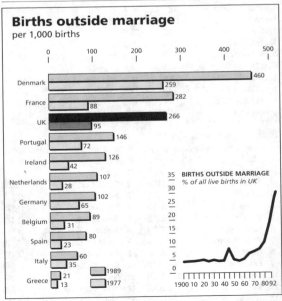

Births outside marriage
per 1,000 births

	1989	1977
Denmark	460	259
France	282	88
UK	266	95
Portugal	146	72
Ireland	126	42
Netherlands	107	28
Germany	102	65
Belgium	89	31
Spain	80	23
Italy	60	35
Greece	21	13

BIRTHS OUTSIDE MARRIAGE
% of all live births in UK

b Includes women who are divorced, separated or whose marital status is not known.

Income and wealth

From Dover to Derry

Average weekly gross household income, real 1992 prices[a]*, £*

	1985–86	1986–87	1988–89	1989–90	1990–91	1992
UK	319.4	333.4	353.5	350.8	363.1	342.9
England	324.7	342.6	362.9	361.5	373.0	350.5
Wales	287.1	281.8	297.6	289.0	294.9	294.6
Scotland	297.8	289.0	311.6	304.8	317.8	313.7
Northern Ireland	273.2	282.6	265.3	255.6	284.2	281.3
North	265.9	268.7	307.6	291.7	286.0	285.1
Yorkshire & Humberside	273.9	284.9	303.0	289.4	306.4	303.2
North West	288.6	315.4	314.7	318.2	332.9	317.1
West Midlands	295.7	306.4	320.8	325.0	331.5	304.2
East Midlands	307.7	308.6	325.4	342.3	352.8	344.4
East Anglia	318.1	299.9	358.8	357.1	352.9	350.2
Greater London	…	…	…	…	458.9	392.9
Rest of South East[b]	381.3	411.6	435.7	434.3	445.3	416.0
South West	329.6	341.2	357.4	348.6	369.1	346.5

Low and high incomes

% of households by weekly income, 1992

	Under £80	£80–£175	£175–375	£375–£649	£650+
UK	12.3	21.8	30.5	24.2	11.4
England	11.6	21.3	30.5	24.4	12.2
Wales	15.4	27.0	29.5	20.8	7.3
Scotland	15.2	22.4	30.8	23.8	7.8
Northern Ireland	16.5	26.7	28.9	21.4	6.6
North	16.5	25.7	30.4	20.0	7.4
Yorkshire & Humberside	12.2	25.5	29.7	26.0	6.7
North West	14.8	24.3	30.2	20.1	10.7
West Midlands	11.8	23.8	32.8	24.0	7.6
East Midlands	9.8	19.3	33.9	27.0	10.2
East Anglia	9.6	18.9	32.9	27.4	11.1
Greater London	12.6	19.0	27.7	24.3	16.3
Rest of South East	8.6	17.5	29.4	26.0	18.5
South West	11.1	21.3	31.2	25.4	11.1

Rich London, poor Wales

Average gross weekly earnings, April 1993, £

1	Greater London	461.2
2	South East	411.6
3	North West	334.6
4	South West	333.2
5	Scotland	333.0
6	East Anglia	326.4
7	West Midlands	324.6
8	North	321.8
9	East Midlands	317.2
10	Yorkshire & Humberside	316.9
11	Northern Ireland	313.6
12	Wales	308.3

Personal disposable income per head 1992, £

1	London	9,133
2	South East	8,030
3	Scotland	7,617
4	East Anglia	7,577
5	South West	7,171
6	Yorkshire & Humberside	7,150
7	North West	7,146
8	East Midlands	7,112
9	West Midlands	7,040
10	North	7,040
11	Northern Ireland	6,755
12	Wales	6,442

Most to dispose of
Distribution of disposable household income, quintile groups of individuals
Net income before housing costs

	Bottom fifth	Next fifth	Middle fifth	Next fifth	Top fifth
1979	10	14	18	23	35
1987	9	13	17	23	39
1990–91	7	12	17	23	41

Net income after housing costs

	Bottom fifth	Next fifth	Middle fifth	Next fifth	Top fifth
1979	10	14	18	23	35
1987	8	12	17	23	40
1990–91	6	12	17	23	43

How the wealth is held
Net wealth of the personal sector by type, %

	1971	1981	1992
Dwellings	26	36	33
Other fixed assets	10	10	5
Non-marketable tenancy rights	12	12	8
Building society shares and deposits	7	8	8
National savings, notes and coins and bank deposits	13	10	10
Stocks, shares and unit trusts	23	8	9
Life assurance and pension funds	15	16	31
Other financial assets net of liabilities	-6	0	-4
Total £bn	172	740	2,300

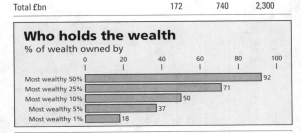

Who holds the wealth
% of wealth owned by

Most wealthy 50%	92
Most wealthy 25%	71
Most wealthy 10%	50
Most wealthy 5%	37
Most wealthy 1%	18

Marketable wealth less value of dwelling
% of wealth owned by

	1976	1981	1986	1989	1991
Most wealthy 1%	29	26	25	28	28
Most wealthy 5%	47	45	46	53	50
Most wealthy 10%	57	56	58	66	63
Most wealthy 25%	73	74	75	81	79
Most wealthy 50%	88	87	89	94	92
Total wealth, £bn[c]	280	565	955	1,578	1,694

a Adjusted for national consumer price inflation.
b Includes Greater London 1985–86 and 1989–90.
c Includes value of dwellings.

Consumerism

Consumer goods
% households owning, 1991–92 (1980–81 in brackets)

	Microwave oven	Washing machine	Tumble dryer	Dish-washer	Fridge-freezer[a]
UK	57	87 (77)	48 (22)	15 (4)	84 (47)
England	57	87 (76)	49 (22)	15 (4)	84 (48)
Wales	62	88 (81)	46 (23)	12 (2)	85 (50)
Scotland	53	90 (83)	49 (24)	12 (3)	79 (39)
Northern Ireland[b]	49	87 (70)	34	14	70
North	60	91 (88)	45 (19)	8 (1)	81 (42)
Yorkshire & Humberside	56	88 (84)	48 (24)	10 (2)	79 (40)
North West	57	87 (77)	46 (21)	12 (2)	83 (40)
West Midlands	59	87 (77)	48 (21)	11 (2)	84 (42)
East Midlands	57	89 (84)	50 (22)	14 (3)	85 (45)
East Anglia	53	87 (80)	49 (27)	14 (5)	84 (59)
South East	56	85 (69)	50 (23)	20 (6)	87 (55)
Greater London	49	79 (61)	43 (20)	15 (4)	83 (50)
Rest of South East	59	88 (75)	54 (25)	22 (7)	89 (59)
South West	59	86 (72)	50 (22)	20 (5)	87 (54)

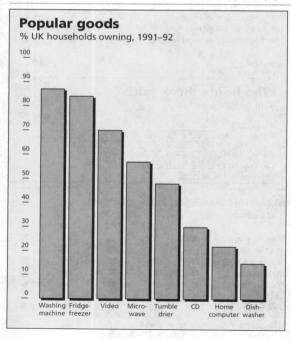

Popular goods
% UK households owning, 1991–92

a 1980-81 deep freezers.

Telephone	Television	CD player	Video	Home computer	Central heating
88 (73)	98 (97)	30	70	22	82 (59)
89 (74)	98 (97)	30	70	22	82 (52)
84 (67)	98 (98)	24	67	22	84 (51)
84 (74)	98 (97)	26	69	19	80 (39)
81 (57)	97 (91)	18	61	17	85 (64)
82 (64)	99 (98)	26	69	22	92 (64)
86 (68)	98 (97)	25	65	19	72 (52)
86 (71)	99 (98)	28	70	22	78 (54)
87 (71)	98 (97)	28	72	20	77 (54)
87 (73)	99 (98)	30	70	22	88 (65)
90 (73)	98 (98)	31	69	23	85 (68)
92 (80)	98 (96)	35	72	24	86 (62)
91 (79)	98 (95)	32	70	20	82 (54)
93 (80)	99 (97)	37	73	26	87 (67)
92 (72)	98 (96)	30	68	22	82 (57)

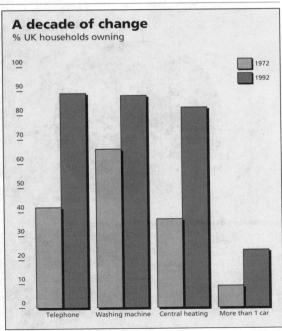

A decade of change
% UK households owning

1972
1992

Telephone   Washing machine   Central heating   More than 1 car

b 1991/92 and 1992/93.

Consumer spending and saving

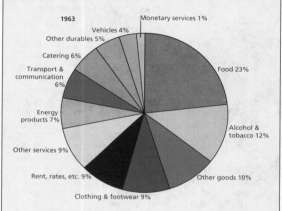

How spending habits have changed
consumer expenditure

1963

- Monetary services 1%
- Vehicles 4%
- Other durables 5%
- Catering 6%
- Transport & communication 6%
- Energy products 7%
- Other services 9%
- Rent, rates, etc. 9%
- Clothing & footwear 9%
- Food 23%
- Alcohol & tobacco 12%
- Other goods 10%

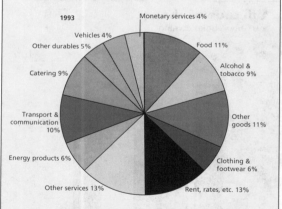

1993

- Monetary services 4%
- Vehicles 4%
- Other durables 5%
- Catering 9%
- Transport & communication 10%
- Energy products 6%
- Other services 13%
- Food 11%
- Alcohol & tobacco 9%
- Other goods 11%
- Clothing & footwear 6%
- Rent, rates, etc. 13%

CONSUMER EXPENDITURE AT CURRENT MARKET PRICES, £m

	1940	1950	1960	1970	1980	1990	1992
Transport & communication	5	7	7	10	16	18	17
Housing	11	9	10	13	14	14	15
Food	30	29	28	20	17	12	12
Recreation, entertainment & education	3	4	5	5	9	10	10
Alcoholic beverages	8	8	6	7	7	6	6
Clothing	11	11	10	9	7	6	6
Household goods & services	6	9	12	11	7	6	6
Fuel & power	5	4	4	5	5	4	4
Tobacco	6	8	7	5	4	2	3
Other	17	11	12	14	14	22	22

a Includes insurance, catering, other services and adjustments for tourists'
  expenditure and expenditure abroad.

How bills are paid
%

	1976	1981	1984	1989	1990	1991	1992
Cash	93	88	86	80	78	78	76
Non-cash	7	12	14	20	22	22	24
Non-cash payments:							
Cheque	68	68	64	55	52	50	46
Standing order/ direct debit	21	20	22	23	23	24	25
Plastic cards	7	9	13	18	20	23	25
of which:							
Credit/charge card	6	8	12	15	15	14	14
Retailer card	...	1	...	1	1	1	1
Debit card	0	0	0	2	4	8	11
Other	2	2	1	4	4	3	4

Savings by class
% of adults

	AB	C1	C2	DE
Building society account	78	70	68	49
Bank account	94	87	83	66
Premium Bonds	45	34	25	15
Unit trusts	19	13	6	2
Shares	27	14	8	4
Government privatisation shares	23	13	7	3
National Savings Bank investment/ ordinary account	11	13	10	7
National Savings certificates/ bonds	14	12	3	4

Savings by age and sex
% of adults

	16–34	34–64	65+	Males	Females
Building society account	62	68	62	63	65
Bank account	77	85	77	83	79
Premium Bonds	16	35	34	28	28
Unit trusts	4	13	7	11	7
Shares	8	16	9	14	9
Government privatisation shares	5	14	12	13	8
National Savings Bank investment/ ordinary account	10	10	10	10	10
National Savings certificates/ bonds	5	7	13	8	7

A history of prices

Prices since 1900

*Actual prices and (**in bold**) revalued to 1994 prices, £*

	1900	1930	1960	1990	1994
Railway fare: London to	1.66	5.00	8.40	59.00	69.00
Glasgow 2nd class return	**76.34**	**179.64**	**96.57**	**67.83**	**69.00**
Atlantic crossing by ship	12.33[a]	16.00[b]	67.00	970.00	1,020.00
(to New York): cheapest	**774.90**	**594.16**	**770.30**	**1,115.21**	**1,020.00**
Cunard ticket available					
Atlantic crossing by air:	...	...	154.35	323.00	268.00
London to New York (return)	...	...	**1,774.56**	**371.35**	**268.00**
cheapest ticket available					
London to Nairobi by air: (return)	...	178.20	199.30	517.00	615.00
cheapest ticket available		**6,395.20**	**2,291.35**	**594.39**	**615.00**
Bottle of whisky including tax	0.18[c]	0.71[d]	1.95[e]	8.80	10.80
	7.75	**23.35**	**22.20**	**10.12**	**10.80**
Car:	225[f]	170	494	6,180	7,095
Ford, cheapest model	**11,771**	**6,108**	**5,680**	**7,105**	**7,095**
Monet painting of	793[g]	1,744[h]	20,000	4,000,000	3,500,000
Waterloo Bridge, *Effet de*	**39,660**	**77,195**	**22,994**	**4,598,795**	**3,500,000**
soleil (oil on canvas 1903)					
English dinner at The Savoy:	0.38[i]	0.78	2.38	28.75	38.00
soup, main course,	**17.48**	**28.03**	**27.36**	**33.05**	**38.00**
pudding, coffee					
Top of the range camera:	20.00	18.60	145.00	1,200.00	1,430
Sanderson, Leica, Nikon	**919.76**	**668.26**	**1,667.06**	**1,380.00**	**1,430**
Telephone call: 3 minutes	0.25[j]	0.33	0.13	0.41	0.10
London to Glasgow	**10.27**	**11.85**	**1.49**	**0.47**	**0.10**
Telephone call: 3 minutes	...	15.00	3.00	2.33	1.43
London to New York	...	**538.92**	**34.49**	**2.68**	**1.43**
Opera ticket at Covent Garden:	0.13	0.33	0.18	3.00	4.00
least expensive	**5.98**	**11.85**	**2.07**	**3.45**	**4.00**
Opera ticket at Covent Garden:	1.50	1.40	2.10	101.00	117.00
most expensive	**68.98**	**50.30**	**24.14**	**116.12**	**117.00**
Household coal per short ton	1.18	1.24	4.22	120.66	160.00
	54.27	**44.55**	**48.52**	**138.72**	**160.00**
The Economist	0.03	0.05	0.08	1.60	2.00
	1.38	**1.79**	**0.86**	**1.84**	**2.00**
Theatre ticket: Theatre Royal,	0.08[k]	0.08[l]	0.30	7.50	8.50
least expensive	**2.14**	**2.97**	**3.45**	**8.62**	**8.50**
Theatre ticket: Theatre Royal,	0.60[k]	0.75[l]	1.50	25.00	30.00
most expensive	**16.07**	**27.86**	**17.25**	**28.74**	**30.00**
Gold per oz	4.24	4.25	12.56	209.16[m]	239.19
	194.99	**152.69**	**144.40**	**240.47**	**239.19**
Hotel room:	...	1.50	6.00	189.00	195.00
Hyde Park Hotel, single	...	**53.90**	**68.98**	**217.29**	**195.00**
Most expensive Jaguar,	...	310[h]	2197	43,200	58,800
two-seater	...	**13,722**	**25,259**	**49,667**	**58,800**
Pair of men's handmade shoes	0.84[n]	1.99	4.98[o]	125.00	165.00
	34.49	**71.50**	**83.02**	**143.71**	**165.00**
Standard Dunhill pipe	0.38[p]	1.25	8.38	108.00	130.00
	16.82	**44.99**	**96.34**	**124.17**	**130.00**

Men's suit:	...	4.20[q]	30.00	269.00	269.00
Daks 2-piece	...	**114.53**	**344.91**	**309.27**	**269.00**
Taxi ride, one mile	0.30	0.11	0.11	1.60	1.85
	1.38	**1.44**	**1.30**	**1.84**	**1.85**
Lighter, gold-plated	1.75[r]	2.25	7.25	185.00	195.00
	47.90	**80.84**	**83.35**	**212.69**	**195.00**
Potatoes per 7lbs	0.02	0.02	0.08	0.91	1.26
	0.82	**0.89**	**0.92**	**1.05**	**1.26**

Actual and (in bold) revalued to 1994 prices, pence

Bread:	0.5	0.7	2.4	42	52
unsliced loaf per 400g	**21**	**31**	**28**	**48**	**52**
Milk per pint	0.7	1.2	3.3	30	36
	30	**44**	**38**	**34**	**36**
Postage stamp:	0.42	0.42	1.25	22	25
London to Scotland	**20**	**20**	**15**	**25**	**25**
Postage stamp:	0.01	0.63	1.25	37	41
London to America	**0.46**	**22**	**14**	**43**	**41**
The Times	0.83[n]	0.83	3.3	35	20
	34	**30**	**38**	**40**	**20**
Underground ticket:	0.83	0.63	2.08	70	90
Victoria to South Kensington	**38**	**23**	**24**	**80**	**90**
Mars bar	...	0.8	2.5	21	28
	...	**36**	**29**	**24**	**28**

Note: all food prices are July 1914 average instead of 1900, and 1933 instead of 1930.

a 1895.
b 1934.
c 1906.
d 1939.
e 1961.
f 1904.
g 1905.
h 1932.
i 1900 price includes fourth course of fish.
j 1912.
k 1922.
l 1935.
m Average for third quarter.
n 1913.
o 1949.
p 1910.
q 1938.
r 1926.
s 1933.

Food and drink

The weekly diet
Estimated household consumption, ounces per person per week, GB

	1965	1975	1985	1993
Cheese	3.20	3.79	3.91	3.85
Butter	6.10	5.63	2.83	1.41
Margarine	3.04	2.60	3.76	2.79[a]
Beef and veal	8.08	9.32	6.51	4.68
Mutton and lamb	5.90	4.25	3.27	2.33
Pork	2.80	2.73	3.45	2.83
Poultry	3.51	5.73	6.90	8.16[a]
Fish	5.79	4.47	4.91	5.10
Fresh green vegetables	14.32	11.58	9.78	8.46
Fresh potatoes	53.24	43.9	40.96	30.88
Fresh fruit	18.79	17.51	18.53	21.75
Other fresh vegetables & frozen vegetables	15.23	17.05	21.67	23.74
Bread	40.6	33.67	20.99	26.70
Tea	2.61	2.18	1.74	1.37[a]
Instant coffee	0.26	0.50	0.54	0.49[a]
Sugar	17.56	11.29	8.41	5.51[a]
Liquid whole milk[b]	4.85	4.76	3.32	1.51
Other milk[b]	0.31	0.33	0.79	1.81
Eggs[c]	4.78	4.14	3.15	1.92

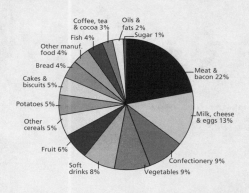

Spending on food
% of domestic spending, UK

Coffee, tea & cocoa 3%
Oils & fats 2%
Sugar 1%
Fish 4%
Other manuf. food 4%
Bread 4%
Cakes & biscuits 5%
Potatoes 5%
Other cereals 5%
Fruit 6%
Soft drinks 8%
Vegetables 9%
Confectionery 9%
Meat & bacon 22%
Milk, cheese & eggs 13%

	£m
Meat and bacon	9,958
Milk, cheese and eggs	6,017
Confectionery	4,081
Vegetables	3,852
Soft drinks	3,503
Fruit	2,911
Other cereals	2,481
Potatoes	2,194

	£m
Cakes and biscuits	2,059
Bread	2,007
Other manufactured food	1,906
Fish	1,663
Coffee, tea and cocoa	1,244
Oils and fats	1,081

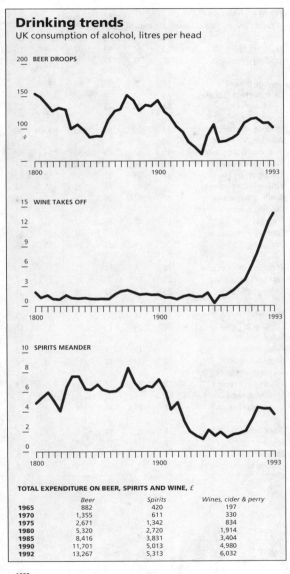

Drinking trends
UK consumption of alcohol, litres per head

BEER DROOPS

WINE TAKES OFF

SPIRITS MEANDER

TOTAL EXPENDITURE ON BEER, SPIRITS AND WINE, £			
	Beer	*Spirits*	*Wines, cider & perry*
1965	882	420	197
1970	1,355	611	330
1975	2,671	1,342	834
1980	5,320	2,720	1,914
1985	8,416	3,831	3,404
1990	11,701	5,013	4,980
1992	13,267	5,313	6,032

a 1992.
b Pints per person per week.
c Number per person per week.

Leisure

What people do
% population who do at least once a week, 1993

	All	16–24	25–34	35–44	45–59	60+
Watching TV	97	97	99	97	97	96
Reading newspapers	80	71	77	83	85	82
Reading books	59	58	45	64	55	69
Listening to CDs, tapes or records	58	88	73	54	57	37
Drinking alcohol at home	49	39	55	53	48	48
Watching videos of recorded programmes	46	60	48	52	46	33
Playing with children	43	39	70	62	32	24
Playing with pets	40	33	35	53	50	32
Visiting pub in evening	39	69	46	39	43	13
Reading magazines	38	41	35	38	36	41
Reading special interest magazines	37	48	33	42	41	28
Cooking for pleasure	36	28	40	36	36	37
Gardening	34	8	22	36	51	45
Watching other videos	28	55	41	37	14	6
Fast food restaurant	22	50	33	23	11	2
Sewing or knitting	20	8	13	19	25	31
Religious meeting	18	14	17	13	18	26
Exercise at home	16	24	18	15	13	11
Pub at lunchtime	16	18	21	16	17	12
Voluntary work	15	13	17	13	13	13
Billiards/snooker	11	22	12	11	9	3
Aerobics/yoga/keep fit (away from home)	10	17	12	10	5	7
Specialist games computer/console	10	29	14	8	3	2
Home computer	8	10	15	8	7	4
Jogging	7	9	11	9	6	–
Darts	5	8	1	9	6	2
Evening classes	4	2	3	5	7	2

% population who do at least once a quarter, 1993

	All	16–24	25–34	35–44	45–59	60+
Going to the pub	61	75	74	69	63	35
Eating out as an occasion	58	55	61	62	61	53
Long walk for pleasure	48	44	45	55	50	47
Eating take-away at home	46	66	63	55	37	20
Holiday in UK	46	40	41	47	53	47
Motoring for pleasure	42	36	43	39	44	45
Eating out – fast food	41	71	54	51	28	15
Home entertaining	38	31	43	37	44	33
Visiting the library	36	31	28	44	40	38
Board games playing	31	36	40	45	22	17
Holiday abroad	30	30	30	36	31	26
Going to the cinema	29	56	40	30	19	7
Sports centre	28	42	35	34	21	14
Short break holiday	28	30	24	30	30	29
Going to a disco or nightclub	27	71	36	24	14	4
Swimming	22	26	32	28	19	8
Spectator sports	20	32	26	28	14	6
Historic building	19	11	19	24	21	20
Playing individual sport	18	26	23	26	14	8
Theatre	18	13	17	25	21	16
Museum/art gallery	17	17	17	20	21	14
Visited a fun fair	15	31	23	19	6	1
Team sport playing	15	30	18	21	8	4
Eating take-away at another place	14	30	21	13	10	3
Exhibition	11	11	10	12	16	6
Theme park visiting	11	13	16	19	6	4
Betting shop	10	15	9	12	12	4
Bingo	10	11	9	8	12	9
Pop or rock concert	8	22	10	6	3	1
Classical concert or opera	6	2	4	8	8	7
Camping/caravanning	6	6	6	8	7	5
Fishing	4	5	4	7	5	2
Circus visiting	3	2	9	4	1	–
Horse racing	2	2	–	5	3	1

Newspapers and magazines

Daily papers
January–July average circulation, '000s

	Daily Telegraph	Financial Times	Guardian	Independent	Times
1940	...	...	...	...	...
1945	...	...	...	...	195
1950	...	58	140	...	254
1955	...	79	156	...	222
1960	1,177	122	199	...	263
1965	1,351	152	276	...	258
1970	1,402	175	303	...	402
1975	1,353	186	336	...	327
1980	1,446	198	375	...	316
1985	1,221	229	487	...	480
1990	1,086	292	433	414	432
1991	1,075	289	431	394	406
1992	1,044	292	418	377	390
1993	1,025	290	416	347	366
1994[b]	1,014	297	401	275	508

Sunday papers
January–June average circulation, '000s

	Independent on Sunday	Observer	Sunday Telegraph	Sunday Times	Mail on Sunday
1940	...	241	...	...	...
1945	...	299	...	...	...
1950	...	422	...	...	...
1955	...	564	...	606	...
1960	...	704	...	943	...
1965	...	829	662	1,275	...
1970	...	848	756	1,464	...
1975	...	761	757	1,396	...
1980	...	1,018	1,032	1,419	...
1985	...	746	690	1,258	1,605
1990	352[a]	567	587	1,187	1,889
1991	385	579	576	1,177	1,940
1992	385	541	562	1,203	1,960
1993	385	509	578	1,224	2,030
1994[b]	328	495	633	1,205	1,972

Magazines
UK circulation figures from start of ABC membership, first half of year yearly average, '000s

	The Economist	Time	Newsweek
1975	58.7	...	...
1980	70.4	65.5	32.5
1985	79.9	59.4	30.3
1990	96.5	71.2	31.9
1993	104.0	96.6	31.6

Daily Express	Daily Mail	Daily Mirror	Star	Sun	Today
...	...	...	...	...	...
3,127	1,752	...	...	...	...
4,116	2,245	4,567	...	2,071	...
4,036	2,068	4,725	...	1,759	...
4,143	2,066	4,565	...	1,407	...
3,981	2,325	4,957	...	1,361	...
3,607	1,917	4,697	...	1,509	...
2,894	1,730	4,018	...	3,435	...
2,325	1,985	3,651	1,033	3,837	...
1,875	1,828	3,272	1,435	4,066	...
1,562	1,670	3,130	919	3,937	581
1,565	1,720	2,957	879	3,693	490
1,538	1,689	2,868	808	3,588	495
1,497	1,775	2,680	773	3,517	538
1,358	1,797	2,497	742	4,102	595

News of the World	People	Sunday Express	Sunday Mirror	Sunday Sport
1,555	...	...	...	...
2,027	...	...	...	...
8,444	5,089	2,967	5,094	...
7,971	5,075	3,235	5,539	...
6,456	5,323	3,556	5,275	...
6,175	5,509	4,187	5,022	...
6,215	5,242	4,281	4,885	...
5,646	4,219	3,786	4,284	...
4,472	3,900	3,100	3,856	...
4,787	3,090	2,405	3,211	...
5,036	2,588	1,727	2,911	452
4,808	2,338	1,623	2,806	371
4,725	2,130	1,692	2,768	316
4,620	2,032	1,727	2,674	258
4,769	2,006	1,544	2,580	275

Business Week	New Statesman	Private Eye	The Spectator
...	37.3	...	...
4.4	34.0	...	15.7
5.9	24.3	226.5	19.3
8.0	...	197.6	25.6
10.3	18.4c	190.6	35.7

a July–December.
b February–July.   c 1992.

Television

Viewing trends
Daily hours of viewing per household

	Total hours	ITV	BBC1	BBC2	C4	Satellite
1969	4.5	2.4	2.1	...	...	...
1972	4.8	2.7	1.9	0.3	...	...
1976	5.1	2.7	2.1	0.4	...	...
1980	5.1	2.5	2.0	0.6	...	...
1982	4.9	2.4	1.9	0.6	...	...
1986	5.3	2.4	1.9	0.6	0.5	...
1990	5.1	2.3	1.9	0.5	0.5	...
1993	6.0	2.3	1.9	0.6	0.7	0.4

Box-watching hours
Monthly average daily hours of viewing per person, 1993

	BBC1	BBC2	ITV	C4	Satellite	Total
January	1.22	0.23	1.44	0.28	0.13	4.10
February	1.20	0.25	1.37	0.28	0.14	4.03
March	1.15	0.21	1.34	0.26	0.13	3.49
April	1.11	0.25	1.28	0.26	0.13	3.43
May	1.06	0.20	1.22	0.23	0.11	3.22
June	0.59	0.22	1.17	0.22	0.12	3.13
July	1.00	0.25	1.15	0.21	0.13	3.14
August	1.03	0.25	1.13	0.22	0.14	3.16
September	1.08	0.18	1.25	0.23	0.13	3.28
October	1.11	0.21	1.31	0.23	0.15	3.41
November	1.19	0.22	1.35	0.25	0.16	3.57
December	1.27	0.23	1.35	0.25	0.16	4.05
Average	1.12	0.23	1.28	0.24	0.14	3.40

Channel ratings
% average monthly share of audience, 1993

	BBC1	BBC2	ITV	C4	Satellite
January	33	9	41	11	5
February	33	10	40	11	6
March	33	9	41	11	6
April	32	11	40	12	6
May	33	10	41	11	6
June	31	11	40	12	6
July	31	13	39	11	7
August	32	13	37	11	7
September	33	9	41	11	6
October	32	9	41	10	7
November	33	9	40	11	7
December	35	9	39	10	6

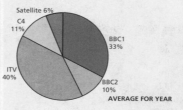

Satellite 6%
C4 11%
BBC1 33%
ITV 40%
BBC2 10%

AVERAGE FOR YEAR

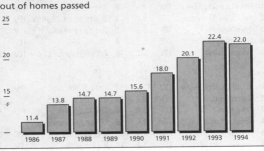

The growth of cable
UK cable market penetration, % of homes connected
out of homes passed

Year	Value
1986	11.4
1987	13.8
1988	14.7
1989	14.7
1990	15.6
1991	18.0
1992	20.1
1993	22.4
1994	22.0

Cable areas
penetration of broadband networks with 2,500+ homes
connected Jan 1994, % homes connected out of
homes passed

Area	%
Northampton	53.8
Kingston & Richmond	43.8
Birmingham	37.6
Harlow	35.7
Swindon	32.5
Enfield	30.0
Edinburgh	27.3
Leicester	27.3
Glenrothes	26.5
South Liverpool	26.2
Nottingham	26.0

Franchises	Homes connected	Franchises	Homes connected
1 Birmingham	56,489	7 Leicester	6,986
2 Swindon	21,459	8 Kingston & Richmond	5,622
3 Enfield	17,390	9 Nottingham	5,253
4 South Liverpool	16,442	10 Glenrothes	4,971
5 Northampton	13,469	11 Harlow	3,184
6 Edinburgh	13,303		

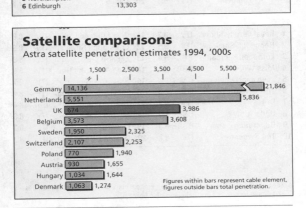

Satellite comparisons
Astra satellite penetration estimates 1994, '000s

Country	Cable element	Total penetration
Germany	14,136	21,846
Netherlands	5,551	5,836
UK	674	3,986
Belgium	3,573	3,608
Sweden	1,950	2,325
Switzerland	2,107	2,253
Poland	770	1,940
Austria	930	1,655
Hungary	1,034	1,644
Denmark	1,063	1,274

Figures within bars represent cable element,
figures outside bars total penetration.

Television: top programmes

Most viewed programmes[a]
m

1960

1	Royal Variety Show	ITV	8.1
2	Armchair Theatre	ITV	7.7
3	Take Your Pick	ITV	7.5
4	No Hiding Place	ITV	7.2
5	Wagon Train	ITV	7.2
6	Army Game	ITV	7.2
7	Bootsie and Snudge	ITV	7.1
8	Sunday Palladium	ITV	7.0
9	The Larkins	ITV	7.0
10	Arthur Haynes Show	ITV	6.9

1965

1	Royal Variety Show	ITV	11.0
2	Coronation Street	ITV	9.7
3	Take Your Pick	ITV	8.8
4	Riviera Police	ITV	8.6
5	No Hiding Place	ITV	8.5
6	Double Your Money	ITV	8.4
7	This Week	ITV	8.4
8	Love Story	ITV	8.4
9	Crane	ITV	8.1
10	Emergency Ward Ten	ITV	8.0
11	The Power Game	ITV	8.0
12	Hello Dolly	ITV	8.0
13	Steptoe and Son	BBC	8.0
14	The Avengers	ITV	8.0
15	Music of Lennon & McCartney	ITV	7.9
16	It's Tarbuck	ITV	7.8
17	Miss World	BBC	7.8
18	Here Comes the Pops	ITV	7.6
19	Blackmail	ITV	7.6
20	Professional Boxing	ITV	7.3

1970

1	Miss World	BBC	10.6
2	Benny Hill Show	ITV	9.3
3	Eurovision Song Contest	BBC	9.2
4	This is Your Life	ITV	8.9
5	Coronation Street	ITV	8.9
6	News at Ten	ITV	8.7
7	Steptoe and Son	BBC	8.7
8	Royal Variety Show	BBC	8.5
9	Apollo 13 Splashdown	ITV	8.3
10	Kate	ITV	8.2
11	On the Buses	ITV	8.2
12	633 Squadron	BBC	8.2
13	News at Ten	ITV	8.2
14	Max	ITV	8.1
15	Morecambe & Wise	BBC	8.0
16	Please Sir!	ITV	8.0
17	The Dustbinmen	ITV	8.0
18	Opportunity Knocks	ITV	7.9
19	A Family at War	ITV	7.9
20	Callan	ITV	7.8

1975

1	Royal Variety Show	ITV	10.3
2	Benny Hill Show	ITV	9.5
3	European Football	BBC	9.4
4	Miss World	BBC	9.4
5	Love thy Neighbour	ITV	9.3
6	This is Your Life	ITV	9.3
7	Dr No	ITV	9.2
8	Dad's Army	BBC	8.9
9	Generation Game	BBC	8.9
10	The Sweeney	ITV	8.8
11	Cilla's Comedy Six	ITV	8.8
12	Coronation Street	ITV	8.8
13	Edward the Seventh	ITV	8.8
14	Man About the House	ITV	8.8
15	Bless this House	ITV	8.7
16	Tommy Cooper Hour	ITV	8.4
17	The Two Ronnies	BBC	8.4
18	My Old Man	ITV	8.3
19	News at Ten	ITV	8.3
20	Upstairs, Downstairs	ITV	8.3

a Soap operas are only featured with their highest entry in the 20. Omnibus editions and repeat broadcasts are included in this figure.

1980

1	Live and Let Die	ITV	23.5
2	To the Manor Born	BBC	21.6
3	Dallas	BBC	20.3
4	This is Your Life	ITV	19.8
5	My Wife Next Door	ITV	19.3
6	Jim'll Fix It	BBC	19.2
7	Blankety Blank	BBC	19.1
8	Coronation Street	ITV	19.0
9	Dick Emery Show	BBC	18.9
10	All Creatures Great and Small	BBC	18.7
11	Morecambe & Wise	ITV	18.7
12	The Two Ronnies	BBC	18.6
13	Paint Your Wagon	ITV	18.5
14	Robin's Nest	ITV	18.4
15	Generation Game	BBC	18.3
16	Benny Hill Show	ITV	18.1
17	Dick Emery Show	ITV	18.1
18	Keep it in the Family	ITV	18.1
19	Little and Large	ITV	18.1
20	George and Mildred	ITV	17.8

1985

1	EastEnders	BBC	23.6
2	Coronation Street	ITV	21.4
3	Wish You Were Here	ITV	19.0
4	Open All Hours	BBC	19.0
5	Last of the Summer Wine	ITV	18.8
6	Prince and Princess of Wales	ITV	18.6
7	It'll Be Alright on the Night	ITV	18.6
8	The Two Ronnies	BBC	18.5
9	That's Life	BBC	18.4
10	Crossroads	ITV	18.1
11	Hollywood Wives	ITV	18.0
12	Boxing	ITV	18.0
13	Night of 100 Stars	ITV	17.7
14	Game for a Laugh	ITV	17.6
15	Superman II	ITV	17.6
16	Fresh Fields	ITV	17.5
17	Dr No	ITV	17.5
18	From Russia with Love	ITV	17.3
19	Goldfinger	ITV	17.0
20	Only Fools and Horses	ITV	16.9

1990

1	Coronation Street	ITV	22.8
2	EastEnders	BBC	20.8
3	Neighbours	BBC	20.6
4	Only Fools and Horses	BBC	18.0
5	It'll Be Alright on the Night	ITV	17.9
6	E.T.	BBC	17.5
7	A View to a Kill	ITV	16.9
8	Generation Game	BBC	16.7
9	World Cup (W. Germany v England)	BBC	16.7
10	News and Weather	BBC	16.6
11	Inspector Morse	ITV	16.2
12	Octopussy	ITV	15.9
13	Blind Date	ITV	15.8
14	Wish You Were Here	ITV	15.8
15	This is Your Life	ITV	15.7
16	The Bill	ITV	15.3
17	For Your Eyes Only	ITV	15.2
18	Watching	ITV	14.8
19	Strike it Lucky	ITV	14.6
20	Bergerac	BBC	14.2

1993

1	Coronation Street	ITV	20.7
2	One Foot in the Algarve	BBC	20.0
3	Only Fools and Horses	BBC	19.6
4	Birds of a Feather	BBC	19.4
5	Inspector Morse	ITV	18.8
6	Ghost	BBC	18.5
7	One Foot in the Grave	BBC	18.4
8	You've Been Framed	ITV	18.3
9	EastEnders	BBC	17.8
10	Heartbeat	ITV	17.8

Video

The rise and peaks of video
Video rental

	Units sold[a]	Value	Consumer retail	Value
	m	£m	transactions, m	£m
1986	4.2	125	300	375
1987	4.5	135	320	410
1988	5.2	155	350	470
1989	6.2	185	385	555
1990	7.4	185	365	550
1991	6.7	170	330	540
1992	…	400	317	511
1993	…	528	328	643

Video sales

	Video sell-through		Blank cassettes	
	Units sold	Value	Units sold	Value
	m	£m	m	£m
1986	6	70	35	160
1987	10	100	37	160
1988	18	175	55	204
1989	37	320	56	184
1990	41	365	59	184
1991	51	444	65	195
1992	48	400	…	…
1993	60	…	…	…

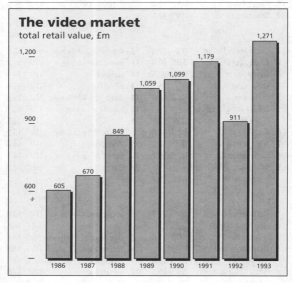

The video market
total retail value, £m

1986	1987	1988	1989	1990	1991	1992	1993
605	670	849	1,059	1,099	1,179	911	1,271

a Units sold by distributors to video outlets.

Music sales

The domestic market

UK sales, '000s

	Singles	LPs	Tapes	CDs	Retail value, $m
1972	46.2	59.3	8.1	...	258
1973	54.6	81.0	15.5	...	379
1974	62.7	89.5	20.2	...	486
1975	56.9	91.6	20.2	...	531
1976	56.9	83.8	18.2	...	459
1977	62.1	81.7	19.6	...	475
1978	88.8	86.0	21.2	...	680
1979	89.1	74.5	23.6	...	845
1980	77.8	67.4	25.2	...	1022
1981	77.3	64.0	28.9	...	867
1982	78.6	57.8	31.5	...	809
1983	74.0	54.3	35.8	0.3	745
1984	77.0	54.1	45.3	0.9	734
1985	73.8	53.0	55.4	3.1	862
1986	67.4	52.3	69.6	8.4	1,089
1987	63.4	52.2	74.4	18.2	1,499
1988	60.1	50.2	80.9	29.2	1,973
1989	61.2	37.9	83.0	41.7	1,981
1990	58.4	24.5	74.3	50.9	2,118
1991	56.3	12.9	66.8	62.8	2,155
1992	53.0	6.7	56.4	70.5	1,998
1993	56.2	5.0	55.7	92.9	1,976

World music sales

	Sales, $m			1993 % share
	1973	*1983*	*1993*	
UK	258	745	1,976	6.5
USA	2,001	3,814	9,833	32.3
Japan	700	1,322	5,082	16.7
Germany[b]	430	897	2,691	8.8
France	314	669	1,849	6.1

b Western.

Cinema and theatre

New British films

	Titles produced	Production cost, £m, 1992 prices	Average budget, £m, 1992 prices
1981	24	113.3	4.7
1982	40	240.6	6.0
1983	51	409.4	8.0
1984	53	420.0	7.9
1985	54	394.4	7.3
1986	41	234.7	5.7
1987	55	265.5	4.8
1988	48	227.0	4.7
1989	30	125.9	4.2
1990	60	238.7	4.0
1991	59	252.3	4.3
1992	47	220.4	3.9
1993	69	…	…

Who funds them

	1990		1991		1992	
	£000s	%	£000s	%	£000s	%
British Screen	4,865	19.6	4,559	19.5	2,700	10.5
European Co-production Fund	…	…	250	1.1	2,043	8.0
Channel Four	5,524	22.2	3,933	16.8	4,709	18.4
Other UK investors	7,497	30.2	4,057	17.3	2,546	9.9
EU investors	3,384	13.6	5,948	25.4	7,878	30.7
US investors	1,822	7.3	4,223	18.1	3,697	14.4
Other	1,756	7.1	421	1.8	2,069	8.1
Total	24,848	100.0	23,391	100.0	25,642	100.0

Cinema visits: a British revival
Millions

	1983	1988	1992/3
UK	64	84	113
France	191[a]	125	133[b]
Germany	125	109	106
Italy	162	93	84
Japan	170	145	126
USA	1,197	1,085	1,100
EU	659	559	558

Average no. admissions per capita

	1983	1988	1992/3
UK	1.2	1.5	1.9
France	…	2.2	2.3
Germany	2.0	1.8	1.3
Italy	2.9	1.6	1.4
Japan	1.4	1.2	1.0
USA	5.1	4.4	4.4
EU	2.3	1.7	1.6

a 1984.   b 1993 provisional.

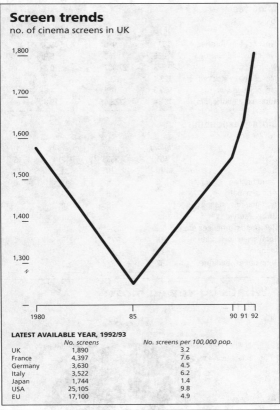

Screen trends
no. of cinema screens in UK

LATEST AVAILABLE YEAR, 1992/93

	No. screens	No. screens per 100,000 pop.
UK	1,890	3.2
France	4,397	7.6
Germany	3,630	4.5
Italy	3,522	6.2
Japan	1,744	1.4
USA	25,105	9.8
EU	17,100	4.9

London theatres

	Paid attendances in West End theatres, m	Gross box office office revenue, £m 1993 prices	No. productions opening
1983	8.9	110.1	201
1984	10.0	132.7	203
1985	10.8	153.0	256
1986	10.2	161.2	213
1987	10.9	178.9	212
1988	10.9	183.3	228
1989	10.9	187.2	237
1990	11.3	198.4	187
1991	10.9	196.8	192
1992	10.9	197.9	193
1993	11.5	215.6	198

Books

Libraries
UK

	1975[a]	1992	% change in real terms
No. of public libraries	3,714	4,080	9.9
No. of mobile libraries	655	700	6.9
No. of staff	30,988	27,807	-10.3
No. of books stocked, *m*	123.4	133.1	7.9
No. of issues, *m*	589.3	561.2	-4.8
Total expenditure, £m	161.4	778.4	19.0

Library expenditure
1992/3, £m

	National	Public	University	HE & FE[b]
Staff	51	383	112	43
Books	10	110	31	13
Periodicals	3	6	41	6
Audio-visual	…	9	3	…
Automated systems	…	16	10	…
On-line services	…	…	1	…
Overheads, premises etc.	…	254	15	…
Total gross expenditure	115	778	213	71
Income	23	51	11	…
Total net expenditure	92	727	202	…

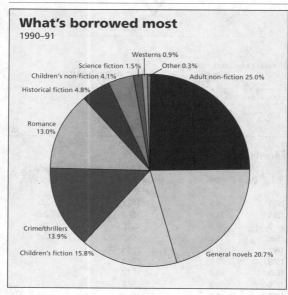

What's borrowed most
1990–91

- Adult non-fiction 25.0%
- General novels 20.7%
- Children's fiction 15.8%
- Crime/thrillers 13.9%
- Romance 13.0%
- Historical fiction 4.8%
- Children's non-fiction 4.1%
- Science fiction 1.5%
- Westerns 0.9%
- Other 0.3%

a Data for 1975 may be greater than listed due to low response rates from Scotland and Northern Ireland.
b Higher education and further education.

What is published
Titles published, 1992 (% change on previous year)

Fiction	8,076	(2.9)	Social sciences	2,312	(47.0)
Children's books	7,006	(13.8)	Travel	2,089	(24.6)
History	3,620	(44.2)	Law	1,811	(32.3)
Economics	3,374	(31.7)	Political science	1,753	(-9.5)
Medicine	3,235	(25.9)	Social welfare	1,656	(101.0)
Religion	2,630	(6.7)	Education	1,621	(17.9)
Management	2,621	(14.4)	Art	1,590	(0.2)
Computers	2,587	(25.4)	Engineering	1,545	(22.6)
Biography	2,574	(17.3)	Psychology	1,231	(-7.4)
School textbooks	2,340	(-18.6)	Other	22,827	(17.8)
Literature	2,337	(25.8)	Total	78,835	(16.4)

Book markets compared
1993

		Total value, $m	Value per capita, $	Title output per m inhabitants	Estimated total value, $m
1	USA	22.500	89	205	26,000
2	Japan	9,130	74	294	10,000
3	Germany	8,340	102	953	9,475
4	UK	3,570	62	1,114	3,900
5	France	3,540	62	735	3,850
6	Spain	3,185	83	935	3,480
7	Italy	2,410	42	435	2,550
8	South Korea	2,210	51	917	2,500
9	Canada	1,515	56	724	1,700
10	China	1,510	1	64	2,000
11	Australia	920	52	674	1,000
12	Netherlands	905	60	916	930
13	Brazil	900	6	130	1,050
14	Austria	740	95	1,336	800
15	Sweden	705	81	1,406	800
16	India	650	<1	17	750
17	Switzerland	560	82	2,061	600
18	Norway	485	113	875	525
19	Denmark	475	92	2,156	525
20	Belgium	440	44	686	470
21	Finland	335	66	2,035	375
22	Portugal	235	22	595	260
23	South Africa	175	4	130	200
24	Ireland	145	41	756	160
25	New Zealand	135	40	1,062	150
26	Hungary	105	10	803	120

Sport

Attendances

	Soccer[a]			Cricket[c]		Tennis	Golf[d]
	England	Scotland[b]		Test	County	Wimbledon	Open
	m	m		'000s	'000s	'000s	'000s
1960/61	28.6	…	1965	…	…	277[e]	33
1965/66	27.2	4.1	1970	…	…	284	73
1970/71	28.2	4.2	1975	…	…	339	76
1975/76	24.9	3.7	1980	…	…	334	132
1980/81	21.9	2.9	1981	…	…	358	112
1981/82	20.0	3.0	1982	…	…	316	132
1982/83	18.8	3.0	1983	…	…	360	142
1983/84	18.4	3.1	1984	296.5	…	395	193
1984/85	17.8	2.8	1985	372.2	296.8	395	142
1985/86	16.5	3.2	1986	285.2	328.1	400	134
1986/87	17.4	4.0	1987	234.6	313.8	396	139
1987/88	18.0	4.6	1988	245.8	304.7	411	207
1988/89	18.5	4.1	1989	343.0	369.6	400	161
1989/90	19.5	3.9	1990	269.2	332.4	348	209
1990/91	19.5	3.8	1991	316.8	363.3	378	192
1991/92	20.5	3.8	1992	306.7	298.7	373	150
1992/93	20.7	4.1	1993	370.7	306.3	393	124
1993/94	21.7	4.0	1994	…	…	378	135[f]

Rugby

International Championship winners

1947	Wales/England	1963	England	1979	Wales
1948	Ireland	1964	Scotland/Wales	1980	England
1949	Ireland	1965	Wales	1981	France
1950	Wales	1966	Wales	1982	Ireland
1951	Ireland	1967	France	1983	France/Ireland
1952	Wales	1968	France	1984	Scotland
1953	England	1969	Wales	1985	Ireland
1954	Eng/France/Wales	1970	France	1986	France/Scotland
1955	France/Wales	1971	Wales	1987	France
1956	Wales	1972	[g]	1988	Wales/France
1957	England	1973	Quintuple tie	1989	France
1958	England	1974	Ireland	1990	Scotland
1959	France	1975	Wales	1991	England
1960	France/England	1976	Wales	1992	England
1961	France	1977	France	1993	France
1962	France	1978	Wales	1994	Wales

a Figures may have been affected by changes to league system and introduction of
  Premier League.
b Includes cup ties.
c Cricket attendances are affected by play at different venues and are totals for all
  days in all tests or first class games. County figures do not include members.
d Golf figures may be affected by change of venue for each Open Championship.
e 1966.
f Approximately.
g Fixtures uncompleted.
h Year in which season ended.
i Cups now named after sponsors.

Cricket
County Championship winners

1946	Yorkshire	**1963**	Yorkshire	**1980**	Middlesex
1947	Middlesex	**1964**	Worcestershire	**1981**	Nottinghamshire
1948	Glamorgan	**1965**	Worcestershire	**1982**	Middlesex
1949	Middx/Yorks	**1966**	Yorkshire	**1983**	Essex
1950	Lancs/Surrey	**1967**	Yorkshire	**1984**	Essex
1951	Warwickshire	**1968**	Yorkshire	**1985**	Middlesex
1952	Surrey	**1969**	Glamorgan	**1986**	Essex
1953	Surrey	**1970**	Kent	**1987**	Nottinghamshire
1954	Surrey	**1971**	Surrey	**1988**	Worcestershire
1955	Surrey	**1972**	Warwickshire	**1989**	Worcestershire
1956	Surrey	**1973**	Hampshire	**1990**	Middlesex
1957	Surrey	**1974**	Worcestershire	**1991**	Essex
1958	Surrey	**1975**	Leicestershire	**1992**	Essex
1959	Yorkshire	**1976**	Middlesex	**1993**	Middlesex
1960	Yorkshire	**1977**	Middx/Kent	**1994**	Warwickshire
1961	Hampshire	**1978**	Kent		
1962	Yorkshire	**1979**	Essex		

Football

	League champions	*F.A. Cup winners*	*League Cup winners*
1966	Liverpool	Everton	W. Bromwich Albion
1967	Manchester United	Tottenham Hotspur	Queens Park Rangers
1968	Manchester City	W. Bromwich Albion	Leeds United
1969	Leeds United	Manchester City	Swindon Town
1970	Everton	Chelsea	Manchester City
1971	Arsenal	Arsenal	Tottenham Hotspur
1972	Derby County	Leeds United	Stoke City
1973	Liverpool	Sunderland	Tottenham Hotspur
1974	Leeds United	Liverpool	Wolves
1975	Derby County	West Ham United	Aston Villa
1976	Liverpool	Southampton	Manchester City
1977	Liverpool	Manchester United	Aston Villa
1978	Nottingham Forest	Ipswich Town	Nottingham Forest
1979	Liverpool	Arsenal	Nottingham Forest
1980	Liverpool	West Ham United	Wolves
1981	Aston Villa	Tottenham Hotspur	Liverpool
1982	Liverpool	Tottenham Hotspur	Liverpool
1983	Liverpool	Manchester United	Liverpool
1984	Liverpool	Everton	Liverpool
1985	Everton	Manchester United	Norwich City
1986	Liverpool	Liverpool	Oxford United
1987	Everton	Coventry City	Arsenal
1988	Liverpool	Wimbledon	Luton Town
1989	Arsenal	Liverpool	Nottingham Forest
1990	Liverpool	Manchester United	Nottingham Forest
1991	Arsenal	Tottenham Hotspur	Sheffield Wednesday
1992	Leeds United	Liverpool	Manchester United
1993	Manchester United	Arsenal	Arsenal
1994	Manchester United	Manchester United	Aston Villa

Holidays and outings

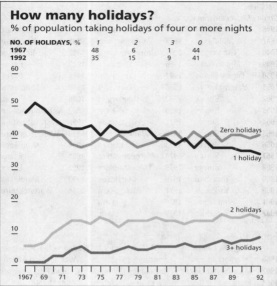

How many holidays?
% of population taking holidays of four or more nights

NO. OF HOLIDAYS, %	1	2	3	0
1967	48	6	1	44
1992	35	15	9	41

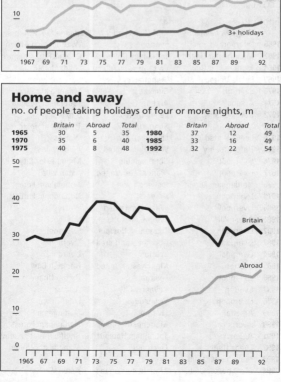

Home and away
no. of people taking holidays of four or more nights, m

	Britain	Abroad	Total		Britain	Abroad	Total
1965	30	5	35	**1980**	37	12	49
1970	35	6	40	**1985**	33	16	49
1975	40	8	48	**1992**	32	22	54

Heritage appeal

Historic properties, no. of paid admissions

1990

1	Tower of London	2,296,683
2	Roman Baths and Pump Room, Bath	950,472
3	State Apartments, Windsor Castle	855,239
4	Stonehenge, Wiltshire	703,221
5	Warwick Castle	685,000
6	Shakespeare's birthplace, Stratford	603,899
7	Leeds Castle, Kent	540,483
8	Tower Bridge, London	527,766
9	Hampton Court Palace	520,995
10	Blenheim Palace, Woodstock	511,630
11	Beaulieu, Hampshire	493,216
12	Chatsworth House, Derbyshire	421,663
13	The Cutty Sark, Greenwich	411,000
14	St George's Chapel, Windsor	372,068
15	Anne Hathaway's Cottage, Shottery	365,286
16	HMS Victory, Portsmouth	340,000
17	The Mary Rose, Portsmouth	333,126
18	Royal Pavilion, Brighton	314,443
19	Hever Castle, Kent	303,094
20	Fountains Abbey, North Yorkshire	300,067
21	Dover Castle, Kent	271,978
22	Castle Howard, North Yorkshire	222,876
23	Christ Church College, Oxford	220,000
24	St Michael's Mount, Marazion	194,793
25	Polesden Lacey, Surrey	192,738
26	Quarry Bank Mill, Styal	187,841

1993

1	Tower of London	2,332,468
2	St Paul's Cathedral, London	1,900,000
3	Roman Baths and Pump Room, Bath	898,142
4	State Apartments, Windsor Castle	813,059
5	Warwick Castle	751,026
6	Stonehenge, Wiltshire	668,607
7	Shakespeare's birthplace, Stratford	606,697
8	Hampton Court Palace	576,664
9	Leeds Castle, Kent	533,000
10	Beaulieu, Hampshire	481,223
11	Blenheim Palace, Woodstock	479,974
12	Chatsworth House, Derbyshire	402,261
13	Buckingham Palace, London	377,000
14	HMS Victory, Portsmouth	371,220
15	Anne Hathaway's Cottage, Shottery	329,091
16	Royal Pavilion, Brighton	327,476
17	St George's Chapel, Windsor	325,000
18	Dover Castle, Kent	304,802
19	Fountains Abbey, North Yorkshire	285,823
20	The Mary Rose, Portsmouth	285,435
21	Hever Castle, Kent	281,628
22	The Cutty Sark, Greenwich	262,223
23	Christ Church College, Oxford	258,996
24	Cabinet War Rooms, London	220,996
25	Harewood House, West Yorkshire	208,690
26	Polesden Lacey, Surrey	204,873
27	Quarry Bank Mill, Styal	202,290

Pets

Dog, cat and budgerigar ownership

	Total, m			Households owning, m		
	Dog	Cat	Budgerigar	Dog	Cat	Budgerigar
1965	4.7	4.1	3.3	…	…	…
1975	5.7	4.5	2.9	…	…	…
1980	5.6	4.9	2.1	4.8	3.7	1.3
1985	6.3	6.1	1.8	5.0	4.1	1.1
1990	7.4	6.8	1.7	5.9	4.6	1.1
1991	7.3	6.9	1.5	5.9	4.7	0.9
1992	7.3	7.0	1.4	5.8	4.7	0.9
1993	6.9	7.1	1.5	5.4	4.6	0.9

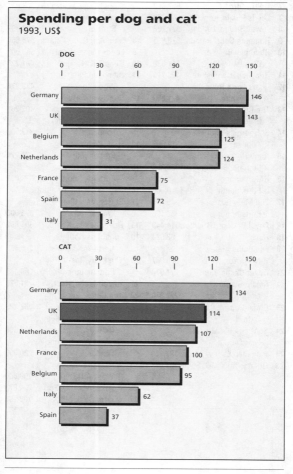

Spending per dog and cat
1993, US$

DOG

Germany	146
UK	143
Belgium	125
Netherlands	124
France	75
Spain	72
Italy	31

CAT

Germany	134
UK	114
Netherlands	107
France	100
Belgium	95
Italy	62
Spain	37

Part XIII
GOVERNMENT

General elections

Votes and seats since 1955

	1955	1959	1964
Conservatives			
Votes recorded, '000	13,311	13,763	12,002
Share of vote, %	49.7	49.4	43.4
Seats	345	366	304
Labour			
Votes recorded, '000	12,418	12,216	12,206
Share of vote, %	46.4	43.8	44.1
Seats	277	258	317
Liberal Democrat			
Votes recorded, '000	722	1,643	3,099
Share of vote, %	2.7	5.9	11.2
Seats	6	6	9
Others			
Votes recorded, '000	309	241	349
Share of vote, %	1.1	1.0	1.3
Seats	2	0	0
Total electorate	**34,852**	**35,397**	**35,894**

	1979	1983	1987
Conservatives			
Votes recorded, '000	13,698	13,013	13,736
Share of vote	43.9	42.4	42.3
Seats	339	397	376
Labour			
Votes recorded, '000	11,510	8,461	10,030
Share of vote	37.0	27.6	30.8
Seats	269	209	229
Liberal Democrat			
Votes recorded, '000	4,314	7,776	7,341
Share of vote	13.8	25.4	22.6
Seats	11	23	22
Others			
Votes recorded, '000	1,700	1,420	1,422
Share of vote	5.3	4.6	4.2
Seats	16	21	23
Total electorate	**41,573**	**42,704**	**43,666**

1966	1970	Feb 1974	Oct 1974	1992
11,418	13,174	11,929	10,429	14,093
41.9	46.4	37.8	35.8	41.9
253	330	297	277	336
13,066	12,186	11,661	11,407	11,563
47.9	43.0	37.0	39.2	34.4
363	288	301	319	271
2,328	2,124	6,057	5,347	6,003
8.5	7.5	19.3	18.3	17.8
12	6	14	13	20
453	875	1,695	2,008	1,961
1.6	3.1	5.8	6.7	5.8
2	6	23	26	24
35,957	**39,615**	**40,256**	**40,256**	**43,725**

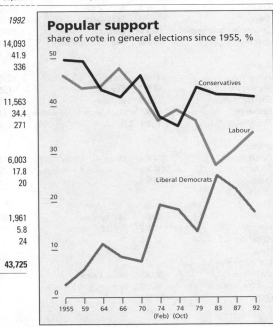

Popular support
share of vote in general elections since 1955, %

Conservatives

Labour

Liberal Democrats

50

40

30

20

10

0

1955 59 64 66 70 74 (Feb) 74 (Oct) 79 83 87 92

Parliamentary constituencies

How many electors?
Parliamentary electors, m

	UK	England	Wales	Scotland	N. Ireland
1984	42.99	35.80	2.15	3.96	1.08
1985	43.13	35.94	2.14	3.97	1.08
1986	43.39	36.16	2.16	3.99	1.09
1987	43.66	36.39	2.18	3.99	1.10
1988	43.71	36.45	2.18	3.97	1.11
1989	43.61	36.36	2.19	3.93	1.12
1990	43.67	36.39	2.21	3.94	1.13
1991	43.55	36.30	2.21	3.91	1.13
1992	43.73	36.44	2.22	3.93	1.14
1993	43.71	36.41	2.22	3.93	1.15

Biggest constituencies
No. of parliamentary electors, 1993

UK

Isle of Wight	101,652	Westbury	89,088
Huntingdon	94,292	North Wiltshire	88,264
East Hampshire	93,619	North Colchester	88,123
Eastleigh	93,465	Wokingham	87,795
The Wrekin	92,951	Dudley West	87,742
East Berkshire	92,357	South Colchester & Maldon	87,404
Devizes	91,555	Bridlington	86,627
Swindon	91,291	South Suffolk	86,540
Cirencester & Tewkesbury	90,549	Horsham	85,897
Ryedale	89,098	Mid Worcestershire	85,785

England

Isle of Wight	101,652	East Berkshire	92,357
Huntingdon	94,292	Devizes	91,555
East Hampshire	93,619	Swindon	91,291
Eastleigh	93,465	Cirencester & Tewkesbury	90,549
The Wrekin	92,951	Ryedale	89,098

Wales

Pembroke	74,314	Clwyd North West	68,172
Carmarthen	69,704	Ceredigion & Pembroke N.	67,686
Delyn	68,645		

Scotland

Gordon	82,654	East Lothian	67,541
Inverness, Nairn & Lochaber	70,955	Banff & Buchan	66,721
Kincardine & Deeside	68,218		

Northern Ireland

South Down	78,583	Lagan Valley	74,852
East Londonderry	78,239	Fermanagh & South Tyrone	72,277
Foyle	77,101		

How average are they?
Parliamentary constituencies as % of average electorate, 1993

	England	Wales	Scotland	N. Ireland
Less than 50%	0	0	1	0
50 but less than 60%	0	1	2	0
60 but less than 70%	8	0	1	0
70 but less than 80%	40	1	2	2
80 but less than 90%	88	6	14	2
90 but less than 100%	106	8	12	1
100 but less than 110%	149	13	19	8
110 but less than 120%	93	8	14	4
120 but less than 130%	31	1	6	0
130 but less than 140%	8	0	0	0
140 but less than 150%	1	0	0	0
150 but less than 160%	0	0	1	0
Total	524	38	72	17
Average electorate	69,487	58,490	54,603	67,836

Smallest constituencies
No. of parliamentary electors, 1993

UK

Western Isles	23,127	Montgomery	42,137
Caithness & Sutherland	31,113	Surbiton	43,947
Orkney & Shetland	32,052	Roxburgh & Berwickshire	44,201
Meirionnydd Nant Conwy	32,826	Glasgow, Cathcart	44,623
Glasgow, Provan	36,625	Kensington	44,649
Tweeddale, Ettrick & L'dale	40,220	Chelsea	44,858
Glasgow, Garscadden	40,975	Newham North West	45,557

England

Surbiton	43,947	Greenwich	48,253
Kensington	44,649	Coventry South East	48,400
Chelsea	44,858	Liverpool Riverside	48,496
Newham North West	45,557	Knowsley North	48,951
Hammersmith	48,112	Hendon South	49,308

Wales

Meirionnydd Nant Conwy	32,826	Cynon Valley	50,026
Montgomery	42,137	Newport East	51,576
Caernarfon	47,031		

Scotland

Western Isles	23,127	Glasgow, Provan	36,625
Caithness & Sutherland	31,113	Tweeddale, Ettrick & L'dale	40,220
Orkney & Shetland	32,052	Glasgow, Garscadden	40,975

Northern Ireland

Belfast South	52,316	Belfast West	55,401
Belfast East	53,213	East Antrim	64,649
Belfast North	55,169		

Ministers

Prime ministers

Sir Robert Walpole	Apr 1721	Earl of Derby	Jun 1866
Earl of Wilmington	Feb 1741	Benjamin Disraeli	Feb 1868
Henry Pelham	Aug 1743	William Ewart Gladstone	Dec 1868
Duke of Newcastle	Mar 1754	Benjamin Disraeli	Feb 1874
Duke of Devonshire	Nov 1756	William Ewart Gladstone	Apr 1880
Duke of Newcastle	Jul 1757	Marquess of Salisbury	Jun 1885
Earl of Bute	May 1762	William Ewart Gladstone	Feb 1886
George Grenville	Apr 1763	Marquess of Salisbury	Jul 1886
Marquess of Rockingham	Jul 1765	William Ewart Gladstone	Aug 1892
Earl of Chatham	Jul 1766	Earl of Rosebery	Mar 1894
Duke of Grafton	Oct 1768	Marquess of Salisbury	Jun 1895
Lord North	Jan 1770	Arthur James Balfour	Jul 1902
Marquess of Rockingham	Mar 1782	Sir Henry Campbell-Bannerman	
Earl of Shelburne	Jul 1782		Dec 1905
Duke of Portland	Apr 1783	Herbert Henry Asquith	Apr 1908
William Pitt	Dec 1783	David Lloyd George	Dec 1916
Henry Addington	Mar 1801	Andrew Bonar Law	Oct 1922
William Pitt	May 1804	Stanley Baldwin	May 1923
Lord Grenville	Feb 1806	James Ramsay MacDonald	
Duke of Portland	Mar 1807		Jan 1924
Spencer Perceval	Oct 1809	Stanley Baldwin	Nov 1924
Earl of Liverpool	Jun 1812	James Ramsay MacDonald	
George Canning	Apr 1827		Jun 1929
Viscount Goderich	Aug 1827	Stanley Baldwin	Jun 1935
Duke of Wellington	Jan 1828	Neville Chamberlain	May 1937
Earl Grey	Nov 1830	Winston Churchill	May 1940
Viscount Melbourne	Jul 1834	Clement Attlee	Jul 1945
Duke of Wellington	Nov 1834	Winston Churchill	Oct 1951
Sir Robert Peel	Dec 1834	Sir Anthony Eden	Apr 1955
Viscount Melbourne	Apr 1835	Harold Macmillan	Jan 1957
Sir Robert Peel	Aug 1841	Sir Alec Douglas-Home	Oct 1963
Lord John Russell	Jun 1846	Harold Wilson	Oct 1964
Earl of Derby	Feb 1852	Edward Heath	Jun 1970
Earl of Aberdeen	Dec 1852	Harold Wilson	Feb 1974
Viscount Palmerston	Feb 1855	James Callaghan	Apr 1976
Earl of Derby	Feb 1858	Margaret Thatcher	May 1979
Viscount Palmerston	Jun 1859	John Major	Nov 1990
Earl Russell	Oct 1865		

Chancellors of the Exchequer

Sir M. Hicks-Beach	1900	S. Baldwin	Oct 1922
Marquess of Lansdowne	Nov 1900	N. Chamberlain	Aug 1923
C. Ritchie	Aug 1902	P. Snowden	Jan 1924
A. Chamberlain	Oct 1903	W. Churchill	Nov 1924
H. Asquith	Dec 1905	P. Snowden	Jun 1929
D. Lloyd-George	Apr 1908	N. Chamberlain	Nov 1931
R. McKenna	May 1915	Sir J. Simon	May 1937
A. Bonar Law	Dec 1916	Sir K. Wood	May 1940
A. Chamberlain	Jan 1919	Sir J. Anderson	Sep 1943
Sir R. Horne	Apr 1921	H. Dalton	Jul 1945

Sir S. Cripps	Nov 1947	R. Jenkins	Nov 1967
H. Gaitskell	Oct 1950	I. Macleod	Jun 1970
R. Butler	Oct 1951	A. Barber	Jul 1970
H. Macmillan	Dec 1955	D. Healey	Mar 1974
P. Thorneycroft	Jan 1957	Sir G. Howe	May 1979
D. Heathcoat Amory	Jan 1958	N. Lawson	Jun 1983
S. Lloyd	Jul 1960	J. Major	Oct 1989
R. Maudling	Jul 1962	N. Lamont	Nov 1990
J. Callaghan	Oct 1964	K. Clarke	May 1993

Foreign ministers

Marquess of Salisbury (3rd)	1900	S. Lloyd	Dec 1955
Sir E. Grey (Vt)	Dec 1905	Earl of Home	Jul 1960
A. Balfour	Dec 1916	R. Butler	Oct 1963
Earl Curzon (M)	Oct 1919	P. Gordon Walker	Oct 1964
R. MacDonald	Jan 1924	M. Stewart	Jan 1965
(Sir) A. Chamberlain	Nov 1924	G. Brown	Aug 1966
A. Henderson	Jun 1929	M. Stewart	Mar 1968
Marquess of Reading	Aug 1931	Sir A. Douglas-Home	Jun 1970
Sir J. Simon	Nov 1931	J. Callaghan	Mar 1974
Sir S. Hoare	Jun 1935	A. Crosland	Apr 1976
A. Eden	Dec 1935	D. Owen	Feb 1977
Vt Halifax	Feb 1938	Lord Carrington	May 1979
A. Eden	Dec 1940	F. Pym	Apr 1982
E. Bevin	Jul 1945	Sir G. Howe	Jun 1983
H. Morrison	Mar 1951	J. Major	Jul 1989
(Sir) A. Eden	Oct 1951	D. Hurd	Oct 1989
H. Macmillan	Apr 1955		

Home ministers

Sir M. White-Ridley	1900	Sir D. Somervell	May 1945
C. Ritchie	Nov 1900	C. Ede	Aug 1945
A. Akers-Douglas	Aug 1902	Sir D. Maxwell-Fyfe	Oct 1951
H. Gladstone	Dec 1905	G. Lloyd-George	Oct 1954
W. Churchill	Feb 1910	R. Butler	Jan 1957
R. McKenna	Oct 1911	H. Brooke	Jul 1962
Sir J. Simon	May 1915	Sir F. Soskice	Oct 1964
Sir H. Samuel	Jan 1916	R. Jenkins	Dec 1965
Sir G. Cave (Vt)	Dec 1916	J. Callaghan	Nov 1967
E. Shortt	Jan 1919	R. Maudling	Jun 1970
W. Bridgeman	Oct 1922	R. Carr	Jul 1972
A. Henderson	Jan 1924	R. Jenkins	Mar 1974
Sir W. Joynson-Hicks	Nov 1924	M. Rees	Sep 1976
J. Clynes	Jun 1929	W. Whitelaw	May 1979
H. Samuel	Aug 1931	L. Brittan	Jun 1983
Sir J. Gilmour	Sep 1932	D. Hurd	Sep 1985
Sir J. Simon	Jun 1935	D. Waddington	Oct 1989
Sir S. Hoare	May 1937	K. Baker	Nov 1990
Sir J. Anderson	Sep 1939	K. Clarke	Apr 1992
H. Morrison	Oct 1940	M. Howard	May 1993

Monarchs

Kings and queens

Saxons and Danes

Egbert	802
Ethelwulf	839
Ethelbald	855
Ethelbert	860
Ethelred	866
Alfred (the Great)	871
Edward I (the Elder)	899
Athelstan	925
Edmund I (the Magnificent)	939
Edred	946
Edwy	955
Edgar (the Peaceable)	959
Edward II (the Martyr)	975
Ethelred II (the Unready)[a]	979
Sweyn	1013
Edmund II (Ironside)[b]	1016
Canute	1016
Harold I[c]	1037
Hardicanute[c]	1040
Edward III (the Confessor)	1042
Harold II	1066
Edgar Atheling[d]	1066

House of Normandy

William I	1066
William II	1087
Henry I	1100
Stephen	1113

House of Plantagenet

Henry II	1154
Richard I	1189
John	1199
Henry III	1216
Edward I	1272
Edward II	1307
Edward III	1327
Richard II	1377

House of Lancaster

Henry IV	1399
Henry V	1413
Henry VI	1422

House of York

Edward IV	1461
Henry VI	1470
Edward IV	1471
Edward V	1483
Richard III	1483

House of Tudor

Henry VII	1485
Henry VIII	1509
Edward VI	1547
Jane[e]	1553
Mary I	1553
Elizabeth I	1558

House of Stuart

James I (VI of Scotland)	1603
Charles I	1625
Charles II	1649

Commonwealth[f]	1649

Charles II	1660
James II	1685
William III and Mary II	1689
William III	1694
Anne	1702

House of Hanover

George I	1714
George II	1727
George III	1760
George IV	1820
William IV	1830
Victoria	1837

House of Saxe-Coburg and Gotha

Edward VII	1901

House of Windsor

George V	1910
Edward VIII[g]	1936
George VI	1936
Elizabeth II	1952

a Restored (in Canute's absence) on Sweyn's death in 1014.
b Divided the kingdom with Canute for seven months.
c Ruled jointly 1035–37.
d October–December.
e 10–19 July.
f Oliver Cromwell, Lord Protector 1653–58; Richard Cromwell, Lord Protector 1658–59.
g January–December.

Sources

The land and the environment
CSO, *Regional Trends*
Countryside Commission
Department of the Environment, *Digest of Environmental Protection and Water Statistics*
OECD, *Environmental Data*
Whitaker's Almanac

Population
CSO, *Annual Abstract of Statistics*
CSO, *Regional Trends*
B.R. Mitchell, *British Historical Statistics*
OPCS
UNDP, *Human Development Report*

The economy
The Bank of England
CSO, *Economic Trends; Annual Abstract of Statistics; Regional Trends; The Pink Book*
Datastream
Dresdner Bank Statistical Survey
The Economist , *One Hundred Years of Economic Statistics*
GATT
IMF, *International Financial Statistics*
B.R. Mitchell, *British Historical Statistics*
OECD, *Economic Outlook; Main Economic Indicators; National Accounts*
Times Newspapers Ltd, *The British Economy, Key Statistics 1900–1970*
UN Development Program, *Human Development Report*

Government finance
Bank of England
HM Treasury
Inland revenue
B.R. Mitchell, *British Historical Statistics*
OECD, *Economic Outlook*

Labour
Department of Employment
Crawford's Directory of City Connections
B.R. Mitchell, *British Historical Statistics*
TUC

Business and finance
The Banker

CBI
CSO, *The Blue Book; Financial Statistics*
Datastream
Gallup
London Stock Exchange, *Stock Exchange Quarterly*
Morgan Stanley Capital International
National stockmarkets
The Patent Office
The Times 1000

Tourism and transport
British Tourist Authority
Civil Aviation Authority
Department of Transport, *Road Accidents Great Britain; Transport Statistics Great Britain; Transport Statistics Report*
International Civil Aviation Organisation
International Road Federation, *World Road Statistics*
World Tourism Organisation

Housing
Building Societies Association
Census Reports
Council of Mortgage Lenders
CSO, *Family Expenditure Survey; Financial Statistics; Regional Trends; Social Trends; Economic Trends*
Department of Employment
Department of Environment
Department of Environment, Northern Ireland
Finance and Personnel Department of Northern Ireland
General Household Survey
General Register Office Scotland
General Register Office Northern Ireland
Northern Ireland Housing Executive
Mitchell B.R., *British Historical Statistics*
OPCS
Scottish Development Department
Scottish Office Environment Department
Welsh Office

Health
CSO, *Family Expenditure Survey; Regional Trends; Social Trends*
General Household Survey and Northern Ireland Continuous Household Survey

General Register Office Scotland
General Register Office Northern Ireland
Government Actuaries Department
Department of Health and Social Services, Department of Northern Ireland
Health and Safety Executive
Home Office
MAFF National Food Survey
National Health Service in Scotland, Directorate of Information Services
OECD Health Data
OPCS
Public Health Laboratory Service, Communicable Disease Surveillance Centre
Scottish Centre for Infection and Environmental Health
Scottish Health Service Common Services Agency
Scottish Office
UN, *World Population Prospects*
Welsh Office
World Bank Development Report

Education
CSO, *Regional Trends; Social Trends*
Department of Education Statistical Bulletin, press releases
Eton College
HMSO, *Education Statistics for the United Kingdom*
Independent Schools Information Service, *Annual Census 1994*
The Times Higher Education Supplement

Crime and punishment
CSO, *Regional Trends*
Council of Europe, Directorate of Legal Affairs
Home Office, *Criminal Statistics England and Wales; Prison Statistics*

People and culture
Audit Bureau of Circulation
Bank of England
The Bookseller
British Airways
British Coal
British Film Institute, *Film and Television Yearbook*
British Screen

British Telecom
Cable and Satellite Europe
Cable and Satellite Express
The Cable Television Association
Centre National de la Cinématographie
Chartered Institute for Public Finance and Accountancy
CSO, *Regional Trends; Social Trends*
Cunard
Datamonitor Food Databases
Department of Employment, *New Earnings Survey*
Dunhill
Euromonitor
The Football League
Ford Motor Company
General Household Survey
Harbord.J. and Wright.J.. *40 Years of British Television*
Hyde Park Hotel
International Federation of the Phonographic Industry
Jaguar Cars
Liverpool University
London Regional Transport
Mars (UK)
Metropolitan Police
OPCS
Pet Food Manufacturers' Association
The Premier League
Royal Opera House
Rothman's Football Yearbook
Rothman's Rugby Union Yearbook
Savoy Hotel
Scotch Whisky Association
Scottish Football League
Simpson (Piccadilly)
Society of London Theatres
Sotheby's
Taylor Nelson AGB/BARB/AGB Television
Test and County Cricket Board
Theatre Royal, Drury Lane
The Times
Wisden Cricketers' Almanack

Government
Anthony King et al., *Britain at the Polls*
R. Allison, S Riddell, *The Royal Encyclopaedia*
OPCS, *Electoral Statistics*
Vacher's Parliamentary Companion